The Pop Culture Tradition

BY EDWARD M. WHITE

The Writer's Control of Tone

The Pop Culture Tradition READINGS WITH ANALYSIS FOR WRITING

EDITED BY *Edward M. White*

CALIFORNIA STATE COLLEGE, SAN BERNARDINO

 W · W · NORTON & COMPANY · INC · NEW YORK

FIRST EDITION

Library of Congress Cataloging in Publication Data
White, Edward Michael, 1933–   comp.
    The Pop Culture Tradition.
    Includes bibliographical references.
    1. Readers—Popular culture.   I. Title.
PE1127.P6W5   808.4   76–152310
ISBN 0–393–09969–5

    3 4 5 6 7 8 9 0

Contents

v

Introduction

WRITING AND PERCEPTION · *I am a wretched artist. Once, on a dare, I studied figure drawing, and turned out a series of misshapen sketches which sent the others in the class into howls of laughter. But I refused to quit. So I followed the instructor's advice, turned away from the model, and began to work from the skeleton hanging in the corner of the room. Hour after hour, I studied the bone structure of the body in different positions. After many dreary hours communing with the skeleton, I finally returned to the model, who was decidedly better viewing.*

My drawings were still pretty awful, but no longer wildly funny. I had learned to see the structure and shape under the skin, and so had a much better sense of what the model's body was really doing in a pose; in a sense, by studying the concealed structure I had gained an awareness of the meaning of the surface. No doubt, if I had studied the arrangement and positions of the muscles, my sketches would have improved even more. But I went no further; I am, after all, a writer, not an artist, and I had gained the competence I wanted, despite my lack of talent.

But when I returned to my typewriter, I was struck by the analogy between my experience as a beginning artist and my practice as a writer. For the job of a writer is to focus upon the surface of what he is writing about in order to see and understand the meaning behind the surface. The really good figure-painters, after all, not only understand the muscles and bones under the skin, but manage to convey the meaning of a life in a portrait. The writer too is never content with surfaces. Nor is his reader.

Of course, as we live our daily lives we cannot constantly peer into the deep meaning of things. If we are to go about our business, we can't stop to consider every aspect of everything we see. All of us, almost all of the time, must rest content with the outsides of things, with the surfaces and categories that we let stand for the things themselves. Otherwise we might never get past the first flower or snowflake we see in the morning.

But when we sit down to write, or paint, whoever we may be, we take on the role of "seer," someone who has seen more deeply than others and who, for that reason, has something to say for others to hear. It is only when we have some perceptions that matter, when we see the structure and meaning below the surface, that we have essays worth the writing and the reading.

ANALYSIS · *I have planned this book to help you write better essays by developing an ability to see behind and around and into your subject. Analysis calls for full perception by the careful examination of the important parts of your subject. Writers and teachers borrow the term "analysis" from the chemistry lab because breaking something down—a chemical compound, a clock, a comic strip, a poem —into its parts is one of the best ways to understand what it is. You find out what makes a clock tick by taking it apart to look at the machinery; if you understand what you are doing, it still ticks when you put it back together, though it may never seem quite as simple as it was.*

Analysis is largely a matter of describing parts and how they fit into a whole. Thus George Orwell, writing on Donald McGill's mildly dirty postcards, needs to give details of color, design, language; Harvey Cox speaks of Playboy's advertisements, then fiction, then photography; Tom Wolfe describes Las Vegas architecture, dress, eating, and drinking. Analysis of a poem calls for attention to tone, metaphor, meanings of important words. Any analysis you do will ask you to describe important parts of your subject, to examine what is there in detail.

But analysis also asks you to notice what is not *apparent, what is* not *stated. Very often, the most important fact about an argument is not what it says but what it takes for granted. What is omitted from or only implied by a poem or story is often more significant than the words printed. What is assumed and implied by a writer, an artist, a work of art, or popular art is often difficult to discover, even though the assumptions and implications may be more important than the overt intention. Thus Orwell describes what relationships the McGill postcards do not portray, Cox perceives the religious attitude behind the Playboy Philosophy, Wolfe looks for the despair behind the Las Vegas "casualties." Analysis of what is there can be mere description for its own sake, which is often pretty dull and can be pointless. But when you look closely at what is assumed and implied, what lies before and after what is shown, you start to ask what it all means: what is it telling you about yourself and your world? Your analysis can then develop into the kind of essay which, like the essays in this book, makes interesting statements about all our lives as well as about the specific material being analyzed.*

This book is a collection of essays, stories, and poems, all of which are in one way or another analyses. Each selection asks you, as a reader and a writer, to observe and understand the way the author is analyzing his subject. Thus Orwell's essay proceeds from careful description of the McGill postcards ("chiefly hedge-sparrow's egg tint and Post Office red") to an examination of their values ("this is obscene, if you like, but it is not immoral") to a discussion of the nature of man ("what they are doing is to give expression to the Sancho Panza view of life"); this is one kind of organization that you might choose to use as you write your own analyses. At the same time, Orwell makes a series of assumptions that call for analysis themselves; his distinctions between "obscenity," "vulgarity," and "immorality," or his definition of man's true nature call for careful attention and fine discriminations.

Analysis, then, asks you to see as much as you can; this book collects a group of writers who have seen deeply into various subjects, most of them familiar to us all. The study of these selections, and the experience of writing similar analyses should sharpen your perceptions and help you find ways to use evidence to demonstrate what you see.

ART AND POPULAR ART · *Art is centrally concerned with special and individual perception, development of new modes of seeing, and hence demands attentive analysis as one way of experiencing its meaning. The popular arts, generally devoted to perpetuation of accepted ways of seeing things, call for analysis for the opposite reason—they tell us what our cultural myths are, and define in that way what we normally accept as true. Writing analyses of art and popular art, and examining closely others' analyses of these arts, are two excellent ways to develop an ability to see deeply and write perceptively.*

Of course, almost everyone who has been through school has written numbers of papers on literature. The reasoning behind such assignments is sound: literature not only presents fresh and unique ways of envisioning experience but serves as a model for the intelligent and sensitive use of language. You may, however, be surprised to see King Kong, Playboy, Uncle Remus, and the Beatles presented here for serious discussion and analysis.

But popular art is unusually appropriate material for the study of analysis—in some ways even more appropriate than the "fine" arts. Popular art is generally accessible—it is everywhere about us— and familiar; it is interesting for what it is and for what it unconsciously reveals about the culture it expresses. In a sense, to examine our popular art is to examine the forces that have helped make us what we are. Its assumptions tend to be our own, and hence hard to distinguish; its implications tend to be so large that we grasp them with difficulty. If you can see clearly something that has been before your eyes all your life, and write perceptively about it, you are ready to examine very difficult matters indeed.

The limitations of popular art, its lack of interest in new or unconventional ideas and styles, finally drive us to art. As we grow up, we abandon Superman *for* Macbeth, *or the film* Easy Rider; *we put aside* True Confessions *for* Romeo and Juliet, *or* Lolita. *But some popular art continues to interest us for what it reveals. Indeed, some popular art is more artful than we suspect, and sometimes it sees with a clarity that is hidden to more sophisticated eyes. Finally, the line between popular art and art is a fuzzy one, and an attempt to define that line by careful analysis of specific works could lead to one of the best essay topics to be taken from this book.*

ORGANIZATION · *The first section of this book asks you to attend to assumptions, the unstated and generally powerful ideas and premises which are felt to be so obviously true that they need not be written. The analyses in this section try to make clear the moral attitudes and values that lie concealed behind various forms of popular art; the stories and the poems talk about the moral effects of art on the artist and on those responding to art. The assumptions that these writers discover in their subjects and the assumptions that the writers themselves make are what lead to the form and meaning of what follows.*

The second section examines implication, the unstated, often unrecognized meanings and conclusions that follow from stated ideas. Most of the selections analyze children's literature, with a serious intention, to discern what this literature suggests about the meaning and form of our world. Thus the writers generally attempt to uncover the implied conclusions about what sort of adults the young readers of these tales will become; what, these writers ask, is the picture of reality the tales dramatize? In a sense, children's literature presents a myth, a working model of what the world is like, which is well worth looking at. But the myths we believe in are the hardest for us to see and understand.

The last section looks specifically at some ways of arranging evidence to defend or deny the artistry of some form of art. The writers here bring various definitions and standards, assumptions and implications, analyses and arguments to the issue in order to make their cases. Analysis leads to demonstration, and the emphasis here is on the ways of using evidence, particularly that derived from analysis, to construct an argument.

The Appendix contains a fresh approach to a definition of the responsible use of sources. Here I demonstrate by discussion and example the stages of responsibility in the use of a quotation, one likely to appear in a paper derived from the materials in Part Three. The emphasis is not on mechanics or footnote form, but on the way to use supporting quotations as one form of evidence, with respect for yourself and your own ideas, as well as for the source. The student paper in the Appendix shows how attention to assumptions, implications, and the appropriate use of evidence can help shape an essay as it moves from first draft to finished copy.

Throughout, my intention has been to move from simpler to more complex essays and ideas. As in the first volume of this series, which focuses upon the control of tone, the emphasis is consistently on the writer's specific job in creating an essay. And while the selections here are all worth reading for their own sakes, they have been collected and arranged here primarily for the purpose of helping you gain additional skill in the perception and demonstration of interesting ideas through analysis.

STUDENT WRITING · *The basic assumption behind this book is that you will write better if you see more clearly what you are writing about; the observation and practice of analysis give you experience in observing carefully, describing what you see in detail, presenting and organizing evidence for the ideas you develop from this close observation.*

Each section of the book suggests its own topic. The first section calls for analysis of the assumptions present in a form of popular art, in an analysis of popular art, or in a work of art. The second section asks you to return to the stories and other art you used to enjoy (secretly?) as a child in order to see now the version of values and reality they offered you along with entertainment. The last section calls for a study of the shadowy line between art and popular art; here you might be asked to present evidence leading to conclusions about the value and meaning of what you examine.

I hope some instructors will use the third section of this text, in combination with the Appendix, as an occasion for discussion of and practice in the use of sources. Most composition courses continue to require a long research paper in order to teach this necessary skill. But perhaps a shorter paper, using a few sources on an interesting subject that is integral to the course, will be as likely to do the job as a long project on unfamiliar material. After all, the essential matter is to help students understand the usefulness of other people's ideas as support for (rather than substitute for) their own assertions. If those reading and commenting upon student papers ask for careful rewriting, the experience of using sources creatively may become familiar, as it should, as one additional way of accumulating and using evidence.

Part One UNDERSTANDING

ASSUMPTIONS: ART AND SOCIETY

The essays in this section all include a great deal of detailed, precise description:

> Who does not know the "comics" of the cheap stationers' windows, the penny or twopenny coloured postcards with their endless succession of fat women in tight bathing-dresses and their crude drawing and unbearable colours, chiefly hedge-sparrow's egg tint and Post Office red? —ORWELL

> Sometimes in Life or Look *we see a double-page photograph of some family standing on the lawn among its possessions: station-wagon, swimming-pool, power-cruiser, sports-car, tape-recorder, television sets, radios, cameras, power lawn-mower, garden tractor, lathe, barbecue-set, sporting equipment, domestic appliances—all of the gleaming, grotesquely imaginative paraphernalia of its existence. It was hard to get everything on two pages, soon it will need four.* —JARRELL

> Everybody at the craps table was staring in consternation to think that anybody would try to needle a tough, hip, elite soldat *like a Las Vegas craps dealer. The gold lamé odalisques of Los Angeles were staring. The Western sports, fifty-eight-year-old men who wear Texas string ties, were staring. The old babes at the slot machines, holding Dixie Cups full of nickles, were staring at the craps tables, but cranking away the whole time.* —WOLFE

The precise concrete nouns here give the descriptions their particularity and strength. Orwell's postcards are not just blue and red, but "hedge-sparrow's egg tint and Post Office red." Jarrell's catalogue of goods brings the familiar advertisement vividly to mind. Wolfe's elderly women in the hotel lounges become "old babes at the slot machines," and he notices the nickles in "Dixie Cups."

Such precision and particularity of description often calls for simple but important facts: the circulation figures for Playboy, the location of the shops selling McGill postcards, and so on. Sometimes size is important, or shape, or color, or length. Perhaps it is a typical story, or advertisement, or table of contents that needs to be summarized. Sometimes it is necessary to describe what is not being analyzed as a way of distinguishing and clarifying: "they are not to be confused with the various other types of comic illustrated postcard, such as the sentimental ones dealing with puppies and kittens. . . ." Just what should be described, and just how it should be described, is a matter of tone, determined by what you have to say about your particular subject to your particular reader. But clear, concrete, detailed description is the first requirement for perceptive writing on popular art.

The best way to support description is by including examples in your essay. You will notice that most of the essays in this book provide a great deal of such quotation, sometimes including whole paragraphs or sections of material. Orwell describes the postcard jokes as "obscene"; then he includes sample jokes so you can see what he means. Cox gives us the ominous words of "The Playboy Advisor": " 'you goofed!' " Thirty hernias begin Wolfe's description of Las Vegas; he makes us hear the aimless noise before the analysis begins.

One of the most typical problems with first drafts of papers is the failure to include the description and quotation I have been describing. Your reader needs to know precisely what it is you are talking about, and what evidence you have for saying what you do. Description and quotation let us as readers see and experience that which is to be analyzed; they also are the most obvious kinds of evidence for what you as a writer have to say. But they cannot stand alone. Description, however detailed, and quotation, however interesting or typical, are only, well, description and quotation. And, necessary though they are, no one reads for that alone. We read, and write, finally and basically, because there is something interesting to be said or something worthwhile to be heard. Meaning is what matters, and perceptive writing uses description and quotation only because they are effective ways to demonstrate meaning.

This section of the text asks you to examine assumptions as one important way to discover meaning in your topic. After seeing carefully and describing concretely what is before your eyes, you need to see through the surface into the reasons for the surface. What, the question becomes, do those who create this material take for granted, just assume to be true? Why do they show and write what they do? Each of the essays here looks long and hard at basic assumptions, the assumptions which determine what is shown and how it is shown.

Thus Orwell, after locating and describing the McGill postcards, defines the world as it is assumed to be in the cards:

> Marriage only benefits the woman. Every man is plotting seduction and every woman is plotting marriage. . . . No woman ever remains single voluntarily. Sex appeal vanishes at about the age of twenty-five. . . . There is no such thing as a happy marriage. . . . No man ever gets the better of a woman in argument.

Harvey Cox sees the same assumptions at work in Playboy's advertisements that appear in its fold-out:

> Most of the advertisements reinforce the sex-accessory identification in another way by attributing female characteristics to the items they sell. Thus a full page ad for the MG assures us that this car is not only "the smoothest pleasure machine" on the road and that having one is a "love-affair," but most importantly, "you drive it—it doesn't drive you." The ad ends with the equivocal question, "Is it a date?"

Assumptions are so powerful because they are—by definition— neither stated nor examined. They have a kind of coercive force; they ask you to accept as true what everybody knows to be true, even if it happens to be false, or partly false. Perceptive writers resist this coercion in order to examine the assumptions that so often determine what things mean. Jarrell's particular quarrel with the media is based on what he sees as a debasing vision of Man as Consumer: "if anyone wishes to paint the genesis of things in our society, he will paint a picture of God holding out to Adam a checkbook or credit card or Charge-A-Plate." The vision of marriage in the McGill postcards, the image of the girl friend in Playboy, can be seen most clearly when the assumptions behind them can be isolated and stated; finally, the postcards or the magazine are worth discussing only because the assumptions behind them are so interesting.

Assumptions operate in many different and special ways. Sometimes it is an assumed definition that needs to be examined closely (e.g., "God is dead"—what is meant by "God"?); sometimes social attitudes call for analysis (e.g., "If you're not part of the solution, you're part of the problem"). Sometimes religious or political or even generational assumptions are significant: if you don't trust anyone over thirty, does that mean you do trust everyone under thirty? But when you analyze popular art, particular assumptions tend to blend into a general, assumed vision of the way the world is put together. It is for this reason that these writers can speak of the "worlds" of the McGill postcards or Playboy magazine; you could do the same with, say, movie magazines, or teen comics, or TV situation comedies. Millions of viewers and readers who want to believe in the myths purveyed by the popular arts keep these arts flourishing; no popular art can survive unless it gives its audience a conception of life that satisfies the audience's needs. Thus the popular artist—as opposed to the traditional "fine" artist—appears as one with his audience, seeing the world as this audience does, assuming the same values and attitudes.

The stories and poems that conclude this section deal with the same kinds of assumptions the essayists examine. Updike's A & P is in some ways a dramatization of what Jarrell describes; the Kafka tale and the Shakespeare sonnet ask you to consider carefully assumptions about the artist's relationship to his audience. But the stories and poems move beyond description, beyond analysis, to create a new vision of what the world is like. One way to discover some differences between art and popular art is to examine the basic assumptions in these works and contrast them with what is assumed to be true in the simpler worlds of the earlier pieces.

George Orwell

THE ART OF DONALD MC GILL

Who does not know the "comics" of the cheap stationers' windows, the penny or twopenny coloured postcards with their endless succession of fat women in tight bathing-dresses and their crude drawing and unbearable colours, chiefly hedge-sparrow's egg tint and Post Office red?

This question ought to be rhetorical, but it is a curious fact that many people seem to be unaware of the existence of these things, or else to have a vague notion that they are something to be found only at the seaside, like nigger minstrels or peppermint rock. Actually they are on sale everywhere—they can be bought at nearly any Woolworth's, for example—and they are evidently produced in enormous numbers, new series constantly appearing. They are not to be confused with the various other types of comic illustrated postcard, such as the sentimental ones dealing with puppies and kittens or the Wendyish, sub-pornographic ones which exploit the love-affairs of children. They are a genre of their own, specialising in very "low" humour, the mother-in-law, baby's nappy, policemen's boots type of joke, and distinguishable from all the other kinds by having no artistic pretensions. Some half-dozen publishing houses issue them, though the people who draw them seem not to be numerous at any one time.

I have associated them especially with the name of Donald Mc-Gill because he is not only the most prolific and by far the best of contemporary postcard artists, but also the most representative, the most perfect in the tradition. Who Donald McGill is, I do not know. He is apparently a trade name, for at least one series of postcards is issued simply as "The Donald McGill Comics", but he is also unquestionably a real person with a style of drawing which is recognisable at a glance. Anyone who examines his postcards in bulk will notice that many of them are not despicable even as drawings, but it would be mere dilettantism to pretend that they have any direct aesthetic value. A comic postcard is simply an illustration to a joke, invariably a "low" joke, and it stands or falls by its ability to raise a laugh. Beyond that it has only "ideological" interest. Mc-Gill is a clever draughtsman with a real caricaturist's touch in the drawing of faces, but the special value of his postcards is that they are so completely typical. They represent, as it were, the norm of the comic postcard. Without being in the least imitative, they are exactly what comic postcards have been any time these last forty years, and from them the meaning and purpose of the whole genre can be inferred.

Get hold of a dozen of these things, preferably McGill's—if you pick out from a pile the ones that seem to you funniest, you will probably find that most of them are McGill's—and spread them out on a table. What do you see?

Your first impression is of overpowering vulgarity. This is quite apart from the ever-present obscenity, and apart also from the hideousness of the colours. They have an utter lowness of mental atmosphere which comes out not only in the nature of the jokes but, even more, in the grotesque, staring, blatant quality of the drawings. The designs, like those of a child, are full of heavy lines and empty spaces, and all the figures in them, every gesture and attitude, are deliberately ugly, the faces grinning and vacuous, the women monstrously parodied, with bottoms like Hottentots. Your second impression, however, is of indefinable familiarity. What do these things remind you of? What are they so like? In the first place, of course, they remind you of the barely different postcards which you probably gazed at in your childhood. But more than this, what you are really looking at is something as traditional as Greek tragedy, a sort of sub-world of smacked bottoms and scrawny mothers-in-law which is a part of western European consciousness. Not that the jokes, taken one by one, are necessarily stale. Not being debarred from smuttiness, comic postcards repeat themselves less often than the joke columns in reputable magazines, but their basic subject-matter, the *kind* of joke they are aiming at, never varies. A few are genuinely witty, in a Max Millerish style. Examples:

> "I like seeing experienced girls home."
> "But I'm not experienced!"
> "You're not home yet!"

> "I've been struggling for years to get a fur coat. How did you get yours?"
> "I left off struggling."

> Judge: "You are prevaricating, sir. Did you or did you not sleep with this woman?"
> Co-respondent: "Not a wink, my lord!"

In general, however, they are not witty but humorous, and it must be said for McGill's postcards, in particular, that the drawing is often a good deal funnier than the joke beneath it. Obviously the outstanding characteristic of comic postcards is their obscenity, and I must discuss that more fully later. But I give here a rough analysis of their habitual subject-matter, with such explanatory remarks as seem to be needed:

Sex · More than half, perhaps three-quarters, of the jokes are sex jokes, ranging from the harmless to the all but unprintable. First favourite is probably the illegitimate baby. Typical captions: "Could you exchange this lucky charm for a baby's feeding-bottle?" "She didn't ask me to the christening, so I'm not going to the wedding." Also newlyweds, old maids, nude statues and women in bathing-dresses. All of these are *ipso facto* funny, mere mention of them being enough to raise a laugh. The cuckoldry joke is very seldom exploited, and there are no references to homosexuality.

Conventions of the sex joke:

a. Marriage only benefits the woman. Every man is plotting seduction and every woman is plotting marriage. No woman ever remains unmarried voluntarily.

b. Sex-appeal vanishes at about the age of twenty-five. Well-preserved and good-looking people beyond their first youth are never represented. The amorous honeymooning couple reappear as the grim-visaged wife and shapeless, mustachioed, red-nosed husband, no intermediate stage being allowed for.

Home Life · Next to sex, the henpecked husband is the favourite joke. Typical caption: "Did they get an X-ray of your wife's jaw at the hospital?"—"No, they got a moving picture instead."

Conventions:

a. There is no such thing as a happy marriage.

b. No man ever gets the better of a woman in argument.

Drunkenness · Both drunkenness and teetotalism are *ipso facto* funny.

Conventions:

a. All drunken men have optical illusions.

b. Drunkenness is something peculiar to middle-aged men. Drunken youths or women are never represented.

WC Jokes · There is not a large number of these. Chamberpots are *ipso facto* funny, and so are public lavatories. A typical postcard, captioned "A Friend in Need", shows a man's hat blown off his head and disappearing down the steps of a ladies' lavatory.

Inter-working-class Snobbery · Much in these postcards suggests
that they are aimed at the better-off working class and poorer middle
class. There are many jokes turning on malapropisms, illiteracy,
dropped aitches and the rough manners of slum-dwellers. Countless
postcards show draggled hags of the stage-char-woman type exchang-
ing "unladylike" abuse. Typical repartee: "I wish you were a statue
and I was a pigeon!" A certain number produced since the war treat
evacuation from the anti-evacuee angle. There are the usual jokes
about tramps, beggars and criminals, and the comic maidservant appears fairly frequently. Also the comic navvy, bargee, etc; but there
are no anti-trade-union jokes. Broadly speaking, everyone with
much over or much under £5 a week is regarded as laughable. The
"swell" is almost as automatically a figure of fun as the slum-dweller.
Stock Figures · Foreigners seldom or never appear. The chief lo-
cality joke is the Scotsman, who is almost inexhaustible. The
lawyer is always a swindler, the clergyman always a nervous idiot
who says the wrong thing. The "knut" or "masher" still appears,
almost as in Edwardian days, in out-of-date-looking evening clothes
and an opera hat, or even with spats and a knobby cane. Another
survival is the Suffragette, one of the big jokes of the pre-1914
period and too valuable to be relinquished. She has reappeared,
unchanged in physical appearance, as the Feminist lecturer or
Temperance fanatic. A feature of the last few years is the complete
absence of anti-Jew postcards. The "Jew joke", always somewhat
more ill-natured than the "Scotch joke", disappeared abruptly soon
after the rise of Hitler.
Politics · Any contemporary event, cult or activity which has
comic possibilities (for example, "free love", feminism, ARP, nud-
ism) rapidly finds its way into the picture postcards, but their
general atmosphere is extremely old-fashioned. The implied political outlook is a radicalism appropriate to about the year 1900. At
normal times they are not only not patriotic, but go in for a mild
guying of patriotism, with jokes about "God save the King", the
Union Jack etc. The European situation only began to reflect itself
in them at some time in 1939, and first did so through the comic
aspects of ARP. Even at this date few postcards mention the war
except in ARP jokes (fat woman stuck in the mouth of Anderson
shelter: wardens neglecting their duty while young woman un-
dresses at window she had forgotten to black out, etc etc). A few
express anti-Hitler sentiments of a not very vindictive kind. One,
not McGill's, shows Hitler, with the usual hypertrophied backside,
bending down to pick a flower. Caption: "What would *you* do,
chums?" This is about as high a flight of patriotism as any postcard
is likely to attain. Unlike the twopenny weekly papers, comic postcards are not the product of any great monopoly company, and

evidently they are not regarded as having any importance in form-ing public opinion. There is no sign in them of any attempt to induce an outlook acceptable to the ruling class.

Here one comes back to the outstanding, all-important feature of comic postcards—their obscenity. It is by this that everyone re-members them, and it is also central to their purpose, though not in a way that is immediately obvious.

A recurrent, almost dominant motif in comic postcards is the woman with the stuck-out behind. In perhaps half of them, or more than half, even when the point of the joke has nothing to do with sex, the same female figure appears, a plump "voluptuous" figure with the dress clinging to it as tightly as another skin and with breasts or buttocks grossly over-emphasized, according to which way it is turned. There can be no doubt that these pictures lift the lid off a very widespread repression, natural enough in a country whose women when young tend to be slim to the point of skimpi-ness. But at the same time the McGill postcard—and this applies to all other postcards in this genre—is not intended as pornography but, a subtler thing, as a skit on pornography. The Hottentot figures of the women are caricatures of the Englishman's secret ideal, not portraits of it. When one examines McGill's postcards more closely, one notices that his brand of humour only has meaning in relation to a fairly strict moral code. Whereas in papers like *Esquire*, for instance, or *La Vie Parisienne*, the imaginary background of the jokes is always promiscuity, the utter breakdown of all stan-dards, the background of the McGill postcard is marriage. The four leading jokes are nakedness, illegitimate babies, old maids and newly married couples, none of which would seem funny in a really dissolute or even "sophisticated" society. The postcards deal-ing with honeymoon couples always have the enthusiastic indecency of those village weddings where it is still considered screamingly funny to sew bells to the bridal bed. In one, for example, a young bridegroom is shown getting out of bed the morning after his wedding night. "The first morning in our own little home, darling!" he is saying; "I'll go and get the milk and paper and bring you a cup of tea." Inset is a picture of the front doorstep; on it are four newspapers and four bottles of milk. This is obscene, if you like, but it is not immoral. Its implication—and this is just the implica-tion that *Esquire* or the *New Yorker* would avoid at all costs—is that marriage is something profoundly exciting and important, the biggest event in the average human being's life. So also with jokes about nagging wives and tyrannous mothers-in-law. They do at least imply a stable society in which marriage is indissoluble and family loyalty taken for granted. And bound up with this is something I noted earlier, the fact that there are no pictures, or hardly any, of good-looking people beyond their first youth. There is the "spooning" couple and the middle-aged, cat-and-dog couple, but nothing in between. The liaison, the illicit but more or less decorous love-affair which used to be the stock joke of French comic papers, is not a postcard subject. And this reflects, on a comic level, the working-class outlook which takes it as a matter of course that youth and adventure—almost, indeed, individual life—end with marriage. One of the few authentic class-differences, as opposed to class-distinctions, still existing in England is that the working classes age very much earlier. They do not live less long, provided that they survive their childhood, nor do they lose their physical activity earlier, but they do lose very early their youthful appearance. This fact is observable everywhere, but can be most easily verified by watching one of the higher age groups registering for military service; the middle- and upper-class members look, on average, ten years younger than the others. It is usual to attribute this to the harder lives that the working classes have to live, but it is doubtful whether any such difference now exists as would account for it. More probably the truth is that the working classes reach middle age earlier because they accept it earlier. For to look young after, say, thirty is largely a matter of wanting to do so. This generalisation is less true of the better-paid workers, especially those who live in council houses and labour-saving flats, but it is true enough even of them to point to a difference of outlook. And in this, as usual, they are more traditional, more in accord with the Christian past than the well-to-do women who try to stay young at forty by means of physical jerks, cosmetics and avoidance of child-bearing. The impulse to cling to youth at all costs, to attempt to preserve your sexual attraction, to see even in middle age a future for yourself and not merely for your children, is a thing of recent growth and has only precariously established itself. It will probably disappear again when our standard of living drops and our birth-rate rises. "Youth's a stuff will not endure" expresses the normal, traditional attitude. It is this ancient wisdom that McGill and his colleagues are reflecting, no doubt unconsciously, when they allow for no transition stage between the honeymoon couple and those glamourless figures, Mum and Dad.

I have said that at least half McGill's postcards are sex jokes, and a proportion, perhaps ten per cent, are far more obscene than anything else that is now printed in England. Newsagents are occasionally prosecuted for selling them, and there would be many more prosecutions if the broadest jokes were not invariably protected by double meanings. A single example will be enough to show how this is done. In one postcard, captioned "They didn't believe her", a young woman is demonstrating, with her hands held apart, something about two feet long to a couple of open-mouthed acquaintances. Behind her on the wall is a stuffed fish in a glass case, and beside that is a photograph of a nearly naked athlete. Obviously it is not the fish that she is referring to, but this could never be proved. Now, it is doubtful whether there is any paper in England that would print a joke of this kind, and certainly there is no paper that does so habitually. There is an immense amount of pornography of a mild sort, countless illustrated papers cashing in on women's legs, but there is no popular literature specialising in the "vulgar", farcical aspect of sex. On the other hand, jokes exactly like McGill's are the ordinary small change of the revue and music-hall stage, and are also to be heard on the radio, at moments when the censor happens to be nodding. In England the gap between what can be said and what can be printed is rather exceptionally wide. Remarks and gestures which hardly anyone objects to on the stage would raise a public outcry if any attempt were made to reproduce them on paper. (Compare Max Miller's * stage patter with his weekly column in the *Sunday Dispatch*.) The comic post-cards are the only existing exception to this rule, the only medium in which really "low" humour is considered to be printable. Only in postcards and on the variety stage can the stuck-out behind, dog and lamp-post, baby's nappy type of joke be freely exploited. Remembering that, one sees what function these postcards, in their humble way, are performing.

What they are doing is to give expression to the Sancho Panza view of life, the attitude to life that Miss Rebecca West once

---

* Reviewing *Applesauce*, a variety show, in *Time and Tide*, 7 September 1940, Orwell wrote: "Anyone wanting to see something really vulgar should visit the Holborn Empire, where you can get quite a good matinée seat for three shillings. Max Miller, of course, is the main attraction.

Max Miller, who looks more like a Middlesex Street hawker than ever when he is wearing a tail coat and a shiny top hat, is one of a long line of English comedians who have specialised in the Sancho Panza side of life, in real *lowness*. To do this probably needs more talent than to express nobility. Little Tich was a master at it. There was a music-hall farce which Little Tich used to act in, in which he was supposed to be factotum to a crook solicitor. The solicitor is giving him his instructions:

'Now, our client who's coming this morning is a widow with a good figure. Are you following me?'
Little Tich: 'I'm ahead of you.'

"As it happens, I have seen this farce acted several times with other people in the same part, but I have never seen anyone who could approach the utter baseness that Little Tich could get into these simple words. There is a touch of the same quality in Max Miller. Quite apart from the laughs they give one, it is important that such comedians should exist. They express something which is valuable in our civilization and which might drop out of it in certain circumstances. To begin with, their genius is entirely masculine. A woman cannot be low without being disgusting, whereas a good male comedian can give the impression of something irredeemable and yet innocent, like a sparrow. Again, they are intensely national. They remind one how closely-knit the civilisation of England is, and how much it resembles a family, in spite of its out-of-date class distinctions. The startling obscenities which occur in *Applesauce* are only possible because they are expressed in *doubles entendres* which imply a common background in the audience. Anyone who had not been brought up on the *Pink 'Un* would miss the point of them. So long as comedians like Max Miller are on the stage and the comic coloured postcards which express approximately the same view of life are in the stationers' windows, one knows that the popular culture of England is surviving. . . ."

summed up as "extracting as much fun as possible from smacking be-
hinds in basement kitchens". The Don Quixote-Sancho Panza combination, which of course is simply the ancient dualism of body and
soul in fiction form, recurs more frequently in the literature of the
last four hundred years than can be explained by mere imitation. It
comes up again and again, in endless variations, Bouvard and
Pécuchet, Jeeves and Wooster, Bloom and Dedalus, Holmes and
Watson (the Holmes-Watson variant is an exceptionally subtle one,
because the usual physical characteristics of two partners have been
transposed). Evidently it corresponds to something enduring in our
civilisation, not in the sense that either character is to be found in
a "pure" state in real life, but in the sense that the two principles,
noble folly and base wisdom, exist side by side in nearly every human being. If you look into your own mind, which are you, Don
Quixote or Sancho Panza? Almost certainly you are both. There is
one part of you that wishes to be a hero or a saint, but another part
of you is a little fat man who sees very clearly the advantages of
staying alive with a whole skin. He is your unofficial self, the voice
of the belly protesting against the soul. His tastes lie towards safety,
soft beds, no work, pots of beer and women with "voluptuous"
figures. He it is who punctures your fine attitudes and urges you to
look after Number One, to be unfaithful to your wife, to bilk your
debts, and so on and so forth. Whether you allow yourself to be
influenced by him is a different question. But it is simply a lie to
say that he is not part of you, just as it is a lie to say that Don
Quixote is not part of you either, though most of what is said and
written consists of one lie or the other, usually the first.

But though in varying forms he is one of the stock figures of
literature, in real life, especially in the way society is ordered, his
point of view never gets a fair hearing. There is a constant world-
wide conspiracy to pretend that he is not there, or at least that
he doesn't matter. Codes of law and morals, or religious systems,
never have much room in them for a humorous view of life. Whatever is funny is subversive, every joke is ultimately a custard pie,
and the reason why so large a proportion of jokes centre round
obscenity is simply that all societies, as the price of survival, have
to insist on a fairly high standard of sexual morality. A dirty joke is
not, of course, a serious attack upon morality, but it is a sort of
mental rebellion, a momentary wish that things were otherwise. So
also with all other jokes, which always centre round cowardice, laziness, dishonesty or some other quality which society cannot afford to
encourage. Society has always to demand a little more from human
beings than it will get in practice. It has to demand faultless discipline and self-sacrifice, it must expect its subjects to work hard, pay
their taxes, and be faithful to their wives, it must assume that men

think it glorious to die on the battlefield and women want to wear themselves out with child-bearing. The whole of what one may call official literature is founded on such assumptions. I never read the proclamations of generals before battle, the speeches of fuehrers and prime ministers, the solidarity songs of public schools and left-wing political parties, national anthems, Temperance tracts, papal encyclicals and sermons against gambling and contraception, without seeming to hear in the background a chorus of raspberries from all the millions of common men to whom these high sentiments make no appeal. Nevertheless the high sentiments always win in the end, leaders who offer blood, toil, tears and sweat always get more out of their followers than those who offer safety and a good time. When it comes to the pinch, human beings are heroic. Women face childbed and the scrubbing brush, revolutionaries keep their mouths shut in the torture chamber, battleships go down with their guns still firing when their decks are awash. It is only that the other element in man, the lazy, cowardly, debt-bilking adulterer who is inside all of us, can never be suppressed altogether and needs a hearing occasionally.

The comic postcards are one expression of his point of view, a humble one, less important than the music halls, but still worthy of attention. In a society which is still basically Christian they naturally concentrate on sex jokes; in a totalitarian society, if they had any freedom of expression at all, they would probably concentrate on laziness or cowardice, but at any rate on the unheroic in one form or another. It will not do to condemn them on the ground that they are vulgar and ugly. That is exactly what they are meant to be. Their whole meaning and virtue is in their unredeemed lowness, not only in the sense of obscenity, but lowness of outlook in every direction whatever. The slightest hint of "higher" influences would ruin them utterly. They stand for the worm's-eye view of life, for the music-hall world where marriage is a dirty joke or a comic disaster, where the rent is always behind and the clothes are always up the spout, where the lawyer is always a crook and the Scotsman always a miser, where the newlyweds make fools of themselves on the hideous beds of seaside lodging houses and the drunken, red-nosed husbands roll home at four in the morning to meet the linen-nightgowned wives who wait for them behind the front door, poker in hand. Their existence, the fact that people want them, is symptomatically important. Like the music halls, they are a sort of saturnalia, a harmless rebellion against virtue. They express only one tendency in the human mind, but a tendency which is always there and will find its own outlet, like water. On the whole, human beings want to be good, but not too good, and not quite all the time. For:

there is a just man that perishes in his righteousness, and
there is a wicked man that prolongeth his life in his wickedness. Be not righteous over much; neither make thyself
over wise; why shouldst thou destroy thyself? Be not over-
much wicked, neither be thou foolish: why shouldst thou
die before thy time?

In the past the mood of the comic postcard could enter into
the central stream of literature, and jokes barely different from
McGill's could casually be uttered between the murders in Shakespeare's tragedies. That is no longer possible, and a whole category
of humour, integral to our literature till 1800 or thereabouts, has
dwindled down to these ill-drawn postcards, leading a barely legal
existence in cheap stationers' windows. The corner of the human
heart that they speak for might easily manifest itself in worse forms,
and I for one should be sorry to see them vanish.

GEORGE ORWELL (1903–1950) *is best known for* Animal Farm
(1946), *a short satire on Soviet Russian history, and the grim political vision of* 1984 (1948). *But throughout the 1940s he was one of
England's leading essayists and journalists, and became known for
his writings on social, political, and literary matters. Popular art was
an enduring interest for him; analyses of such art gave him the opportunity to discuss the issues of human behavior and language that
mattered to him. An earlier essay in this area is* "Boys' Weeklies"
(1939), *a description and analysis of schoolboy stories; the political
and social assumptions that govern these tales struck Orwell as important, even dangerous:* "These papers exist because of a specialized
demand, because boys at certain ages find it necessary to read about
Martians, death-rays, grizzly bears and gangsters. They get what
they are looking for, but they get it wrapped up in the illusions
which their future employers think suitable for them." *As late as
1944, Orwell wrote a comparison between types of English detective
stories,* "Raffles and Miss Blandish"; *he portrays the amoral but
gentlemanly code of Raffles as much superior to a* "half-understood
import from America," *in which* "the cult of power tends to be
mixed up with a love of cruelty and wickedness for their own sakes.
. . . It is a day dream appropriate to a totalitarian age."

*"The Art of Donald McGill" appeared in 1941. McGill himself
died at the age of eighty-seven in 1962, after turning out no fewer*

than 12,500 cards and selling 200 million copies. "I am really rather Victorian in my outlook," he said of himself.

1. A major problem Orwell faces here, and one common to writers on popular art, is the usual unthinking reaction to such a topic: why should he write about, and ask a reader to read about, apparently trivial stuff? Orwell deals with this problem in many ways throughout the essay; for example, in the fifth paragraph he says, "what you are really looking at is something as traditional as Greek tragedy. . . ." What does he mean by this? Find and describe other passages which speak to the importance of the topic, and the relationship of writer to reader.

2. How does Orwell give you a clear picture of what the McGill postcards look like? Find and analyze specific passages designed to help you see the cards in your mind.

3. When Orwell moves to analysis of the cards, he gives a list of seven areas (sex, home life, drunkenness, etc.) in which the McGill assumptions seem important and consistent. Choose several of these areas and show how Orwell provides evidence for the assumptions he isolates.

4. In the fifth paragraph, Orwell distinguishes between vulgarity and obscenity. Later on, describing the honeymoon postcard, he says, "This is obscene, if you like, but it is not immoral." What are the differences between "vulgarity," "obscenity," and "immorality" in this essay? How do these distinctions relate to the defense of the cards at the end of the essay?

5. Describe the evidence that Orwell brings to support his argument that the cards perform a valuable function. What assumptions does Orwell himself make in the last few paragraphs, those defining the nature of man? If Orwell's defense of the McGill cards does not convince you of their value, what arguments can you bring to support your own point of view, and how would you argue against his conclusions?

Harvey Cox

PLAYBOY'S DOCTRINE OF MALE

Sometime this month over one million American young men will place sixty cents on a counter somewhere and walk away with a copy of *Playboy*, one of the most spectacular successes in the entire history of American journalism. When one remembers that every copy will probably be seen by several other people in college dormitories and suburban rumpus rooms, the total readership in any one month easily exceeds that of all the independent religious magazines, serious political and cultural journals, and literary periodicals put together.

What accounts for this uncanny reception? What factors in American life have combined to allow *Playboy*'s ambitious young publisher, Hugh Hefner, to pyramid his jackpot into a chain of night clubs, TV spectaculars, bachelor tours to Europe and special discount cards? What impact does *Playboy* really have?

Clearly *Playboy*'s astonishing popularity is not attributable solely to pin-up girls. For sheer nudity its pictorial art cannot compete with such would-be competitors as *Dude* and *Escapade*. Rather, *Playboy* appeals to a highly mobile, increasingly affluent group of young readers, mostly between eighteen and thirty, who want much more from their drugstore reading than bosoms and thighs. They need a total image of what it means to be a man. And Mr. Hefner's *Playboy* has no hesitancy about telling them.

Why should such a need arise? David Riesman has argued that the responsibility for character formation in our society has shifted from the family to the peer group and to the mass media peer group surrogates. Things are changing so rapidly that one who is equipped by his family with inflexible, highly internalized values becomes unable to deal with the accelerated pace of change and with the varying contexts in which he is called upon to function. This is especially true in the area of consumer values toward which the "other-directed person" is increasingly oriented.

A *Guidebook to Identity* · Within the confusing plethora of mass media signals and peer group values, *Playboy* fills a special need.

Reprinted with permission of Macmillan Publishing Co., Inc. From *The Secular City*, Revised Edition, by Harvey Cox. Copyright © Harvey Cox 1965, 1966.

For the insecure young man with newly acquired time and money on his hands who still feels uncertain about his consumer skills, *Playboy* supplies a comprehensive and authoritative guidebook to this foreboding new world to which he now has access. It tells him not only who to be; it tells him *how* to be it, and even provides consolation outlets for those who secretly feel that they have not quite made it.

In supplying for the other-directed consumer of leisure both the normative identity image and the means for achieving it, *Playboy* relies on a careful integration of copy and advertising material. The comic book that appeals to a younger generation with an analogous problem skillfully intersperses illustrations of incredibly muscled men and excessively mammalian women with advertisements for body-building gimmicks and foam rubber brassiere supplements. Thus the thin-chested comic book readers of both sexes are thoughtfully supplied with both the ends and the means for attaining a spurious brand of maturity. *Playboy* merely continues the comic book tactic for the next age group. Since within every identity crisis, whether in 'teens or twenties, there is usually a sexual identity problem, *Playboy* speaks to those who desperately want to know what it means to be a *man*, and more specifically a *male*, in today's world.

Both the image of man and the means for its attainment exhibit a remarkable consistency in *Playboy*. The skilled consumer is cool and unruffled. He savors sports cars, liquor, high fidelity and book club selections with a casual, unhurried aplomb. Though he must certainly *have* and *use* the latest consumption item, he must not permit himself to get too attached to it. The style will change and he must always be ready to adjust. His persistent anxiety that he may mix a drink incorrectly, enjoy a jazz group that is passé, or wear last year's necktie style is comforted by an authoritative tone in *Playboy* beside which papal encyclicals sound irresolute.

"Don't hesitate," he is told, "this assertive, self-assured weskit is what every man of taste wants for the fall season." Lingering doubts about his masculinity are extirpated by the firm assurance that "real men demand this ruggedly masculine smoke" (cigar ad). Though "the ladies will swoon for you, no matter what they promise, don't give them a puff. This cigar is for men only." A fur-lined canvas field jacket is described as "the most masculine thing since the cave man." What to be and how to be it are both made unambiguously clear.

But since being a male necessitates some kind of relationship to females, *Playboy* fearlessly confronts this problem too, and solves it by the consistent application of the same formula. Sex becomes one of the items of leisure activity that the knowledgeable con-

sumer of leisure handles with his characteristic skill and detach-
ment. The girl becomes a desirable, indeed an indispensable "Playboy accessory."

Recreational Sex · In a question-answering column entitled: "The
Playboy Advisor," queries about smoking equipment (how to break
in a meerschaum pipe), cocktail preparation (how to mix a "Yellow
Fever") and whether or not to wear suspenders with a vest, alternate
with questions about what to do with girls who complicate the
cardinal principle of casualness, either by suggesting marriage or by
some other impulsive gesture toward permanent relationship. The
infallible answer from the oracle never varies: sex must be contained,
at all costs, within the entertainment-recreation area. Don't let her
get "serious."

After all, the most famous feature of the magazine is its monthly
fold-out photo of a *play*mate. She is the symbol par excellence of
recreational sex. When play time is over, the playmate's function
ceases, so she must be made to understand the rules of the game.
As the crew-cut young man in a *Playboy* cartoon says to the rumpled
and disarrayed girl he is passionately embracing, "Why speak of
love at a time like this?"

The magazine's fiction purveys the same kind of severely de-
partmentalized sex. Although the editors have recently dressed up
the contents of *Playboy* with contributions by Hemingway, Bemel-
mans and even a Chekhov translation, the regular run of stories
relies on a repetitious and predictable formula. A successful young
man, either single or somewhat less than ideally married—a figure
with whom readers have no difficulty identifying—encounters a
gorgeous and seductive woman who makes no demands on him
except sex. She is the prose duplication of the cool-eyed but hot-
blooded playmate of the fold-out page.

Don't Get Involved! · Drawing heavily on the phantasy life of all
young Americans, the writers utilize for their stereotyped heroines
the hero's school teacher, his secretary, an old girl friend, or the
girl who brings her car into the garage where he works. The happy
issue is always a casual but satisfying sexual experience with no en-
tangling alliances whatever. Unlike the women he knows in real
life, the *Playboy* reader's fictional girl friends know their place and
ask for nothing more. They present no danger of permanent involvement. Like any good accessory, they are detachable and disposable.

Many of the advertisements reinforce the sex-accessory identification in another way by attributing female characteristics to the
items they sell. Thus a full page ad for the MG assures us that
this car is not only "the smoothest pleasure machine" on the road
and that having one is a "love-affair," but most importantly, "you
drive it—it doesn't drive you." The ad ends with the equivocal

question, "Is it a date?"

Playboy insists that its message is one of liberation. Its gospel frees us from captivity to the puritanical "hat-pin brigade." It solemnly crusades for "frankness" and publishes scores of letters congratulating it for its unblushing "candor." Yet the whole phenomenon of which *Playboy* is only a part vividly illustrates the awful fact of a new kind of tyranny.

Those liberated by technology and increased prosperity to new worlds of leisure now become the anxious slaves of dictatorial tastemakers. Obsequiously waiting for the latest signal on what is cool and what is awkward, they are paralyzed by the fear that they may hear pronounced on them that dread sentence occasionally intoned by "The Playboy Advisor": "you goofed!" Leisure is thus swallowed up in apprehensive competitiveness, its liberating potential transformed into a self-destructive compulsion to consume only what is *au courant*. *Playboy* mediates the Word of the most high into one section of the consumer world, but it is a word of bondage, not of freedom.

Nor will *Playboy*'s synthetic doctrine of man stand the test of scrutiny. Psychoanalysts constantly remind us how deeply seated sexuality is in the human self. But if they didn't remind us, we would soon discover it anyway in our own experience. As much as the human male might like to terminate his relationship with a woman as he snaps off the stereo, or store her for special purposes like a camel's hair jacket, it really can't be done. And anyone with a modicum of experience with women knows it can't be done. Perhaps this is the reason why *Playboy*'s readership drops off so sharply after the age of thirty.

Playboy really feeds on the presence of a repressed fear of involvement with women, which for various reasons is still present in many otherwise adult Americans. So *Playboy*'s version of sexuality grows increasingly irrelevant as authentic sexual maturity is achieved.

A *Futile Doctrine* · The male identity crisis to which *Playboy* speaks has at its roots a deep-set fear of sex, a fear that is uncomfortably combined with fascination. *Playboy* strives to resolve this antinomy by reducing the terrible proportions of sexuality, its power and its passion, to a packageable consumption item. Thus in *Playboy*'s iconography, the nude woman symbolizes total sexual accessibility, but demands nothing from the observer. "You drive it—it doesn't drive you." The terror of sex, which cannot be separated from its ecstacy, is dissolved. But this futile attempt to reduce the *mysterium tremendum* of the sexual fails to solve the problem of being a man. For sexuality is the basic form of all human relationship, and therein lies its terror and its power.

Karl Barth has called this basic relational form of man's life *Mitmensch*, co-humanity. This means that becoming fully human, in this case a human male, necessitates not having the other totally exposed to me and my purposes—while I remain uncommitted—but exposing myself to the risk of encounter with the other by reciprocal self-exposure. The story of man's refusal to be so exposed goes back to the story of Eden and is expressed by man's desire to control the other rather than to *be with* the other. It is basically the fear to be one's self, a lack of the "courage to be."

Thus any theological critique of *Playboy* that focuses on its "lewdness" will misfire completely. *Playboy* and its less successful imitators are not "sex magazines" at all. They are basically anti-sexual. They dilute and dissipate authentic sexuality by reducing it to an accessory, by keeping it at a safe distance.

It is precisely because these magazines are anti-sexual that they deserve the most searching kind of theological criticism. They foster a heretical doctrine of man, one at radical variance with the biblical view. For *Playboy*'s man, others—especially women—are *for* him. They are his leisure accessories, his playthings. For the Bible, man only becomes fully man by being *for* the other.

Moralistic criticisms of *Playboy* fail because its anti-moralism is one of the few places in which *Playboy* is right. But if Christians bear the name of One who was truly man because he was totally *for* the other, and if it is in him that we know who God is and what human life is for, then we must see in *Playboy* the latest and slickest episode in man's continuing refusal to be fully human.

HARVEY COX (1929–   ) *first achieved wide attention when this essay was published in* Christianity and Crisis, *April 17, 1961. He has since published* The Secular City *(1965) and* On Not Leaving It to the Snake *(1967), both of which bring modern religious views to the problems of the city. He has edited* The Church Amid Revolution *(1967) and writes from time to time for many magazines, including* Playboy.

"*Christianity today,*" *Dr. Cox has said, "desperately needs the arts." In addition to teaching in the Harvard Divinity School, he is a research associate in the Harvard University Program on Technology and Society, and a fellow of the Foundation for the Arts, Religion and Culture.*

Playboy's *response to Cox has taken several forms: Hugh Hefner's tome* The Playboy Philosophy *(1962, 1963) uses Cox's argument (partly misunderstood) as a starting place; Hefner feels great*

*satisfaction at "qualifying as a movement, as well as a magazine."
The defense is an assertion of the naturalness of healthy sex. More
recently, the* Playboy *editors point to Cox's association with Hefner
on television panels and his contributions to the magazine, and
quote Cox as admitting his "original view of* Playboy *has changed,
just as* Playboy *itself has changed." Nonetheless, they continue,
"From time to time, readers have sent us texts of sermons or essays
from parish bulletins in which the hand is the hand of the Reverend
So-and-so but the voice is Harvey Cox" (*Playboy, *January 1968, p.
203).*

1. How does Cox seek in his opening paragraph to convince the
   religious readers of Christianity and Crisis *that an article on*
   Playboy *deserves their attention? Where in the third and fifth
   paragraphs does Cox speak of the need to discover underlying assumptions and their importance? How does Cox relate religious
   issues to the assumptions behind* Playboy?
2. Cox begins his analysis of Playboy *not with an attack on its display of nakedness (as you might expect), but with careful description of its advertising. Why? How does the analysis of
   assumptions in the advertising lead to the analysis of sexual assumptions? How does Cox connect the descriptions of the other
   departments of the magazine to his analysis of the advertising?*
3. The last section of the essay sets out to show that Playboy, *despite its claims and intentions, "illustrates the awful fact of a
   new kind of tyranny." What tyranny is Cox speaking about?
   How does it relate to Cox's own assumptions about maturity in
   sexual relationships, and to his summary of the Christian view
   of sex and humanity? How can Cox assert that* Playboy *and its
   imitators "are basically anti-sexual"?*
4. Playboy's *editors in the January 1968 issue dismissed this argument as "based on research about as relevant and up to date as
   the Edsel" (p. 203). Has the magazine so changed by now that
   this essay no longer applies, or are the same assumptions still
   at work?*

Tom Wolfe

LAS VEGAS (WHAT?) LAS VEGAS

(CAN'T HEAR YOU! TOO NOISY) LAS VEGAS!!!!

Hernia, hernia, hernia, hernia, hernia, hernia, hernia, hernia, hernia, hernia, hernia, hernia, hernia, HERNia; hernia, HERNia, hernia, hernia, hernia, hernia, HERNia, HERNia, HERNia; hernia, hernia, hernia, hernia, hernia, hernia, hernia, eight is the point, the point is eight; hernia, hernia, HERNia; hernia, hernia, hernia, hernia, all right, hernia, hernia, hernia, hernia, hard eight, hernia, hernia, hernia, HERNia, hernia, hernia, hernia, HERNia, hernia, hernia, hernia, HERNia, hernia, hernia, hernia, hernia

"What is all this *hernia hernia* stuff?"

This was Raymond talking to the wavy-haired fellow with the stick, the dealer, at the craps table about 3:45 Sunday morning. The stickman had no idea what this big wiseacre was talking about, but he resented the tone. He gave Raymond that patient arch of the eyebrows known as a Red Hook brushoff, which is supposed to convey some such thought as, I am a very tough but cool guy, as you can tell by the way I carry my eyeballs low in the pouches, and if this wasn't such a high-class joint we would take wiseacres like you out back and beat you into jellied madrilene.

At this point, however, Raymond was immune to subtle looks.

The stickman tried to get the game going again, but every time he would start up his singsong, by easing the words out through the nose, which seems to be the style among craps dealers in Las Vegas—"All right, a new shooter . . . eight is the point, the point is eight" and so on—Raymond would start droning along with him in exactly the same tone of voice, "Hernia, hernia, hernia; hernia, HERNia, HERNia, hernia; hernia, hernia, hernia."

Everybody at the craps table was staring in consternation to think that anybody would try to needle a tough, hip, elite *soldat* like a Las Vegas craps dealer. The gold-lamé odalisques of Los Angeles were staring. The Western sports, fifty-eight-year-old men

who wear Texas string ties, were staring. The old babes at the slot
machines, holding Dixie Cups full of nickles, were staring at the
craps tables, but cranking away the whole time.

Raymond, who is thirty-four-years-old and works as an engineer
in Phoenix, is big but not terrifying. He has the sort of thatchwork
hair that grows so low all along the forehead there is no logical
place to part it, but he tries anyway. He has a huge, prognathous
jaw, but it is as smooth, soft and round as a melon, so that Raymond's total effect is that of an Episcopal divinity student.

The guards were wonderful. They were dressed in cowboy uniforms like Bruce Cabot in *Sundown* and they wore sheriff's stars.

"Mister, is there something we can do for you?"

"The expression is 'Sir,'" said Raymond. "You said 'Mister.'
The expression is 'Sir.' How's your old Cosa Nostra?"

Amazingly, the casino guards were easing Raymond out peace-
ably, without putting a hand on him. I had never seen the fellow
before, but possibly because I had been following his progress for
the last five minutes, he turned to me and said, "Hey, do you have
a car? This wild stuff is starting again."

The gist of it was that he had left his car somewhere and he
wanted to ride up the Strip to the Stardust, one of the big hotel-
casinos. I am describing this big goof Raymond not because he is
a typical Las Vegas tourist, although he has some typical symptoms,
but because he is a good example of the marvelous impact Las
Vegas has on the senses. Raymond's senses were at a high pitch of
excitation, the only trouble being that he was going off his nut. He
had been up since Thursday afternoon, and it was now about 3:45
A.M. Sunday. He had an envelope full of pep pills—amphetamine—
in his left coat pocket and an envelope full of Equanils—meprobamate—in his right pocket, or were the Equanils in the left and
the pep pills in the right? He could tell by looking, but he wasn't
going to look anymore. He didn't care to see how many were left.

He had been rolling up and down the incredible electric-sign
gauntlet of Las Vegas' Strip, U.S. Route 91, where the neon and
the par lamps—bubbling, spiraling, rocketing, and exploding in
sunbursts ten stories high out in the middle of the desert—celebrate one-story casinos. He had been gambling and drinking and
eating now and again at the buffet tables the casinos keep heaped
with food day and night, but mostly hopping himself up with
good old amphetamine, cooling himself down with meprobamate,
then hooking down more alcohol, until now, after sixty hours, he
was slipping into the symptoms of toxic schizophrenia.

He was also enjoying what the prophets of hallucinogen call
"consciousness expansion." The man was psychedelic. He was beginning to isolate the components of Las Vegas' unique bombard-

ment of the senses. He was quite right about this *hernia hernia* stuff. Every casino in Las Vegas is, among the other things, a room full of craps tables with dealers who keep up a running singsong that sounds as though they are saying "hernia, hernia, hernia, hernia, hernia" and so on. There they are day and night, easing a running commentary through their nostrils. What they have to say contains next to no useful instruction. Its underlying message is, We are the initiates, riding the crest of chance. That the accumulated sound comes out "hernia" is merely an unfortunate phonetic coincidence. Actually, it is part of something rare and rather grand: a combination of baroque stimuli that brings to mind the bronze gongs, no larger than a blue plate, that Louis XIV, his ruff collars larded with the lint of the foul Old City of Byzantium, personally hunted out in the bazaars of Asia Minor to provide exotic acoustics for his new palace outside Paris.

The sounds of the craps dealer will be in, let's say, the middle register. In the lower register will be the sound of the old babes at the slot machines. Men play the slots too, of course, but one of the indelible images of Las Vegas is that of the old babes at the row upon row of slot machines. There they are at six o'clock Sunday morning no less than at three o'clock Tuesday afternoon. Some of them pack their old hummocky shanks into Capri pants, but many of them just put on the old print dress, the same one day after day, and the old hob-heeled shoes, looking like they might be going out to buy eggs in Tupelo, Mississippi. They have a Dixie Cup full of nickles or dimes in the left hand and an Iron Boy work glove on the right hand to keep the callouses from getting sore. Every time they pull the handle, the machine makes a sound much like the sound a cash register makes before the bell rings, then the slot pictures start clattering up from left to right, the oranges, lemons, plums, cherries, bells, bars, buckaroos—the figure of a cowboy riding a bucking bronco. The whole sound keeps churning up over and over again in eccentric series all over the place, like one of those random-sound radio symphonies by John Cage. You can hear it at any hour of the day or night all over Las Vegas. You can walk down Fremont Street at dawn and hear it without even walking in a door, that and the spins of the wheels of fortune, a boring and not very popular sort of simplified roulette, as the tabs flap to a stop. As an overtone, or at times simply as a loud sound, comes the babble of the casino crowds, with an occasional shriek from the craps tables, or, anywhere from 4 P.M. to 6 A.M., the sound of brass instruments or electrified string instruments from the cocktail-lounge shows.

The crowd and band sounds are not very extraordinary, of course. But Las Vegas' Muzak is. Muzak pervades Las Vegas from the time you walk into the airport upon landing to the last time you leave the casinos. It is piped out to the swimming pool. It is in the drugstores. It is as if there were a communal fear that someone, somewhere in Las Vegas, was going to be left with a totally vacant minute on his hands.

Las Vegas has succeeded in wiring an entire city with this electronic stimulation, day and night, out in the middle of the desert. In the automobile I rented, the radio could not be turned off, no matter which dial you went after. I drove for days in a happy burble of Action Checkpoint News, "Monkey No. 9," "Donna, Donna, the Prima Donna," and picking-and-singing jingles for the Frontier Bank and the Fremont Hotel.

One can see the magnitude of the achievement. Las Vegas takes what in other American towns is but a quixotic inflammation of the senses for some poor salary mule in the brief interval between the flagstone rambler and the automatic elevator downtown and magnifies it, foliates it, embellishes it into an institution.

For example, Las Vegas is the only town in the world whose skyline is made up neither of buildings, like New York, nor of trees, like Wilbraham, Massachusetts, but signs. One can look at Las Vegas from a mile away on Route 91 and see no buildings, no trees, only signs. But such signs! They tower. They revolve, they oscillate, they soar in shapes before which the existing vocabulary of art history is helpless. I can only attempt to supply names—Boomerang Modern, Palette Curvilinear, Flash Gordon Ming-Alert Spiral, McDonald's Hamburger Parabola, Mint Casino Elliptical, Miami Beach Kidney. Las Vegas' sign makers work so far out beyond the frontiers of conventional studio art that they have no names themselves for the forms they create. Vaughan Cannon, one of those tall, blond Westerners, the builders of places like Las Vegas and Los Angeles, whose eyes seem to have been bleached by the sun, is in the back shop of the Young Electric Sign Company out on East Charleston Boulevard with Herman Boernge, one of his designers, looking at the model they have prepared for the Lucky Strike Casino sign, and Cannon points to where the sign's two great curving faces meet to form a narrow vertical face and says:

"Well, here we are again—what do we call that?"

"I don't know," says Boernge. "It's sort of a nose effect. Call it a nose."

Okay, a nose, but it rises sixteen stories high above a two-story building. In Las Vegas no farseeing entrepreneur buys a sign to fit a building he owns. He rebuilds the building to support the biggest sign he can get up the money for and, if necessary, changes the name. The Lucky Strike Casino today is the Lucky Casino, which fits better when recorded in sixteen stories of flaming peach and incandescent yellow in the middle of the Mojave Desert. In the

Young Electric Sign Co. era signs have become the architecture of Las Vegas, and the most whimsical, Yale-seminar-frenzied devices of the two late geniuses of Baroque Modern, Frank Lloyd Wright and Eero Saarinen, seem rather stuffy business, like a jest at a faculty meeting, compared to it. Men like Boernge, Kermit Wayne, Ben Mitchem and Jack Larsen, formerly an artist for Walt Disney, are the designer-sculptor geniuses of Las Vegas, but their motifs have been carried faithfully throughout the town by lesser men, for gasoline stations, motels, funeral parlors, churches, public buildings, flophouses and sauna baths.

Then there is a stimulus that is both visual and sexual—the Las Vegas buttocks décolletage. This is a form of sexually provocative dress seen more and more in the United States, but avoided like Broadway message-embroidered ("Kiss Me, I'm Cold") underwear in the fashion pages, so that the euphemisms have not been established and I have no choice but clinical terms. To achieve buttocks décolletage a woman wears bikini-style shorts that cut across the round fatty masses of the buttocks rather than cupping them from below, so that the outer-lower edges of these fatty masses, or "cheeks," are exposed. I am in the cocktail lounge of the Hacienda Hotel, talking to managing director Dick Taylor about the great success his place has had in attracting family and tour groups, and all around me the waitresses are bobbing on their high heels, bare legs and décolletage-bare backsides, set off by pelvis-length lingerie of an uncertain denomination. I stare, but I am new here. At the White Cross Rexall drugstore on the Strip a pregnant brunette walks in off the street wearing black shorts with buttocks décolletage aft and illusion-of-cloth nylon lingerie hanging fore, and not even the old mom's-pie pensioners up near the door are staring. They just crank away at the slot machines. On the streets of Las Vegas, not only the show girls, of which the town has about two hundred fifty, bona fide, in residence, but girls of every soft, including, especially, Las Vegas' little high-school buds, who adorn what locals seeking roots in the sand call "our city of churches and schools," have taken up the chic of wearing buttocks décolletage step-ins under flesh-tight slacks, with the outline of the undergarment showing through fashionably. Others go them one better. They achieve the effect of having been dipped once, briefly, in Helenca stretch nylon. More and more they look like those wonderful old girls out of Flash Gordon who were wrapped just once over in Baghdad pantaloons of clear polyethylene with only Flash Gordon between them and the insane red-eyed assaults of the minions of Ming. It is as if all the hip young suburban gals of America named Lana, Deborah and Sandra, who gather wherever the arc lights shine and the studs steady their coiffures in the plate-glass reflec-

tion, have convened in Las Vegas with their bouffant hair above
and anatomically stretch-pant-swathed little bottoms, below, here on
the new American frontier. But exactly!

None of it would have been possible, however, without one of
those historic combinations of nature and art that creates an epoch.
In this case, the Mojave Desert plus the father of Las Vegas, the
late Benjamin "Bugsy" Siegel.

Bugsy was an inspired man. Back in 1944 the city fathers of
Las Vegas, their Protestant rectitude alloyed only by the giddy prospect of gambling revenues, were considering the sort of ordinance
that would have preserved the town with a kind of Colonial Wil-
liamsburg dinkiness in the motif of the Wild West. All new
buildings would have to have at least the façade of the sort of place
where piano players used to wear garters on their sleeves in Virginia City around 1880. In Las Vegas in 1944, it should be noted,
there was nothing more stimulating in the entire town than a
Fremont Street bar where the composer of "Deep in the Heart of
Texas" held forth and the regulars downed fifteen-cent beer.

Bugsy pulled into Las Vegas in 1945 with several million dollars
that, after his assassination, was traced back in the general direction of gangster-financiers. Siegel put up a hotel-casino such as Las
Vegas had never seen and called it the Flamingo—all Miami
Modern, and the hell with piano players with garters and whatever
that was all about. Everybody drove out Route 91 just to gape. Such
shapes! Boomerang Modern supports, Palette Curvilinear bars, Hot
Shoppe Cantilever roofs and a scalloped swimming pool. Such
colors! All the new electrochemical pastels of the Florida littoral:
tangerine, broiling magenta, livid pink, incarnadine, fuchsia demure,
Congo ruby, methyl green, viridine, aquamarine, phenosafranine,
incandescent orange, scarlet-fever purple, cyanic blue, tessellated
bronze, hospital-fruit-basket orange. And such signs! Two cylinders
rose at either end of the Flamingo—eight stories high and covered
from top to bottom with neon rings in the shape of bubbles that
fizzed all eight stories up into the desert sky all night long like an
illuminated whisky-soda tumbler filled to the brim with pink
champagne.

The business history of the Flamingo, on the other hand, was
not such a smashing success. For one thing, the gambling operation
was losing money at a rate that rather gloriously refuted all the recorded odds of the gaming science. Siegel's backers apparently
suspected that he was playing both ends against the middle in
collusion with professional gamblers who hung out at the Flamingo
as though they had liens on it. What with one thing and another,
someone decided by the night of June 20, 1947, that Benny Siegel,

lord of the Flamingo, had had it. He was shot to death in Los
Angeles.

Yet Siegel's aesthetic, psychological and cultural insights, like
Cézanne's, Freud's and Max Weber's, could not die. The Siegel
vision and the Siegel aesthetic were already sweeping Las Vegas
like gold fever. And there were builders of the West equal to the
opportunity. All over Las Vegas the incredible electric pastels were
repeated. Overnight the Baroque Modern forms made Las Vegas
one of the few architecturally unified cities of the world—the
style was Late American Rich—and without the bother and bad
humor of a City Council ordinance. No enterprise was too small,
too pedestrian or too solemn for The Look. The Supersonic Car-
wash, the Mercury Jetaway, Gas Vegas Village and Terrible Herbst
gasoline stations, the Para-a-Dice Motel, the Palm Mortuary, the
Orbit Inn, the Desert Moon, the Blue Onion Drive-In—on it went,
like Wildwood, New Jersey, entering Heaven.

The atmosphere of the six-mile-long Strip of hotel-casinos grips
even those segments of the population who rarely go near it. Barely
twenty-five-hundred feet off the Strip, over by the Convention Center, stands Landmark Towers, a shaft thirty stories high, full of
apartments, supporting a huge circular structure shaped like a
space observation platform, which was to have contained the restaurant and casino. Somewhere along the way Landmark Towers went
bankrupt, probably at that point in the last of the many crises
when the construction workers *still* insisted on spending half the
day flat on their bellies with their heads, tongues and eyeballs
hanging over the edge of the tower, looking down into the swimming pool of the Playboy Apartments below, which has a "nudes
only" section for show girls whose work calls for a tan all over.

Elsewhere, Las Vegas' beautiful little high-school buds in their
buttocks-décolletage stretch pants are back on the foam-rubber
upholstery of luxury broughams peeling off the entire chick en-
semble long enough to establish the highest venereal-disease rate
among high-school students anywhere north of the yaws-rotting
shanty jungles of the Eighth Parallel. The Negroes who have done
much of the construction work in Las Vegas' sixteen-year boom are
off in their ghetto on the west side of town, and some of them are
smoking marijuana, eating peyote buttons and taking horse (her-
oin), which they get from Tijuana, I mean it's simple, baby, right
through the mails, and old Raymond, the Phoenix engineer, does
not have the high life to himself.

I am on the third floor of the Clark County Courthouse talking
to Sheriff Captain Ray Gubser, another of these strong, pale-eyed
Western-builder types, who is obligingly explaining to me law

enforcement on the Strip, where the problem is not so much the drunks, crooks or roughhousers, but these nuts on pills who don't want to ever go to bed, and they have hallucinations and try to bring down the casinos like Samson. The county has two padded cells for them. They cool down after three or four days and they turn out to be somebody's earnest breadwinner back in Denver or Minneapolis, loaded with the right credentials and pouring soul and apologiae all over the county cops before finally pulling out of never-never land for good by plane. Captain Gubser is telling me about life and eccentric times in Las Vegas, but I am distracted. The captain's office has windows out on the corridor. Coming down the corridor is a covey of girls, skipping and screaming, giggling along, their heads exploding in platinum-and-neon-yellow bouffants or beehives or raspberry-silk scarves, their eyes appliquéd in black like mail-order decals, their breasts aimed up under their jerseys at the angle of anti-aircraft automatic weapons, and, as they swing around the corner toward the elevator, their glutei maximi are bobbing up and down with their pumps in the inevitable buttocks décolletage pressed out against black, beige and incarnadine stretch pants. This is part of the latest shipment of show girls to Las Vegas, seventy in all, for the "Lido de Paris" revue at the Stardust, to be entitled *Bravo!*, replacing the old show, entitled V*oilà*. The girls are in the county courthouse getting their working papers, and fifteen days from now these little glutei maximi and ack-ack breasts with stars pasted on the tips will be swinging out over the slack jaws and cocked-up noses of patrons sitting at stageside at the Stardust. I am still listening to Gubser, but somehow it is a courthouse where mere words are beaten back like old atonal Arturo Toscanini trying to sing along with the NBC Symphony. There he would be, flapping his little toy arms like Tony Galento shadowboxing with fate, bawling away in the face of union musicians who drowned him without a bubble. I sat in on three trials in the courthouse, and it was wonderful, because the courtrooms are all blond-wood modern and look like sets for TV panel discussions on marriage and the teenager. What the judge has to say is no less formal and no more fatuous than what judges say everywhere, but inside of forty seconds it is all meaningless because the atmosphere is precisely like a news broadcast over Las Vegas' finest radio station, KORK. The newscast, as it is called, begins with a series of electronic wheeps out on that far edge of sound where only quadrupeds can hear. A voice then announces that this is Action Checkpoint News. "The news—all the news—flows first through Action Checkpoint!—then reaches You! at the speed of Sound!" More electronic wheeps, beeps and lulus, and then an item: "Cuban Premier Fidel Castro nearly drowned yesterday." Urp! Wheep! Lulu! No news a KORK announcer has ever brought to Las Vegas at the speed of sound, or could possibly bring, short of word of the annihilation of Los Angeles, could conceivably compete within the brain with the giddiness of this electronic jollification.

The wheeps, beeps, freeps, electronic lulus, Boomerang Modern and Flash Gordon sunbursts soar on through the night over the billowing hernia—hernia sounds and the old babes at the slots— until it is 7:30 A.M. and I am watching five men at a green-topped card table playing poker. They are sliding their Bee-brand cards into their hands and squinting at the pips with a set to the lips like Conrad Veidt in a tunic collar studying a code message from S.S. headquarters. Big Sid Wyman, the old Big-Time gambler from St. Louis, is there, with his eyes looking like two poached eggs engraved with a road map of West Virginia after all night at the poker table. Sixty-year-old Chicago Tommy Hargan is there with his topknot of white hair pulled back over his little pink skull and a mountain of chips in front of his old caved-in sternum. Sixty-two-year-old Dallas Maxie Welch is there, fat and phlegmatic as an Indian Ocean potentate. Two Los Angeles biggies are there exhaling smoke from candela-green cigars into the gloom. It looks like the perfect vignette of every Big Time back room, "athletic club," snooker house and floating poker game in the history of the guys-and-dolls lumpen-bourgeoisie. But what is all this? Off to the side, at a rostrum, sits a flawless little creature with bouffant hair and Stridex-pure skin who looks like she is polished each morning with a rotary buffer. Before her on the rostrum is a globe of coffee on a hot coil. Her sole job is to keep the poker players warmed up with coffee. Meantime, numberless uniformed lackeys are cocked and aimed about the edges to bring the five Big Timers whatever else they might desire, cigarettes, drinks, napkins, eyeglass-cleaning tissues, plug-in telephones. All around the poker table, at a respectful distance of ten feet, is a fence with the most delicate golden pickets. Upon it, even at this narcoleptic hour, lean men and women in their best clothes watching the combat of the titans. The scene is the charmed circle of the casino of the Dunes Hotel. As everyone there knows, or believes, these fabulous men are playing for table stakes of fifteen or twenty thousand dollars. One hundred dollars rides on a chip. Mandibles gape at the progress of the battle. And now Sid Wyman, who is also a vice-president of the Dunes, is at a small escritoire just inside the golden fence signing a stack of vouchers for such sums as $4500, all printed in the heavy Mondrianesque digits of a Burroughs business check-making machine. It is as if America's guys-and-dolls gamblers have somehow been tapped upon the shoulders, knighted, initiated into a new aristocracy.

Las Vegas has become, just as Bugsy Siegel dreamed, the American Monte Carlo—without any of the inevitable upper-class baggage of the Riviera casinos. At Monte Carlo there is still the plush mustiness of the 19th century noble lions—of Baron Bleich-roden, a big winner at roulette who always said, "My dear friends, it is so easy on Black." Of Lord Jersey, who won seventeen maxi-mum bets in a row—on black, as a matter of fact—nodded to the croupier, and said, "Much obliged, old sport, old sport," took his winnings to England, retired to the country and never gambled again in his life. Or of the old Duc de Dinc who said he could win only in the high-toned Club Privé, and who won very heavily one night, saw two Englishmen gaping at his good fortune, threw them every mille-franc note he had in his hands and said, "Here. English-men without money are altogether odious." Thousands of Euro-peans from the lower orders now have the money to go to the Riviera, but they remain under the century-old status pall of the aristocracy. At Monte Carlo there are still Wrong Forks, Deficient Accents, Poor Tailoring, Gauche Displays, Nouveau Richness, Cul-tural Aridity—concepts unknown in Las Vegas. For the grand debut of Monte Carlo as a resort in 1879 the architect Charles Garnier designed an opera house for the Place du Casino; and Sarah Bern-hardt read a symbolic poem. For the debut of Las Vegas as a resort in 1946 Bugsy Siegel hired Abbott and Costello, and there, in a way, you have it all.

I am in the office of Major A. Riddle—Major is his name—the president of the Dunes Hotel. He combs his hair straight back and wears a heavy gold band on his little finger with a diamond sunk into it. As everywhere else in Las Vegas, someone has turned on the air conditioning to the point where it will be remembered, all right, as Las Vegas-style air conditioning. Riddle has an appoint-ment to see a doctor at 4:30 about a crimp in his neck. His secre-tary, Maude McBride, has her head down and is rubbing the back of her neck. Lee Fisher, the P.R. man, and I are turning ours from time to time to keep the pivots from freezing up. Riddle is telling me about "the French war" and moving his neck gingerly. The Stardust bought and imported a version of the Lido de Paris spec-tacular, and the sight of all those sequined giblets pooning around on flamingo legs inflamed the tourists. The Tropicana fought back with the Folies Bergère, the New Frontier installed "Paree Ooh La La," the Hacienda reached for the puppets "Les Poupées de Paris," and the Silver Slipper called in Lili St. Cyr, the stripper, which was going French after a fashion. So the Dunes has bought up the third and last of the great Paris girlie shows, the Casino de Paris.

Lee Fisher says, "And we're going to do things they *can't* top. In this town you've got to move ahead in quantum jumps."

Quantum? But exactly! The beauty of the Dunes' Casino de Paris show is that it will be beyond art, beyond dance, beyond spectacle, even beyond the titillations of the winking crotch. The Casino de Paris will be a behemoth piece of American calculus, like Project Mercury.

"This show alone will cost us two and a half million a year to operate and one and a half million to produce," Major A. Riddle is saying. "The costumes alone will be fantastic. There'll be more than five hundred costumes and—well, they'll be fantastic.

"And this machine—by the time we get through expanding the stage, this machine will cost us $250,000."

"Machine?"

"Yes. Sean Kenny is doing the staging. The whole set moves electronically right in front of your eyes. He used to work with this fellow Lloyd Wright."

"Frank Lloyd Wright?"

"Yes. Kenny did the staging for *Blitz*. Did you see it? Fantastic. Well, it's all done electronically. They built this machine for us in Glasgow, Scotland, and it's being shipped here right now. It moves all over the place and creates smoke and special effects. We'll have everything. You can stage a bombardment with it. You'll think the whole theatre is blowing up.

"You'll have to program it. They had to use the same mechanism that's in the Skybolt Missile to build it. It's called a 'Celson' or something like that. That's how complicated this thing is. They have to have the same thing as the Skybolt Missile."

As Riddle speaks, one gets a wonderful picture of sex riding the crest of the future. Whole tableaux of bare-bottomed Cosmonaughties will be hurtling around the Casino de Paris Room of the Dunes Hotel at fantastic speed in elliptical orbits, a flash of the sequined giblets here, a blur of the black-rimmed decal eyes there, a wink of the crotch here and there, until, with one vast Project Climax for our times, Sean Kenny, who used to work with this fellow Frank Lloyd Wright, presses the red button and the whole yahooing harem, shrieking ooh-la-la amid the din, exits in a mushroom cloud.

The allure is most irresistible not to the young but the old. No one in Las Vegas will admit it—it is not the modern, glamorous notion—but Las Vegas is a resort for old people. In those last years, before the tissue deteriorates and the wires of the cerebral cortex hang in the skull like a clump of dried seaweed, they are seeking liberation.

At eight o'clock Sunday morning it is another almost boringly sunny day in the desert, and Clara and Abby, both about sixty, and their husbands, Earl, sixty-three, and Ernest, sixty-four, come squinting out of the Mint Casino onto Fremont Street.

"I don't know what's wrong with me," Abby says. "Those last three drinks, I couldn't even feel them. It was just like drinking fizz. You know what I mean?"

"Hey," says Ernest, "how about that place back 'ere? We ain't been back 'ere. Come on."

The others are standing there on the corner, squinting and looking doubtful. Abby and Clara have both entered old babehood. They have that fleshy, humped-over shape across the back of the shoulders. Their torsos are hunched up into fat little loaves supported by bony, atrophied leg stems sticking up into their hummocky hips. Their hair has been fried and dyed into improbable designs.

"You know what I mean? After a while it just gives me gas," says Abby. "I don't even feel it."

"Did you see me over there?" says Earl. "I was just going along, nice and easy, not too much, just riding along real nice. You know? And then, boy, I don't know what happened to me. First thing I know I'm laying down fifty dollars. . . ."

Abby lets out a great belch. Clara giggles.

"Gives me gas," Abby says mechanically.

"Hey, how about that place back 'ere?" says Ernest.

". . . Just nice and easy as you please. . . ."

". . . get me all fizzed up. . . ."

"Aw, come on. . . ."

And there at eight o'clock Sunday morning stand four old parties from Albuquerque, New Mexico, up all night, squinting at the sun, belching from a surfeit of tall drinks at eight o'clock Sunday morning, and—marvelous!—there is no one around to snigger at what an old babe with decaying haunches looks like in Capri pants with her heels jacked up on decorated wedgies.

"Where do we *come* from?" Clara said to me, speaking for the first time since I approached them on Fremont Street. "He wants to know where we come from. I think it's past your bedtime, sweets."

"Climb the stairs and go to bed," said Abby.

Laughter all around.

"Climb the stairs" was Abby's finest line. At present there are almost no stairs to climb in Las Vegas. Avalon homes are soon to go up, advertising "Two-Story Homes!" as though this were an incredibly lavish and exotic concept. As I talked to Clara, Abby, Earl and Ernest, it came out that "climb the stairs" was a phrase they brought along to Albuquerque with them from Marshalltown, Iowa, those many years ago, along with a lot of other baggage, such as the entire cupboard of Protestant taboos against drinking, lusting, gambling, staying out late, getting up late, loafing, idling, lollygagging around the streets and wearing Capri pants—all designed to deny a person short-term pleasures so he will center his energies on bigger, long-term goals.

"We was in 'ere"—the Mint—"a couple of hours ago, and that old boy was playing the guitar, you know, 'Walk right in, set right down,' and I kept hearing an old song I haven't heard for twenty years. It has this little boy and his folks keep telling him it's late and he has to go to bed. He keeps saying, 'Don't make me go to bed and I'll be good.' Am I *good*, Earl? Am I *good?*"

The liberated cortex in all its glory is none other than the old babes at the slot machines. Some of them are tourists whose husbands said, *Here is fifty bucks, go play the slot machines*, while they themselves went off to more complex pleasures. But most of these old babes are part of the permanent landscape of Las Vegas. In they go to the Golden Nugget or the Mint, with their Social Security check or their pension check from the Ohio telephone company, cash it at the casino cashier's, pull out the Dixie Cup and the Iron Boy work glove, disappear down a row of slots and get on with it. I remember particularly talking to another Abby—a widow, sixty-two years old, built short and up from the bottom like a fire hydrant. After living alone for twelve years in Canton, Ohio, she had moved out to Las Vegas to live with her daughter and her husband, who worked for the Army.

"They were wonderful about it," she said. "Perfect hypocrites. She kept saying, you know, 'Mother, we'd be delighted to have you, only we don't think you'll *like* it. It's practically a fron*tier* town,' she says. 'It's so *ga*rish,' she says. So I said, I told her, 'Well, if you'd rather I didn't come. . . .' 'Oh, no!' she says. I wish I could have heard what her husband was saying. He calls me 'Mother.' '*Mother*,' he says. Well, once I was here, they figured, well, I *might* make a good baby-sitter and dishwasher and duster and mopper. The children are nasty little things. So one day I was in town for something or other and I just played a slot machine. It's fun—I can't describe it to you. I suppose I lose. I lose a little. And *they* have fits about it. 'For God's sake, Grandmother,' and so forth. They always say '*Grand*mother' when I am supposed to 'act my age' or crawl through a crack in the floor. Well, I'll tell you, the slot machines are a *whole lot* better than sitting in that little house all day. They kind of get you; I can't explain it."

The childlike megalomania of gambling is, of course, from the same cloth as the megalomania of the town. And, as the children of the liberated cortex, the old guys and babes are running up and down the Strip around the clock like everybody else. It is not by chance that much of the entertainment in Las Vegas, especially the second-stringers who perform in the cocktail lounges, will recall for an aging man what was glamorous twenty-five years ago when he had neither the money nor the freedom of spirit to indulge himself in it. In the big theatre-dining room at the Desert Inn, The Painted Desert Room, Eddie Fisher's act is on and he is saying cozily to a florid guy at a table right next to the stage, "Manny, you know you shouldn'a sat this close—you know you're in for it now, Manny, baby," while Manny beams with fright. But in the cocktail lounge, where the idea is chiefly just to keep the razzle-dazzle going, there is Hugh Farr, one of the stars of another era in the West, composer of two of the five Western songs the Library of Congress has taped for posterity, "Cool Water" and "Tumbling Tumbleweed," when he played the violin for the Sons of the Pioneers. And now around the eyes he looks like an aging Chinese savant, but he is wearing a white tuxedo and powder-blue leather boots and playing his sad old Western violin with an electric cord plugged in it for a group called The Country Gentlemen. And there is Ben Blue, looking like a waxwork exhibit of vaudeville, doffing his straw skimmer to reveal the sculptural qualities of his skull. And down at the Flamingo cocktail lounge—Ella Fitzgerald is in the main room—there is Harry James, looking old and pudgy in one of those toy Italian-style show-biz suits. And the Ink Spots are at the New Frontier and Louis Prima is at the Sahara, and the old parties are seeing it all, roaring through the dawn into the next day, until the sun seems like a par lamp fading in and out. The casinos, the bars, the liquor stores are open every minute of every day, like a sempiternal wading pool for the childhood ego. ". . . Don't make me go to bed. . . ."

Finally the casualties start piling up. I am in the manager's office of a hotel on the Strip. A man and his wife, each about sixty, are in there, raging. Someone got into their room and stole seventy dollars from her purse, and they want the hotel to make it up to them. The man pops up and down from a chair and ricochets back and forth across the room, flailing his great pig's-knuckle elbows about.

"What kind of security you call that? Walk right in the goddern room and just help themselves. And where do you think I found your security man? Back around the corner reading a god-dern detective magazine!"

He had scored a point there, but he was wearing a striped polo shirt with a hip Hollywood solid-color collar, and she had on Capri pants, and hooked across their wrinkly old faces they both had rimless, wraparound French sunglasses of the sort young-punk heroes in *nouvelle vague* movies wear, and it was impossible to give any earnest contemplation to a word they said. They seemed to have the great shiny popeyes of a praying mantis.

"Listen, Mister," she is saying, "I don't care about the seventy bucks. I'd lose seventy bucks at your craps table and I wouldn't think nothing of it. I'd play seventy bucks just like that, and it wouldn't mean nothing. I wouldn't regret it. But when they can just walk in—and you don't give a damn—for Christ's sake!"

They are both zeroing in on the manager with their great insect corneas. The manager is a cool number in a white-on-white shirt and silver tie.

"This happened three days ago. Why didn't you tell us about it then?"

"Well, I was gonna be a nice guy about it. Seventy dollars," he said, as if it would be difficult for the brain to grasp a sum much smaller. "But then I found your man back there reading a god-dern detective magazine. *True Detectives* it was. Had a picture on the front of some floozie with one leg up on a chair and her garter showing. Looked like a god-derned athlete's-foot ad. Boy, I went into a slow burn. But when I am burned up, I am *burned up!* You get me, Mister? There he was, reading the god-derned *True Detectives*."

"Any decent hotel would have insurance," she says.

The manager says, "I don't know a hotel in the world that offers insurance against theft."

"Hold on, Mister," he says, "are you calling my wife a liar? You just get smart, and I'm gonna pop you one! I'll pop you one right now if you call my wife a liar."

At this point the manager lowers his head to one side and looks up at the old guy from under his eyebrows with a version of the Red Hook brush-off, and the old guy begins to cool off.

But others are beyond cooling off. Hornette Reilly, a buttery hipped whore from New York City, is lying in bed with a bald-headed guy from some place who has skin like oatmeal. He is asleep or passed out or something. Hornette is relating all this to the doctor over the Princess telephone by the bed.

"Look," she says, "I'm breaking up. I can't tell you how much I've drunk. About a bottle of brandy since four o'clock, I'm not kidding. I'm in bed with a guy. Right this minute. I'm talking on the telephone to you and this slob is lying here like an animal. He's all fat and his skin looks like oatmeal—what's happening to me? I'm going to take some more pills. I'm not kidding, I'm breaking up. I'm going to kill myself. You've got to put me in Rose de Lima.

I'm breaking up, and I don't even know what's happening to me."

"So naturally you want to go to Rose de Lima."

"Well, yeah."

"You can come by the office, but I'm not sending you to Rose de Lima."

"Doctor, I'm not kidding."

"I don't doubt that you're sick, old girl, but I'm not sending you to Rose de Lima to sober up."

The girls do not want to go to the County Hospital. They want to go to Rose de Lima, where the psychiatric cases receive milieu therapy. The patients dress in street clothes, socialize and play games with the staff, eat well and relax in the sun, all paid for by the State. One of the folk heroines of the Las Vegas floozies, apparently, is the call girl who last year was spending Monday through Friday at Rose de Lima and "turning out," as they call it, Saturdays and Sundays on the Strip, to the tune of $200 to $300 a weekend. She looks upon herself not as a whore, or even a call girl, but as a lady of assignation. When some guy comes to the Strip and unveils the little art-nouveau curves in his psyche and calls for two girls to perform arts upon one another, this one consents to be the passive member of the team only. A Rose de Lima girl, she draws the line.

At the County Hospital the psychiatric ward is latched, bolted, wired up and jammed with patients who are edging along the walls in the inner hall, the only place they have to take a walk other than the courtyard.

A big brunette with the remnants of a beehive hairdo and decal eyes and an obvious pregnancy is the liveliest of the lot. She is making eyes at everyone who walks in. She also nods gaily toward vacant places along the wall.

"Mrs. —— is refusing medication," a nurse tells one of the psychiatrists. "She won't even open her mouth."

Presently the woman, in a white hospital tunic, is led up the hall. She looks about fifty, but she has extraordinary lines on her face.

"Welcome home," says Dr. ——.

"This is not my home," she says.

"Well, as I told you before, it has to be for the time being."

"Listen, you didn't analyze me."

"Oh, yes. Two psychiatrists examined you—all over again."

"You mean that time in jail."

"Exactly."

"You can't tell anything from that. I was excited. I had been out on the Strip, and then all that stupid—"

Three-fourths of the 640 patients who clustered into the ward last year were casualties of the Strip or the Strip milieu of Las

Vegas, the psychiatrist tells me. He is a bright and energetic man in a shawl-collared black silk suit with brass buttons.

"I'm not even her doctor," he says. "I don't know her case. There's nothing I can do for her."

Here, securely out of sight in this little warren, are all those who have taken the loop-the-loop and could not stand the centripety. Some, like Raymond, who has been rocketing for days on pills and liquor, who has gone without sleep to the point of anoxia, might pull out of the toxic reaction in two or three days, or eight or ten. Others have conflicts to add to the chemical wackiness. A man who has thrown all his cash to the flabby homunculus who sits at every craps table stuffing the take down an almost hidden chute so it won't pile up in front of the customers' eyes; a man who has sold the family car for next to nothing at a car lot advertising "Cash for your car—*right now*" and then thrown that to the homunculus, too, but also still has the family waiting guiltlessly, guilelessly back home; well, he has troubles.

". . . After I came here and began doing personal studies," the doctor is saying, "I recognized extreme aggressiveness continually. It's not merely what Las Vegas can do to a person, it's the type of person it attracts. Gambling is a very aggressive pastime, and Las Vegas attracts aggressive people. They have an amazing capacity to louse up a normal situation."

The girl, probably a looker in more favorable moments, is pressed face into the wall, cutting glances at the doctor. The nurse tells her something and she puts her face in her hands, convulsing but not making a sound. She retreats to her room, and then the sounds come shrieking out. The doctor rushes back. Other patients are sticking their heads out of their rooms along the hall.

"The young girl?" a quiet guy says to a nurse. "The young girl," he says to somebody in the room.

But the big brunette just keeps rolling her decal eyes.

Out in the courtyard—all bare sand—the light is a kind of light-bulb twilight. An old babe is rocking herself back and forth on a straight chair and putting one hand out in front from time to time and pulling it in toward her bosom.

It seems clear enough to me. "A slot machine?" I say to the nurse, but she says there is no telling.

". . . and yet the same aggressive types are necessary to build a frontier town, and Las Vegas is a frontier town, certainly by any psychological standard," Dr. —— is saying. "They'll undertake anything and they'll accomplish it. The building here has been incredible. They don't seem to care what they're up against, so they do it."

I go out to the parking lot in back of the County Hospital and it doesn't take a second; as soon as I turn on the motor I'm swinging again with Action Checkpoint News, "Monkey No. 9," "Donna, Donna, the Prima Donna," and friendly picking and swinging for the Fremont Hotel and Frontier Federal. Me and my big white car are sailing down the Strip and the Boomerang Modern, Palette Curvilinear, Flash Gordon Ming-Alert Spiral, McDonald's Hamburger Parabola, Mint Casino Elliptical and Miami Beach Kidney sunbursts are exploding in the Young Electric Sign Company's Grand Gallery for all the sun kings. At the airport there was that bad interval between the rental-car stall and the terminal entrance, but once through the automatic door the Muzak came bubbling up with "Song of India." On the upper level around the ramps the slots were cranking away. They are placed like "traps," a word Las Vegas picked up from golf. And an old guy is walking up the ramp, just off the plane from Denver, with a huge plastic bag of clothes slung over the left shoulder and a two-suiter suitcase in his right hand. He has to put the suitcase down on the floor and jostle the plastic bag all up around his neck to keep it from falling, but he manages to dig into his pocket for a couple of coins and get going on the slot machines. All seems right, but walking out to my plane I sense that something is missing. Then I recall sitting in the cocktail lounge of the Dunes at 3 P.M. with Jack Heskett, district manager of the Federal Sign and Signal Corporation, and Marty Steinman, the sales manager, and Ted Blaney, a designer. They are telling me about the sign they are building for the Dunes to put up at the airport. It will be five thousand square feet of free-standing sign, done in flaming-lake red on burning-desert gold. The d—the D—alone in the word Dunes, written in Cyrillic modern, will be practically two stories high. An inset plexiglas display, the largest revolving, trivision plexiglas sign in the world, will turn and show first the Dunes, with its twenty-two-story addition, then the seahorse swimming pool, then the new golf course. The scimitar curves of the sign will soar to a huge roaring diamond at the very top. "You'll be able to see it from an airplane fifteen miles away," says Jack Heskett. "Fifty miles," says Lee Fisher. And it will be sixty-five feet up in the air—because the thing was, somebody was out at the airport and they noticed there was only one display to be topped. That was that shaft about sixty feet high with the lit-up globe and the beacon lights, which is to say, the control tower. Hell, you can only see that forty miles away. But exactly!

———

Tom Wolfe (1931–   ), *a former semi-pro ball player with a Yale Ph.D. in American Studies (1957), has collected some of his magazine articles in two books:* The Kandy-Kolored Tangerine-Flake Streamline Baby *(1965), and* The Pump House Gang *(1966). His most recent book,* Radical Chic and Mau-Mauing the Flak-Catchers *(1970) aims to get below the surface of the relationships between white liberals and black radicals. What he calls "the wowie!" style originated, according to his account, from lack of time to finish an* Esquire *article from his notes: "I just started recording it all and inside of a couple of hours, typing along like a madman."*

As you might expect, Wolfe's style has been attacked as "elaboration rather than development," leaving "facts unchecked, generalizations untested, allusions unverified." But his defenders praise "a hard core of perceptiveness" in his writing; "always he poses and bravely tries to answer the frustrating question 'What (if anything) does it all mean?'"

1. *The "Too Noisy" of the title echoes through the essay, particularly in the first parts. List the noises you are asked to hear, the discrete parts of "the accumulated sound" that Wolfe calls "part of something rare and rather grand. . . ." What does Wolfe want you to think about the noise? What assumptions does he point to when he says about the constant Muzak "It is as if there were a communal fear that someone, somewhere in Las Vegas, was going to be left with a totally vacant minute on his hands"?*

2. *From sound, Wolfe turns to sight. What particular art form distinguishes the appearance of Las Vegas? What drives the author to invent names for this art form: "Boomerang Modern," "McDonald's Hamburger Parabola," etc.? (Compare the invented names of colors: "scarlet-fever purple," "hospital-fruit-basket orange"). When Wolfe calls the originators of this sort of thing "designer-sculptor geniuses," how seriously are we to take him?*

3. *Wolfe is interested in showing the effects of Las Vegas on people. Notice the series of vignettes, like close-ups in a film: Raymond, Sheriff Gubser and the Lido de Paris troupe, the five poker players, Clara and Abby and Earl and Ernest, etc. What happens to people in this city? What are we told about the high-school girls, the construction workers, the Negroes? In what sense are the "old boys" and "old babes" "liberated"? Why is the last section of the essay located in a mad house?*

4. *Wolfe sees Las Vegas as a form of popular art, including various arts (such as architecture, and design), but expanding to a com-*

*plete vision of life. It is a vision that moves beyond Las Vegas:
"It is as if all the hip young suburban gals of America . . . have
convened in Las Vegas. . . ." What are the assumptions behind
this vision of life? What are the values that matter? What do
the sights and sounds impress upon us? In what ways is this a
comic-book world ("More and more they look like those wonderful old girls out of Flash Gordon")? How do the energy and
creativity of this world find expression?*

5. *Compare and contrast Harvey Cox's analysis of Playboy with
Tom Wolfe's of Las Vegas. Be careful to allow for obvious differences in topic and style, but examine closely the ways in
which both authors move below the surface description in order
to analyze assumptions and meaning.*

Randall Jarrell

A SAD HEART AT THE SUPERMARKET

The Emperor Augustus would sometimes say to his Senate: "Words fail me, my Lords; nothing I can say could possibly indicate the depth of my feelings in this matter." But in this matter of mass culture, the mass media, I am speaking not as an emperor but as a fool, a suffering, complaining, helplessly non-conforming poet-or-artist-of-a-sort, far off at the obsolescent rear of things; what I say will indicate the depth of my feelings and the shallowness and one-sidedness of my thoughts. If those English lyric poets who went mad during the eighteenth century had told you why the Age of Enlightenment was driving them crazy, it would have had a kind of documentary interest: what I say may have a kind of documentary interest. *The toad beneath the harrow knows/ Exactly where each tooth-point goes*: if you tell me that the field is being harrowed to grow grain for bread, and to create a world in which there will be no more famines, or toads either, I will say: "I know"; but let me tell you where the tooth-points go, and what the harrow looks like from below.

Advertising men, businessmen speak continually of *media* or *the media* or *the mass media*. One of their trade journals is named, simply, *Media*. It is an impressive word: one imagines Mephistopheles offering Faust *media that no man has ever known*; one feels, while the word is in one's ear, that abstract, overmastering powers, of a scale and intensity unimagined yesterday, are being offered one by the technicians who discovered and control them—offered, and at a price. The word has the clear fatal ring of that new world whose space we occupy so luxuriously and precariously; the world that produces mink stoles, rockabilly records, and tactical nuclear weapons by the million; the world that Attila, Galileo, Hansel and Gretel never knew.

And yet, it's only the plural of *medium*. "*Medium*," says the dictionary, "that which lies in the middle; hence, middle condition or degree . . . A substance through which a force acts or an effect is transmitted . . . That through or by which anything is accomplished; as, an advertising *medium* . . . *Biol.* A nutritive mixture or substance, as broth, gelatin, agar, for cultivating bacteria, fungi, etc."

Let us name *our* trade journal *The Medium*. For all these media —television, radio, movies, newspapers, magazines, and the rest— are a single medium, in whose depths we are all being cultivated. This Medium is of middle condition or degree, mediocre; it lies in the middle of everything, between a man and his neighbor, his wife, his child, his self; it, more than anything else, is the substance through which the forces of our society act upon us, and make us into what our society needs.

And what does it need? For us to need.

Oh, it needs for us to do or be many things: workers, technicians, executives, soldiers, housewives. But first of all, last of all, it needs for us to be buyers; consumers; beings who want much and will want more—who want consistently and insatiably. Find some spell to make us turn away from the stoles, the records, and the weapons, and our world will change into something to us unimaginable. Find some spell to make us see that the product or service that yesterday was an unthinkable luxury today is an inexorable necessity, and our world will go on. It is the Medium which casts this spell—which is this spell. As we look at the television set, listen to the radio, read the magazines, the frontier of necessity is always being pushed forward. The Medium shows us what our new needs are—how often, without it, we should not have known!—and it shows us how they can be satisfied: they can be satisfied by buying something. The act of buying something is at the root of our world; if anyone wishes to paint the genesis of things in our society, he will paint a picture of God holding out to Adam a check-book or credit card or Charge-A-Plate.

But how quickly our poor naked Adam is turned into a consumer, is linked to others by the great chain of buying!

> No outcast he, bewildered and depressed:
> Along his infant veins are interfused
> The gravitation and the filial bond
> Of nature that connect him with the world.

Children of three or four can ask for a brand of cereal, sing some soap's commercial; by the time that they are twelve or thirteen they are not children but teen-age consumers, interviewed, graphed, analyzed. They are well on their way to becoming that ideal figure of our culture, the knowledgeable consumer. Let me define him: the knowledgeable consumer is someone who, when he comes to Weimar, knows how to buy a Weimaraner.

Daisy's voice sounded like money; everything about the knowl-

edgeable consumer looks like or sounds like or feels like money,
and informed money at that. To live is to consume, to understand
life is to know what to consume: he has learned to understand this,
so that his life is a series of choices—correct ones—among the products and services of the world. He is able to choose to consume
something, of course, only because sometime, somewhere, he or
someone else produced something—but just when or where or
what no longer seems to us of as much interest. We may still go to
Methodist or Baptist or Presbyterian churches on Sunday, but the
Protestant ethic of frugal industry, of production for its own sake, is
gone.

Production has come to seem to our society not much more
than a condition prior to consumption. "The challenge of today,"
an advertising agency writes, "is to make the consumer raise his
level of demand." This challenge has been met: the Medium has
found it easy to make its people feel the continually increasing
lacks, the many specialized dissatisfactions (merging into one great
dissatisfaction, temporarily assuaged by new purchases) that it needs
for them to feel. When in some magazine we see the Medium at its
most nearly perfect, we hardly know which half is entertaining and
distracting us, which half making us buy: some advertisement may
be more ingeniously entertaining than the text beside it, but it is
the text which has made us long for a product more passionately.
When one finishes *Holiday* or *Harper's Bazaar* or *House and Garden*
or *The New Yorker* or *High Fidelity* or *Road and Track* or—but
make your own list—buying something, going somewhere seems a
necessary completion to the act of reading the magazine.

Reader, isn't buying or fantasy-buying an important part of your
and my emotional life? (If you reply, *No*, I'll think of you with bitter envy as more than merely human; as deeply un-American.) It is
a standard joke that when a woman is bored or sad she buys something, to cheer herself up; but in this respect we are all women
together, and can hear complacently the reminder of how feminine
this consumer-world of ours has become. One imagines as a characteristic dialogue of our time an interview in which someone is
asking of a vague gracious figure, a kind of Mrs. America: "But
while you waited for the intercontinental ballistic missiles what did
you *do?*" She answers: "I bought things."

She reminds one of the sentinel at Pompeii—a space among
ashes, now, but at his post: she too did what she was supposed to
do. Our society has delivered us—most of us—from the bonds of
necessity, so that we no longer struggle to find food to keep from
starving, clothing and shelter to keep from freezing; yet if the ends
for which we work and of which we dream are only clothes and
restaurants and houses, possessions, consumption, how have we es-

caped?—we have exchanged man's old bondage for a new voluntary one. It is more than a figure of speech to say that the consumer is trained for his job of consuming as the factory-worker is trained for his job of producing; and the first can be a longer, more complicated training, since it is easier to teach a man to handle a tool, to read a dial, than it is to teach him to ask, always, for a name-brand aspirin —to want, someday, a stand-by generator.

What is that? You don't know? I used not to know, but the readers of *House Beautiful* all know, so that now I know. It is the electrical generator that stands in the basement of the suburban house-owner, shining, silent, till at last one night the lights go out, the furnace stops, the freezer's food begins to—

Ah, but it's frozen for good, the lights are on forever; the owner has switched on the stand-by generator.

But you don't see that he really needs the generator, you'd rather have seen him buy a second car? He has two. A second bathroom? He has four. When the People of the Medium doubled everything, he doubled everything; and now that he's gone twice round he will have to wait three years, or four, till both are obsolescent—but while he waits there are so many new needs that he can satisfy, so many things a man can buy. "Man wants but little here below/ Nor wants that little long," said the poet; what a lie! Man wants almost unlimited quantities of almost everything, and he wants it till the day he dies.

Sometimes in *Life* or *Look* we see a double-page photograph of some family standing on the lawn among its possessions: station-wagon, swimming-pool, power-cruiser, sports-car, tape-recorder, television sets, radios, cameras, power lawn-mower, garden tractor, lathe, barbecue-set, sporting equipment, domestic appliances—all the gleaming, grotesquely imaginative paraphernalia of its existence. It was hard to get everything on two pages, soon it will need four. It is like a dream, a child's dream before Christmas; yet if the members of the family doubt that they are awake, they have only to reach out and pinch something. The family seems pale and small, a negligible appendage, beside its possessions; only a human being would need to ask: "Which owns which?" We are fond of saying that something is not just something but "a way of life"; this too is a way of life—our way, the way.

Emerson, in his spare stony New England, a few miles from Walden, could write: "Things are in the saddle/ And ride mankind." He could say more now: that they are in the theater and studio, and entertain mankind; are in the pulpit and preach to mankind. The values of business, in a business society like our own, are reflected in every sphere: values which agree with them are reinforced, values which disagree are cancelled out or have lip service paid to them. In business what sells is good, and that's the end of it—that is what *good* means; if the world doesn't beat a path to your door, your mouse-trap wasn't better. The values of the Medium—which is both a popular business itself and the cause of popularity in other businesses—are business values: money, success, celebrity. If we are representative members of our society, the Medium's values are ours; and even if we are unrepresentative, nonconforming, our hands are—too often—subdued to the element they work in, and our unconscious expectations are all that we consciously reject. Darwin said that he always immediately wrote down evidence against a theory because otherwise, he'd noticed, he would forget it; in the same way, we keep forgetting the existence of those poor and unknown failures whom we might rebelliously love and admire.

If you're so smart why aren't you rich? is the ground-bass of our society, a grumbling and quite unanswerable criticism, since the society's non-monetary values *are* directly convertible into money. Celebrity turns into testimonials, lectures, directorships, presidencies, the capital gains of an autobiography *Told To* some professional ghost who photographs the man's life as Bachrach photographs his body. I read in the newspapers a lyric and perhaps exaggerated instance of this direct conversion of celebrity into money: his son accompanied Adlai Stevenson on a trip to Russia, took snapshots of his father, and sold them (to accompany his father's account of the trip) to *Look* for $20,000. When Liberace said that his critics' unfavorable reviews hurt him so much that he cried all the way to the bank, one had to admire the correctness and penetration of his press-agent's wit—in another age, what might not such a man have become!

Our culture is essentially periodical: we believe that all that is deserves to perish and to have something else put in its place. We speak of planned obsolescence, but it is more than planned, it is felt; is an assumption about the nature of the world. We feel that the present is better and more interesting, more real, than the past, and that the future will be better and more interesting, more real, than the present; but, consciously, we do not hold against the present its prospective obsolescence. Our standards have become to an astonishing degree the standards of what is called the world of fashion, where mere timeliness—being orange in orange's year, violet in violet's—is the value to which all other values are reducible. In our society the word *old-fashioned* is so final a condemnation that someone like Norman Vincent Peale can say about atheism or agnosticism simply that it is old-fashioned; the homely recommendation of the phrase *Give me that good old-time religion* has become, after a few decades, the conclusive rejection of the phrase *old-fashioned atheism.*

All this is, at bottom, the opposite of the world of the arts, where commercial and scientific progress do not exist; where the bone of Homer and Mozart and Donatello is there, always, under the mere blush of fashion; where the past—the remote past, even—is responsible for the way that we understand, value, and act in, the present. (When one reads an abstract expressionist's remark that Washington studios are "eighteen months behind" those of his colleagues in New York, one realizes something of the terrible power of business and fashion over those most overtly hostile to them.) An artist's work and life presuppose continuing standards, values extended over centuries or millennia, a future that is the continuation and modification of the past, not its contradiction or irrelevant replacement. He is working for the time that wants the best that he can do: the present, he hopes—but if not that, the future. If he sees that fewer and fewer people are any real audience for the serious artists of the past, he will feel that still fewer are going to be an audience for the serious artists of the present: for those who, willingly or unwillingly, sacrifice extrinsic values to intrinsic ones, immediate effectiveness to that steady attraction which, the artist hopes, true excellence will always exert.

The past's relation to the artist or man of culture is almost the opposite of its relation to the rest of our society. To him the present is no more than the last ring on the trunk, understandable and valuable only in terms of all the earlier rings. The rest of our society sees only that great last ring, the enveloping surface of the trunk; what's underneath is a disregarded, almost mythical foundation. When Northrop Frye writes that "the preoccupation of the humanities with the past is sometimes made a reproach against them by those who forget that we face the past: it may be shadowy, but it is all that is there," he is saying what for the artist or man of culture is self-evidently true. Yet for the Medium and the People of the Medium it is as self-evidently false: for them the present—or a past so recent, so quick-changing, so soon-disappearing, that it might be called the specious present—is all that is there.

In the past our culture's body of common knowledge—its frame of reference, its possibility of comprehensible allusion—changed slowly and superficially; the amount added to it or taken away from it, in any ten years, was surprisingly small. Now in any ten years a surprisingly large proportion of the whole is replaced. Most of the information people have in common is something that four or five years from now they will not even remember having known. A newspaper story remarks in astonishment that television quiz-programs "have proved that ordinary citizens can be conversant with such esoterica as jazz, opera, the Bible, Shakespeare, poetry, and fisticuffs." You may exclaim: "Esoterica! If the Bible and Shakespeare are esoterica, what is there that's common knowledge?" The answer, I suppose, is that Elfrida von Nordroff and Teddy Nadler—the ordinary citizens on the quiz-programs—are common knowledge; though not for long. Songs disappear in two or three months, celebrities in two or three years; most of the Medium is little felt and soon forgotten. Nothing is as dead as day-before-yesterday's newspaper, the next-to-the-last number on the roulette wheel; but most of the knowledge people have in common and lose in common is knowledge of such newspapers, such numbers. Yet the novelist or poet or dramatist, when he moves a great audience, depends upon the deep feelings, the living knowledge, that the people of that audience share; if so much has become contingent, superficial, ephemeral, it is disastrous for him.

New products and fashions replace the old, and the fact that they replace them is proof enough of their superiority. Similarly, the Medium does not need to show that the subjects which fill it are interesting or timely or important; the fact that they are its subjects makes them so. If *Time, Life,* and the television shows are full of Tom Fool this month, he's no fool. And when he has been gone from them a while, we do not think him a fool—we do not think of him at all. He no longer exists, in the fullest sense of the word *exist:* to be is to be perceived, to be a part of the Medium of our perception. Our celebrities are not kings, romantic in exile, but Representatives who, defeated, are forgotten; they had, always, only the qualities that we delegated to them.

After driving for four or five minutes along the road outside my door, I come to a row of one-room shacks about the size of kitchens, made out of used boards, metal signs, old tin roofs. To the people who live in them an electric dishwasher of one's own is as much a fantasy as an ocean liner of one's own. But since the Medium (and those whose thought is molded by it) does not perceive them, these people are themselves a fantasy. No matter how many millions of such exceptions to the general rule there are, they do not really exist, but have a kind of anomalous, statistical subsistence; our moral and imaginative view of the world is no more affected by them than by the occupants of some home for the mentally deficient a little farther along the road. If some night one of these out-moded, economically deficient ghosts should scratch at my window, I could say only: "Come back twenty or thirty years ago." And if I myself, as an old-fashioned, one-room poet, a friend of "quiet culture," a "meek lover of the good," should go out some night to scratch at another window, shouldn't I hear someone's indifferent or regretful: "Come back a century or two ago"?

When those whose existence the Medium recognizes ring the

chimes of the writer's doorbell, fall through his letter-slot, float out onto his television-screen, what is he to say to them? A man's unsuccessful struggle to get his family food is material for a work of art—for tragedy, almost; his unsuccessful struggle to get his family a stand-by generator is material for what? Comedy? Farce? Comedy on such a scale, at such a level, that our society and its standards seem, almost, farce? And yet it is the People of the Medium—those who struggle for and get, or struggle for and don't get, the generator—whom our society finds representative: they are there, there primarily, there to be treated first of all. How shall the artist treat them? And the Medium itself—an end of life and a means of life, something essential to people's understanding and valuing of their existence, something many of their waking hours are spent listening to or looking at—how is *it* to be treated as subject-matter for art? The artist cannot merely reproduce it; should he satirize or parody it? But by the time the artist's work reaches its audience, the portion of the Medium which it satirized will already have been forgotten; and parody is impossible, often, when so much of the Medium is already an unintentional parody. (Our age might be defined as the age in which real parody became impossible, since any parody had already been duplicated, or parodied, in earnest.) Yet the Medium, by now, is an essential part of its watchers. How can you explain those whom Mohammedans call the People of the Book in any terms that omit the Book? We are people of the television-set, the magazine, the radio, and are inexplicable in any terms that omit them.

Oscar Wilde said that Nature imitates Art, that before Whistler painted them there were no fogs along the Thames. If his statement were not false, it would not be witty. But to say that Nature imitates Art, when the Nature is human nature and the Art that of television, radio, motion-pictures, magazines, is literally true. The Medium shows its People what life is, what people are, and its People believe it: expect people to be that, try themselves to be that. Seeing is believing; and if what you see in *Life* is different from what you see in life, which of the two are you to believe? For many people it is what you see in *Life* (and in the movies, over television, on the radio) that is real life; and everyday existence, mere local or personal variation, is not real in the same sense.

The Medium mediates between us and raw reality, and the mediation more and more replaces reality for us. Many radio-stations have a news-broadcast every hour, and many people like and need to hear it. In many houses either the television set or the radio is turned on during most of the hours the family is awake. It is as if they longed to be established in reality, to be reminded continually of the "real," "objective" world—the created world of the Medium

––rather than to be left at the mercy of actuality, of the helpless contingency of the world in which the radio-receiver or television set is sitting. And surely we can sympathize: which of us hasn't found a similar refuge in the "real," created world of Cézanne or Goethe or Verdi? Yet Dostoievsky's world is too different from Wordsworth's, Piero della Francesca's from Goya's, Bach's from Wolf's, for us to be able to substitute one homogeneous mediated reality for everyday reality in the belief that it *is* everyday reality. For many watchers, listeners, readers, the world of events and celebrities and performers—the Great World—has become the world of primary reality: how many times they have sighed at the colorless unreality of their own lives and families, and sighed for the bright reality of, say, Elizabeth Taylor's. The watchers call the celebrities by their first names, approve or disapprove of "who they're dating," handle them with a mixture of love, identification, envy, and contempt. But however they handle them, they *handle* them: the Medium has given everyone so terrible a familiarity with everyone that it takes great magnanimity of spirit not to be affected by it. These celebrities are not heroes to us, their valets.

Better to have these real ones play themselves, and not sacrifice too much of their reality to art; better to have the watcher play himself, and not lose too much of himself in art. Usually the watcher is halfway between two worlds, paying full attention to neither: half distracted from, half distracted by, this distraction; and able for the moment not to be too greatly affected, have too great demands made upon him, by either world. For in the Medium, which we escape to from work, nothing is ever *work*, makes intellectual or emotional or imaginative demands which we might find it difficult to satisfy. Here in the half-world everything is homogeneous—is, as much as possible, the same as everything else: each familiar novelty, novel familiarity has the same treatment on top and the same attitude and conclusion at bottom; only the middle, the particular subject of the particular program or article, is different. If it *is* different: everyone is given the same automatic "human interest" treatment, so that it is hard for us to remember, unnecessary for us to remember, which particular celebrity we're reading about this time—often it's the same one, we've just moved on to a different magazine.

Francesco Caraccioli said that the English have a hundred religions and one sauce; so do we; and we are so accustomed to this sauce or dye or style of presentation, the aesthetic equivalent of Standard Brands, that a very simple thing can seem obscure or perverse without it. And, too, we find it hard to have to shift from one genre to another, to vary our attitudes and expectations, to use our unexercised imaginations. Poetry disappeared long ago, even for most intellectuals; each year fiction is a little less important. Our age is the age of articles: we buy articles in stores, read articles in magazines, exist among the interstices of articles: of columns, interviews, photographic essays, documentaries; of facts condensed into headlines or expanded into non-fiction best-sellers; of real facts about real people.

Art lies to us to tell us the (sometimes disquieting) truth. The Medium tells us truths, facts, in order to make us believe some reassuring or entertaining lie or half-truth. These actually existing celebrities, of universally admitted importance, about whom we are told directly authoritative facts—how can fictional characters compete with these? These *are* our fictional characters, our Lears and Clytemnestras. (This is ironically appropriate, since many of their doings and sayings are fictional, made up by public relations officers, columnists, agents, or other affable familiar ghosts.) And the Medium gives us such facts, such tape-recordings, such clinical reports not only about the great but also about (representative samples of) the small. When we have been shown so much about so many—*can* be shown, we feel, anything about anybody—does fiction seem so essential as it once seemed? Shakespeare or Tolstoy can show us all about someone, but so can *Life*; and when *Life* does, it's someone real.

The Medium is half life and half art, and competes with both life and art. It spoils its audience for both; spoils both for its audience. For the People of the Medium life isn't sufficiently a matter of success and glamor and celebrity, isn't entertaining enough, distracting enough, *mediated* enough; and art is too difficult or individual or novel, too much a matter of tradition and the past, too much a matter of special attitudes and aptitudes—its mediation sometimes is queer or excessive, and sometimes is not even recognizable as mediation. The Medium's mixture of rhetoric and reality, in which people are given what they know they want to be given in the form in which they know they want to be given it, is something more efficient and irresistible than any real art. If a man has all his life been fed a combination of marzipan and ethyl alcohol —if eating, to him, is a matter of being knocked unconscious by an ice cream soda—can he, by taking thought, come to prefer a diet of bread and wine, apples and well-water? Will a man who has spent his life watching gladiatorial games come to prefer listening to chamber music? And those who produce the bread and the wine and the quartets for him—won't they be tempted either to give up producing them, or else to produce a bread that's half sugar and half alcohol, a quartet that ends with the cellist at the violist's bleeding throat?

Any outsider who has worked for the Medium will have ob-

served that the one thing which seems to its managers most unnatural is for someone to do something naturally, to speak or write
as an individual speaking or writing to other individuals, and not
as a sub-contractor supplying a standardized product to the Medium. It is as if producers and editors and supervisors—middle
men—were particles forming a screen between maker and public,
one which will let through only particles of their own size and
weight (or as they say, the public's). As you look into their strained
puréed faces, their big horn-rimmed eyes, you despair of Creation
itself, which seems for the instant made in their own owl-eyed
image. There are so many extrinsic considerations involved in the
presentation of his work, the maker finds, that by the time it is
presented almost any intrinsic consideration has come to seem
secondary. No wonder that the professional who writes the ordinary
commercial success—the ordinary script, scenario, or best seller—
resembles imaginative writers less than he resembles editors, producers, executives. The supplier has come to resemble those he
supplies, and what he supplies them resembles both. With an
artist you never know what you will get; with him you know what
you will get. He is a reliable source for a standard product. He is
almost exactly the opposite of the imaginative artist: instead of
stubbornly or helplessly sticking to what he sees and feels—to what
is right for him, true to his reality, regardless of what the others
think and want—he gives the others what they think and want,
regardless of what he himself sees and feels.

The Medium represents, to the artist, all that he has learned not
to do: its sure-fire stereotypes seem to him what any true art, true
spirit, has had to struggle past on its way to the truth. The artist
sees the values and textures of this art-substitute replacing those
of his art, so far as most of society is concerned; conditioning the
expectations of what audience his art has kept. Mass culture either
corrupts or isolates the writer. His old feeling of oneness—of
speaking naturally to an audience with essentially similar standards
—is gone; and writers no longer have much of the consolatory feeling that took its place, the feeling of writing for the happy few,
the kindred spirits whose standards are those of the future. (Today
they feel: the future, should there be one, will be worse.) True
works of art are more and more produced away from or in opposition to society. And yet the artist needs society as much as society
needs him: as our cultural enclaves get smaller and drier, more hysterical or academic, one mourns for the artists inside and the public
outside. An incomparable historian of mass culture, Ernest van
den Haag, has expressed this with laconic force: "The artist who,
by refusing to work for the mass market, becomes marginal, cannot
create what he might have created had there been no mass market.

One may prefer a monologue to addressing a mass meeting. But it is still not a conversation."

Even if the rebellious artist's rebellion is whole-hearted, it can never be whole-stomach'd, whole-unconscious'd. Part of him wants to be like his kind, is like his kind; longs to be loved and admired and successful. Our society—and the artist, in so far as he is truly a part of it—has no place set aside for the different and poor and obscure, the fools for Christ's sake: they all go willy-nilly into Limbo. The artist is tempted, consciously, to give his society what it wants—or if he won't or can't, to give it nothing at all; is tempted, unconsciously, to give it superficially independent or contradictory works which are at heart works of the Medium. But it is hard for him to go on serving both God and Mammon when God is so really ill-, Mammon so really well-organized.

"Shakespeare wrote for the Medium of his day; if Shakespeare were alive now he'd be writing *My Fair Lady*; isn't *My Fair Lady*, then, our *Hamlet*? shouldn't you be writing *Hamlet* instead of sitting there worrying about your superego? I need my *Hamlet*!" So society speaks to the artist, reasons with the artist; and after he has written it its *Hamlet* it is satisfied, and tries to make sure that he will never do it again. There are many more urgent needs that it wants him to satisfy: to lecture to it; to be interviewed; to appear on television programs; to give testimonials; to attend book luncheons; to make trips abroad for the State Department; to judge books for Book Clubs; to read for publishers, judge for publishers, be a publisher for publishers; to edit magazines; to teach writing at colleges or conferences; to write scenarios or scripts or articles—articles about his home town for *Holiday*, about cats or clothes or Christmas for *Vogue*, about "How I Wrote *Hamlet*" for anything; to—

But why go on? I once heard a composer, lecturing, say to a poet, lecturing: "They'll pay us to do *anything*, so long as it isn't writing music or writing poems." I knew the reply that as a member of my society I should have made: "As long as they pay you, what do you care?" But I didn't make it: it was plain that they cared . . . But how many more learn not to care, to love what they once endured! It is a whole so comprehensive that any alternative seems impossible, any opposition irrelevant; in the end a man says in a small voice: "I accept the Medium." The Enemy of the People winds up as the People—but where there is no enemy, the people perish.

The climate of our culture is changing. Under these new rains, new suns, small things grow great, and what was great grows small; whole species disappear and are replaced. The American present is very different from the American past: so different that our awareness of the extent of the changes has been repressed, and we regard as ordinary what is extraordinary—ominous perhaps—both for us and for the rest of the world. The American present is many other peoples' future: our cultural and economic example is to much of the world mesmeric, and it is only its weakness and poverty that prevent it from hurrying with us into the Roman future. But at this moment of our power and success, our thought and art are full of a troubled sadness, of the conviction of our own decline. When the President of Yale University writes that "the ideal of the good life has faded from the educational process, leaving only miscellaneous prospects of jobs and joyless hedonism," are we likely to find it unfaded among our entertainers and executives? Is the influence of what I have called the Medium likely to lead us to any good life? to make us love and try to attain any real excellence, beauty, magnanimity? or to make us understand these as obligatory but transparent rationalizations behind which the realities of money and power are waiting?

The tourist Matthew Arnold once spoke about our green culture in terms that have an altered relevance—but are not yet irrelevant—to our ripe one. He said: "What really dissatisfies in American civilization is the want of the *interesting*, a want due chiefly to the want of those two great elements of the interesting, which are elevation and beauty." This use of *interesting*—and, perhaps, this tone of a curator pointing out what is plain and culpable—shows how far along in the decline of the West Arnold came: it is only in the latter days that we ask to be interested. He had found the word, he tells us, in Carlyle. Carlyle is writing to a friend to persuade him not to emigrate to the United States; he asks: "Could you banish yourself from all that is interesting to your mind, forget the history, the glorious institutions, the noble principles of old Scotland—that you might eat a better dinner, perhaps?" We smile, and feel like reminding Carlyle of the history, the glorious institutions, the noble principles of new America—of that New World which is, after all, the heir of the Old.

And yet . . . Can we smile as comfortably, today, as we could have smiled yesterday? Nor could we listen as unconcernedly, if on taking leave of us some other tourist should conclude, with the penetration and obtuseness of his kind:

"I remember reading somewhere: that which you inherit from your fathers you must earn in order to possess. I have been so much impressed with your power and your possessions that I have neglected, perhaps, your principles. The elevation or beauty of your spirit did not equal, always, that of your mountains and skyscrapers: it seems to me that your society provides you with 'all that is interesting to the mind' only exceptionally, at odd hours, in little reservations like those of your Indians. But as for your dinners, I've never seen anything like them: your daily bread comes *flambé*. And yet—wouldn't you say—the more dinners a man eats, the more comforts he possesses, the hungrier and more uncomfortable some part of him becomes: inside every fat man there is a man who is starving. Part of you is being starved to death, and the rest of you is being stuffed to death. But this will change: no one goes on being stuffed to death or starved to death forever.

"This is a gloomy, an equivocal conclusion? Oh yes, I come from an older culture, where things are accustomed to coming to such conclusions; where there is no last-paragraph fairy to bring one, always, a happy ending—or that happiest of all endings, no ending at all. And have I no advice to give you as I go? None. You are too successful to need advice, or to be able to take it if it were offered; but if ever you should fail, it is there waiting for you, the advice or consolation of all the other failures."

———

RANDALL JARRELL (1914–1965) *was a successful teacher, poet, novelist, and editor. He taught at Kenyon College, The University of Texas, Sarah Lawrence, Princeton, and the University of North Carolina; he served as consultant in poetry to the Library of Congress (1956–58); and he won the National Book Award in 1961 for his collection of poems and translations,* The Woman at the Washington Zoo *(1960). His academic novel,* Pictures From an Institution *(1954) is supposedly based on his experiences at Sarah Lawrence. He edited various volumes of poems and stories, wrote a children's book,* The Gingerbread Man *(1963), and served in an editorial capacity for* The Nation, Partisan Review, Yale Review, *and* American Scholar.

Though he was hardly the "old-fashioned, one-room poet" who speaks in this essay, his sense of himself as artist confronting a world unsympathetic to art is consistent in all his work.

1. *This is an essay lamenting the values and assumptions of a large segment of our society; as Jarrell says about planned obsolescence, "it is more than planned, it is felt; is an assumption about the nature of the world." List the particular assumptions Jarrell attributes to "the Medium and the People of the Medium."*

2. *Jarrell assumes the role of "fool" in the first paragraph, and speaks for the artist confronting popular art. What makes him, and, by extension, all real artists, "foolish" before "the Me-*

dium"? What are the assumptions Jarrell claims an artist must make about the nature of the world and his audience? How do these values conflict with the list you drew up for question 1?

3. Explain what Jarrell means when he says, "Art lies to us to tell us the (sometimes disquieting) truth. The Medium tells us truths, facts, in order to make us believe some reassuring or entertaining lie or half-truth."

4. In the second section of this text, another celebrated modern American poet writes about popular art. Look ahead to X. J. Kennedy's essay in praise of King Kong, and contrast his assumptions about popular art with Jarrell's.

5. Choose one or two advertisements from popular periodicals that make interesting assumptions about what Jarrell calls "the nature of the world." Describe the ad or ads you have chosen and demonstrate the assumptions they make and ask you to make. What would Jarrell's reaction to these ads probably be? What is your reaction?

John Updike

A & P

In walks these three girls in nothing but bathing suits. I'm in the third checkout slot, with my back to the door, so I don't see them until they're over by the bread. The one that caught my eye first was the one in the plaid green two-piece. She was a chunky kid, with a good tan and a sweet broad soft-looking can with those two crescents of white just under it, where the sun never seems to hit, at the top of the backs of her legs. I stood there with my hand on a box of HiHo crackers trying to remember if I rang it up or not. I ring it up again and the customer starts giving me hell. She's one of these cash-register-watchers, a witch about fifty with rouge on her cheekbones and no eyebrows, and I know it made her day to trip me up. She'd been watching cash registers for fifty years and probably never seen a mistake before.

By the time I got her feathers smoothed and her goodies into a bag—she gives me a little snort in passing, if she'd been born at the right time they would have burned her over in Salem—by the time I get her on her way the girls had circled around the bread and were coming back, without a pushcart, back my way along the counters, in the aisle between the checkouts and the Special bins. They didn't even have shoes on. There was this chunky one, with the two-piece—it was bright green and the seams on the bra were still sharp and her belly was still pretty pale so I guessed she just got it (the suit)—but there was this one, with one of those chubby berry-faces, the lips all bunched together under her nose, this one, and a tall one, with black hair that hadn't quite frizzed right, and one of these sunburns right across under the eyes, and a chin that was too long—you know, the kind of girl other girls think is very "striking" and "attractive" but never quite makes it, as they very well know, which is why they like her so much—and then the third one, that wasn't quite so tall. She was the queen. She kind of led them, the other two peeking around and making their shoulders round. She didn't look around, not this queen, she just walked straight on slowly, on these long white prima-donna legs. She came

Reprinted from *Pigeon Feathers and Other Stories*, by John Updike, by permission of Alfred A. Knopf, Inc. Copyright © 1962 by John Updike. This story first appeared in *The New Yorker*.

down a little hard on her heels, as if she didn't walk in her bare feet that much, putting down her heels and then letting the weight move along to her toes as if she was testing the floor with every step, putting a little deliberate extra action into it. You never know for sure how girls' minds work (do you really think it's a mind in there or just a little buzz like a bee in a glass jar?) but you got the idea she had talked the other two into coming in here with her, and now she was showing them how to do it, walk slow and hold yourself straight.

She had on a kind of dirty-pink—beige maybe, I don't know—bathing suit with a little nubble all over it and, what got me, the straps were down. They were off her shoulders looped loose around the cool tops of her arms, and I guess as a result the suit had slipped a little on her, so all around the top of the cloth there was this shining rim. If it hadn't been there you wouldn't have known there could have been anything whiter than those shoulders. With the straps pushed off, there was nothing between the top of the suit and the top of her head except just *her*, this clean bare plane of the top of her chest down from the shoulder bones like a dented sheet of metal tilted in the light. I mean, it was more than pretty.

She had sort of oaky hair that the sun and salt had bleached, done up in a bun that was unravelling, and a kind of prim face. Walking into the A & P with your straps down, I suppose it's the only kind of face you *can* have. She held her head so high her neck, coming up out of those white shoulders, looked kind of stretched, but I didn't mind. The longer her neck was, the more of her there was.

She must have felt in the corner of her eye me and over my shoulder Stokesie in the second slot watching, but she didn't tip. Not this queen. She kept her eyes moving across the racks, and stopped, and turned so slow it made my stomach rub the inside of my apron, and buzzed to the other two, who kind of huddled against her for relief, and then they all three of them went up the cat-and-dog-food-breakfast-cereal-macaroni-rice-raisins-seasonings spreads-spaghetti-soft-drinks-crackers-and-cookies aisle. From the third slot I look straight up this aisle to the meat counter, and I watched them all the way. The fat one with the tan sort of fumbled with the cookies, but on second thought she put the package back. The sheep pushing their carts down the aisle—the girls were walking against the usual traffic (not that we have one-way signs or anything)—were pretty hilarious. You could see them, when Queenie's white shoulders dawned on them, kind of jerk, or hop, or hiccup, but their eyes snapped back to their own baskets and on they pushed. I bet you could set off dynamite in an A & P and the people would by and large keep reaching and checking oatmeal off their lists and muttering "Let me see, there was a third thing, began with A, asparagus, no, ah, yes, applesauce!" or whatever it is they do mutter. But there was no doubt, this jiggled them. A few house-slaves in pin curlers even looked around after pushing their carts past to make sure what they had seen was correct.

You know, it's one thing to have a girl in a bathing suit down on the beach, where what with the glare nobody can look at each other much anyway, and another thing in the cool of the A & P, under the fluorescent lights, against all those stacked packages, with her feet paddling along naked over our checkerboard green-and-cream rubber-tile floor.

"Oh Daddy," Stokesie said beside me. "I feel so faint."

"Darling," I said. "Hold me tight." Stokesie's married, with two babies chalked up on his fuselage already, but as far as I can tell that's the only difference. He's twenty-two, and I was nineteen this April.

"Is it done?" he asks, the responsible married man finding his voice. I forgot to say he thinks he's going to be manager some sunny day, maybe in 1990 when it's called the Great Alexandrov and Petrooshki Tea Company or something.

What he meant was, our town is five miles from a beach, with a big summer colony out on the Point, but we're right in the middle of town, and the women generally put on a shirt or shorts or something before they get out of the car into the street. And anyway these are usually women with six children and varicose veins mapping their legs and nobody, including them, could care less. As I say, we're right in the middle of town, and if you stand at our front doors you can see two banks and the Congregational church and the newspaper store and three real-estate offices and about twenty-seven old freeloaders tearing up Central Street because the sewer broke again. It's not as if we're on the Cape; we're north of Boston and there's people in this town haven't seen the ocean for twenty years.

The girls had reached the meat counter and were asking Mc-Mahon something. He pointed, they pointed, and they shuffled out of sight behind a pyramid of Diet Delight peaches. All that was left for us to see was old McMahon patting his mouth and looking after them sizing up their joints. Poor kids, I began to feel sorry for them, they couldn't help it.

*   *   *

Now here comes the sad part of the story, at least my family says it's sad, but I don't think it's so sad myself. The store's pretty empty, it being Thursday afternoon, so there was nothing much to do except lean on the register and wait for the girls to show up

again. The whole store was like a pinball machine and I didn't know
which tunnel they'd come out of. After a while they come around
out of the far aisle, around the light bulbs, records at discount of
the Caribbean Six or Tony Martin Sings or some such gunk you
wonder they waste the wax on, sixpacks of candy bars, and plastic
toys done up in cellophane that fall apart when a kid looks at them
anyway. Around they come, Queenie still leading the way, and holding a little gray jar in her hand. Slots Three through Seven are
unmanned and I could see her wondering between Stokes and me,
but Stokesie with his usual luck draws an old party in baggy gray
pants who stumbles up with four giant cans of pineapple juice
(what do these bums *do* with all that pineapple juice? I've often
asked myself) so the girls come to me. Queenie puts down the jar
and I take it into my fingers icy cold. Kingfish Fancy Herring Snacks
in Pure Sour Cream: 49¢. Now her hands are empty, not a ring or
a bracelet, bare as God made them, and I wonder where the money's
coming from. Still with that prim look she lifts a folded dollar bill
out of the hollow at the center of her nubbled pink top. The jar
went heavy in my hand. Really, I thought that was so cute.

Then everybody's luck begins to run out. Lengel comes in from
haggling with a truck full of cabbages on the lot and is about to
scuttle into that door marked MANAGER behind which he hides all
day when the girls touch his eye. Lengel's pretty dreary, teaches
Sunday school and the rest, but he doesn't miss that much. He
comes over and says, "Girls, this isn't the beach."

Queenie blushes, though maybe it's just a brush of sunburn I
was noticing for the first time, now that she was so close. "My
mother asked me to pick up a jar of herring snacks." Her voice kind
of startled me, the way voices do when you see the people first,
coming out so flat and dumb yet kind of tony, too, the way it ticked
over "pick up" and "snacks." All of a sudden I slid right down her
voice into her living room. Her father and the other men were
standing around in ice-cream coats and bow ties and the women
were in sandals picking up herring snacks on toothpicks off a big
glass plate and they were all holding drinks the color of water with
olives and sprigs of mint in them. When my parents have somebody over they get lemonade and if it's a real racy affair Schlitz in
tall glasses with "They'll Do It Every Time" cartoons stencilled on.

"That's all right," Lengel said. "But this isn't the beach." His
repeating this struck me as funny, as if it had just occurred to him,
and he had been thinking all these years the A & P was a great big
dune and he was the head lifeguard. He didn't like my smiling—as
I say he doesn't miss much—but he concentrates on giving the girls
that sad Sunday-school-superintendent stare.

Queenie's blush is no sunburn now, and the plump one in

plaid, that I liked better from the back—a really sweet can—pipes
up, "We weren't doing any shopping. We just came in for the one
thing."

"That makes no difference," Lengel tells her, and I could see
from the way his eyes went that he hadn't noticed she was wearing
a two-piece before. "We want you decently dressed when you come
in here."

"We *are* decent," Queenie says suddenly, her lower lip pushing, getting sore now that she remembers her place, a place from
which the crowd that runs the A & P must look pretty crummy.
Fancy Herring Snacks flashed in her very blue eyes.

"Girls, I don't want to argue with you. After this come in here
with your shoulders covered. It's our policy." He turns his back.
That's policy for you. Policy is what the kingpins want. What the
others want is juvenile delinquency.

All this while, the customers had been showing up with their
carts but, you know, sheep, seeing a scene, they had all bunched up
on Stokesie, who shook open a paper bag as gently as peeling a
peach, not wanting to miss a word. I could feel in the silence everybody getting nervous, most of all Lengel, who asks me, "Sammy,
have you rung up their purchase?"

I thought and said "No" but it wasn't about that I was thinking.
I go through the punches, 4, 9, GROC, TOT—it's more complicated
than you think, and after you do it often enough, it begins to make
a little song, that you hear words to, in my case "Hello (*bing*) there,
you (*gung*) hap-py *pee*-pul (*splat*)!"—the *splat* being the drawer
flying out. I uncrease the bill, tenderly as you may imagine, it just
having come from between the two smoothest scoops of vanilla I
had ever known were there, and pass a half and a penny into her
narrow pink palm, and nestle the herrings in a bag and twist its
neck and hand it over, all the time thinking.

The girls, and who'd blame them, are in a hurry to get out, so
I say "I quit" to Lengel quick enough for them to hear, hoping
they'll stop and watch me, their unsuspected hero. They keep right
on going, into the electric eye; the door flies open and they flicker
across the lot to their car, Queenie and Plaid and Big Tall Goony-
Goony (not that as raw material she was so bad), leaving me with
Lengel and a kink in his eyebrow.

"Did you say something, Sammy?"

"I said I quit."

"I thought you did."

"You didn't have to embarrass them."

"It was they who were embarrassing us."

I started to say something that came out "Fiddle-de-doo." It's
a saying of my grandmother's, and I know she would have been

pleased.

"I don't think you know what you're saying," Lengel said.

"I know you don't," I said. "But I do." I pull the bow at the back of my apron and start shrugging it off my shoulders. A couple customers that had been heading for my slot begin to knock against each other, like scared pigs in a chute.

Lengel sighs and begins to look very patient and old and gray. He's been a friend of my parents for years. "Sammy, you don't want to do this to your Mom and Dad," he tells me. It's true, I don't. But it seems to me that once you begin a gesture it's fatal not to go through with it. I fold the apron, "Sammy" stitched in red on the pocket, and put it on the counter, and drop the bow tie on top of it. The bow tie is theirs, if you've ever wondered. "You'll feel this for the rest of your life," Lengel says, and I know that's true, too, but remembering how he made that pretty girl blush makes me so scrunchy inside I punch the No Sale tab and the machine whirs "pee-pul" and the drawer splats out. One advantage to this scene taking place in summer, I can follow this up with a clean exit, there's no fumbling around getting your coat and galoshes, I just saunter into the electric eye in my white shirt that my mother ironed the night before, and the door heaves itself open, and outside the sunshine is skating around on the asphalt.

I look around for my girls, but they're gone, of course. There wasn't anybody but some young married screaming with her children about some candy they didn't get by the door of a powder-blue Falcon station wagon. Looking back in the big windows, over the bags of peat moss and aluminum lawn furniture stacked on the pavement, I could see Lengel in my place in the slot, checking the sheep through. His face was dark gray and his back stiff, as if he'd just had an injection of iron, and my stomach kind of fell as I felt how hard the world was going to be to me hereafter.

———

JOHN UPDIKE (1932–   ) *became a staff writer for* The New Yorker *after leaving Harvard, and continues to contribute poetry, articles, and stories to what he calls "the best of possible magazines." His best-known novels are* Rabbit, Run (1960), The Centaur (1963), *and* Couples (1968), *but he prefers his short stories to them; he told a* Paris Review *interviewer in 1968 that "if I had to give anybody one book" of his own, it would be the* Vintage *edition of short stories,* Olinger Stories (1964). *A sequel to* Rabbit, Run—Rabbit, Redux—*was published in 1971.*

In a recollection of his childhood printed in Five Boyhoods *(ed.*

Martin Levin, 1962), Updike hints at an assumption present in many of his writings; from a boyhood tormentor "I received my first impression of the smug, chinkless, irresistible power *of stupidity; it is the most powerful force on earth."*

1. The A & P is first of all a setting for this story. Reread the story and locate several of the detailed descriptions of the supermarket, its merchandise, its machinery, its people. Why does Updike give so many concrete details?

2. By calling the story "A & P," Updike suggests that the supermarket is not only a setting but in some way is central to the idea of the story. What kinds of things, people, and attitudes does he ask you to associate with the A & P? When the narrator says, "I bet you could set off dynamite in an A & P and the people would by and large keep reaching and checking oatmeal off their lists . . . ," he seems to see the A & P as a state of mind as well as a place. What is this state of mind, and where else in the story do you see it in action?

3. The girls say only a few words, yet their presence makes the story. What do they mean to the manager of the store? To the narrator? To the shoppers in the A & P? How many of these meanings are contained in the narrator's description of a girl in a bathing suit "in the cool of the A & P, under the fluorescent lights, against all those stacked packages, with her feet paddling along naked over our checkerboard green-and-cream rubber-tile floor?"

4. Why does the narrator quit his job? What has he learned about the A & P and the way of life it supports and expresses? What is his decision, and the new understanding that led to it, going to do to his life? "I felt how hard the world was going to be to me hereafter," he tells us. Why?

Franz Kafka

A HUNGER ARTIST

During these last decades the interest in professional fasting has markedly diminished. It used to pay very well to stage such great performances under one's own management, but today that is quite impossible. We live in a different world now. At one time the whole town took a lively interest in the hunger artist; from day to day of his fast the excitement mounted; everybody wanted to see him at least once a day; there were people who bought season tickets for the last few days and sat from morning till night in front of his small barred cage; even in the nighttime there were visiting hours, when the whole effect was heightened by torch flares; on fine days the cage was set out in the open air, and then it was the children's special treat to see the hunger artist; for their elders he was often just a joke that happened to be in fashion, but the children stood open-mouthed, holding each other's hands for greater security, marveling at him as he sat there pallid in black tights, with his ribs sticking out so prominently, not even on a seat but down among straw on the ground, sometimes giving a courteous nod, answering questions with a constrained smile, or perhaps stretching an arm through the bars so that one might feel how thin it was, and then again withdrawing deep into himself, paying no attention to anyone or anything, not even to the all-important striking of the clock that was the only piece of furniture in his cage, but merely staring into vacancy with half-shut eyes, now and then taking a sip from a tiny glass of water to moisten his lips.

Besides casual onlookers there were also relays of permanent watchers selected by the public, usually butchers, strangely enough, and it was their task to watch the hunger artist day and night, three of them at a time, in case he should have some secret recourse to nourishment. This was nothing but a formality, instituted to reassure the masses, for the initiates knew well enough that during his fast the artist would never in any circumstances, not even under forcible compulsion, swallow the smallest morsel of food; the honor of his profession forbade it. Not every watcher, of course, was capable of understanding this, there were often groups of night watchers who were very lax in carrying out their duties and deliberately huddled together in a retired corner to play cards with great absorption, obviously intending to give the hunger artist the chance of a little refreshment, which they supposed he could draw from some private hoard. Nothing annoyed the artist more than such watchers; they made him miserable; they made his fast seem unendurable; sometimes he mastered his feebleness sufficiently to sing during their watch for as long as he could keep going, to show them how unjust their suspicions were. But that was of little use; they only wondered at his cleverness in being able to fill his mouth even while singing. Much more to his taste were the watchers who sat close up to the bars, who were not content with the dim night lighting of the hall but focused him in the full glare of the electric pocket torch given them by the impresario. The harsh light did not trouble him at all. In any case he could never sleep properly, and he could always drowse a little, whatever the light, at any hour, even when the hall was thronged with noisy onlookers. He was quite happy at the prospect of spending a sleepless night with such watchers; he was ready to exchange jokes with them, to tell them stories out of his nomadic life, anything at all to keep them awake and demonstrate to them again that he had no eatables in his cage and that he was fasting as not one of them could fast. But his happiest moment was when the morning came and an enormous breakfast was brought them, at his expense, on which they flung themselves with the keen appetite of healthy men after a weary night of wakefulness. Of course there were people who argued that this breakfast was an unfair attempt to bribe the watchers, but that was going rather too far, and when they were invited to take on a night's vigil without a breakfast, merely for the sake of the cause, they made themselves scarce, although they stuck stubbornly to their suspicions.

Such suspicions, anyhow, were a necessary accompaniment to the profession of fasting. No one could possibly watch the hunger artist continuously, day and night, and so no one could produce first-hand evidence that the fast had really been rigorous and continuous; only the artist himself could know that; he was therefore bound to be the sole completely satisfied spectator of his own fast. Yet for other reasons he was never satisfied; it was not perhaps mere fasting that had brought him to such skeleton thinness that many people had regretfully to keep away from his exhibitions, because the sight of him was too much for them, perhaps it was dissatisfaction with himself that had worn him down. For he alone knew, what no other initiate knew, how easy it was to fast. It was the easiest thing in the world. He made no secret of this, yet people

did not believe him; at the best they set him down as modest, most
of them, however, thought he was out for publicity or else was some
kind of cheat who found it easy to fast because he had discovered a
way of making it easy, and then had the impudence to admit the
fact, more or less. He had to put up with all that, and in the course
of time had got used to it, but his inner dissatisfaction always ran-
kled, and never yet, after any term of fasting—this must be granted
to his credit—had he left the cage of his own free will. The longest
period of fasting was fixed by his impresario at forty days, beyond
that term he was not allowed to go, not even in great cities, and
there was good reason for it, too. Experience had proved that for
about forty days the interest of the public could be stimulated by a
steadily increasing pressure of advertisement, but after that the
town began to lose interest, sympathetic support began notably to
fall off; there were of course local variations as between one town
and another or one country and another, but as a general rule forty
days marked the limit. So on the fortieth day the flower-bedecked
cage was opened, enthusiastic spectators filled the hall, a military
band played, two doctors entered the cage to measure the results of
the fast, which were announced through a megaphone, and finally
two young ladies appeared, blissful at having been selected for the
honor, to help the hunger artist down the few steps leading to a
small table on which was spread a carefully chosen invalid repast.
And at this very moment the artist always turned stubborn. True,
he would entrust his bony arms to the outstretched helping hands
of the ladies bending over him, but stand up he would not. Why
stop fasting at this particular moment, after forty days of it? He had
held out for a long time, an illimitably long time; why stop now,
when he was in his best fasting form, or rather, not yet quite in his
best fasting form? Why should he be cheated of the fame he would
get for fasting longer, for being not only the record hunger artist of
all time, which presumably he was already, but for beating his own
record by a performance beyond human imagination, since he felt
that there were no limits to his capacity for fasting? His public pretended to admire him so much, why should it have so little patience
with him; if he could endure fasting longer, why shouldn't the
public endure it? Besides, he was tired, he was comfortable sitting
in the straw, and now he was supposed to lift himself to his full
height and go down to a meal the very thought of which gave him
a nausea that only the presence of the ladies kept him from betray-
ing, and even that with an effort. And he looked up into the eyes of
the ladies who were apparently so friendly and in reality so cruel,
and shook his head, which felt too heavy on its strengthless neck.
But then there happened yet again what always happened. The
impresario came forward, without a word—for the band made

speech impossible—lifted his arms in the air above the artist, as if
inviting Heaven to look down upon its creature here in the straw,
this suffering martyr, which indeed he was, although in quite another sense; grasped him round the emaciated waist, with exaggerated caution, so that the frail condition he was in might be
appreciated; and committed him to the care of the blenching
ladies, not without secretly giving him a shaking so that his legs and
body tottered and swayed. The artist now submitted completely;
his head lolled on his breast as if it had landed there by chance;
his body was hollowed out; his legs in a spasm of self-preservation
clung close to each other at the knees, yet scraped on the ground as
if it were not really solid ground, as if they were only trying to find
solid ground; and the whole weight of his body, a featherweight
after all, relapsed onto one of the ladies, who, looking round for
help and panting a little—this post of honor was not at all what she
had expected it to be—first stretched her neck as far as she could
to keep her face at least free from contact with the artist, then finding this impossible, and her more fortunate companion not coming
to her aid but merely holding extended on her own trembling hand
the little bunch of knucklebones that was the artist's, to the great
delight of the spectators burst into tears and had to be replaced by
an attendant who had long been stationed in readiness. Then came
the food, a little of which the impresario managed to get between
the artist's lips, while he sat in a kind of half-fainting trance, to the
accompaniment of cheerful patter designed to distract the public's
attention from the artist's condition; after that, a toast was drunk to
the public, supposedly prompted by a whisper from the artist in the
impresario's ear; the band confirmed it with a mighty flourish, the
spectators melted away, and no one had any cause to be dissatisfied
with the proceedings, no one except the hunger artist himself, he
only, as always.

So he lived for many years, with small regular intervals of recu-
peration, in visible glory, honored by the world, yet in spite of that
troubled in spirit, and all the more troubled because no one would
take his trouble seriously. What comfort could he possibly need?
What more could he possibly wish for? And if some good-natured
person, feeling sorry for him, tried to console him by pointing out
that his melancholy was probably caused by fasting, it could happen, especially when he had been fasting for some time, that he
reacted with an outburst of fury and to the general alarm began to
shake the bars of his cage like a wild animal. Yet the impresario had
a way of punishing these outbreaks which he rather enjoyed putting
into operation. He would apologize publicly for the artist's behavior, which was only to be excused, he admitted, because of the
irritability caused by fasting; a condition hardly to be understood

by well-fed people; then by natural transition he went on to mention the artist's equally incomprehensible boast that he could fast
for much longer than he was doing; he praised the high ambition,
the good will, the great self-denial undoubtedly implicit in such a
statement; and then quite simply countered it by bringing out
photographs, which were also on sale to the public, showing the
artist on the fortieth day of a fast lying in bed almost dead from
exhaustion. This perversion of the truth, familiar to the artist
though it was, always unnerved him afresh and proved too much
for him. What was a consequence of the premature ending of his
fast was here presented as the cause of it! To fight against this lack
of understanding, against a whole world of non-understanding, was
impossible. Time and again in good faith he stood by the bars listening to the impresario, but as soon as the photographs appeared
he always let go and sank with a groan back on to his straw, and the
reassured public could once more come close and gaze at him.

A few years later when the witnesses of such scenes called them
to mind, they often failed to understand themselves at all. For
meanwhile the aforementioned change in public interest had set
in; it seemed to happen almost overnight; there may have been
profound causes for it, but who was going to bother about that; at
any rate the pampered hunger artist suddenly found himself deserted one fine day by the amusement seekers, who went streaming
past him to other more favored attractions. For the last time the
impresario hurried him over half Europe to discover whether the
old interest might still survive here and there; all in vain; everywhere, as if by secret agreement, a positive revulsion from professional fasting was in evidence. Of course it could not really have
sprung up so suddenly as all that, and many premonitory symptoms which had not been sufficiently remarked or suppressed during the rush and glitter of success now came retrospectively to
mind, but it was now too late to take any countermeasures. Fasting
would surely come into fashion again at some future date, yet that
was no comfort for those living in the present. What, then, was the
hunger artist to do? He had been applauded by thousands in his
time and could hardly come down to showing himself in a street
booth at village fairs, and as for adopting another profession, he
was not only too old for that but too fanatically devoted to fasting.
So he took leave of the impresario, his partner in an unparalleled
career, and hired himself to a large circus; in order to spare his own
feelings he avoided reading the conditions of his contract.

A large circus with its enormous traffic in replacing and recruit-
ing men, animals and apparatus can always find a use for people at
any time, even for a hunger artist, provided of course that he does
not ask too much, and in this particular case anyhow it was not only

the artist who was taken on but his famous and long-known name as well; indeed considering the peculiar nature of his performance, which was not impaired by advancing age, it could not be objected that here was an artist past his prime, no longer at the height of his professional skill, seeking a refuge in some quiet corner of a circus; on the contrary, the hunger artist averred that he could fast as well as ever, which was entirely credible; he even alleged that if he were allowed to fast as he liked, and this was at once promised him without more ado, he could astound the world by establishing a record never yet achieved, a statement which certainly provoked a smile among the other professionals, since it left out of account the change in public opinion, which the hunger artist in his zeal conveniently forgot.

He had not, however, actually lost his sense of the real situation and took it as a matter of course that he and his cage should be stationed, not in the middle of the ring as a main attraction, but outside, near the animal cages, on a site that was after all easily accessible. Large and gaily painted placards made a frame for the cage and announced what was to be seen inside it. When the public came thronging out in the intervals to see the animals, they could hardly avoid passing the hunger artist's cage and stopping there for a moment, perhaps they might even have stayed longer had not those pressing behind them in the narrow gangway, who did not understand why they should be held up on their way towards the excitements of the menagerie, made it impossible for anyone to stand gazing quietly for any length of time. And that was the reason why the hunger artist, who had of course been looking forward to these visiting hours as the main achievement of his life, began instead to shrink from them. At first he could hardly wait for the intervals; it was exhilarating to watch the crowds come streaming his way, until only too soon—not even the most obstinate self-deception, clung to almost consciously, could hold out against the fact—the conviction was borne in upon him that these people, most of them, to judge from their actions, again and again, without exception, were all on their way to the menagerie. And the first sight of them from the distance remained the best. For when they reached his cage he was at once deafened by the storm of shouting and abuse that arose from the two contending factions, which renewed themselves continuously, of those who wanted to stop and stare at him—he soon began to dislike them more than the others —not out of real interest but only out of obstinate self-assertiveness, and those who wanted to go straight on to the animals. When the first great rush was past, the stragglers came along, and these, whom nothing could have prevented from stopping to look at him as long as they had breath, raced past with long strides, hardly even glancing at him, in their haste to get to the menagerie in time. And all too rarely did it happen that he had a stroke of luck, when some father of a family fetched up before him with his children, pointed a finger at the hunger artist and explained at length what the phenomenon meant, telling stories of earlier years when he himself had watched similar but much more thrilling performances, and the children, still rather uncomprehending, since neither inside nor outside school had they been sufficiently prepared for this lesson—what did they care about fasting?—yet showed by the brightness of their intent eyes that new and better times might be coming. Perhaps, said the hunger artist to himself many a time, things would be a little better if his cage were set not quite so near the menagerie. That made it too easy for people to make their choice, to say nothing of what he suffered from the stench of the menagerie, the animals' restlessness by night, the carrying past of raw lumps of flesh for the beasts of prey, the roaring at feeding times, which depressed him continually. But he did not dare to lodge a complaint with the management; after all, he had the animals to thank for the troops of people who passed his cage, among whom there might always be one here and there to take an interest in him, and who could tell where they might seclude him if he called attention to his existence and thereby to the fact that, strictly speaking, he was only an impediment on the way to the menagerie.

A small impediment, to be sure, one that grew steadily less. People grew familiar with the strange idea that they could be expected, in times like these, to take an interest in a hunger artist, and with this familiarity the verdict went out against him. He might fast as much as he could, and he did so; but nothing could save him now, people passed him by. Just try to explain to anyone the art of fasting! Anyone who has no feeling for it cannot be made to understand it. The fine placards grew dirty and illegible, they were torn down; the little notice board telling the number of fast days achieved, which at first was changed carefully every day, had long stayed at the same figure, for after the first few weeks even this small task seemed pointless to the staff; and so the artist simply fasted on and on, as he had once dreamed of doing, and it was no trouble to him, just as he had always foretold, but no one counted the days, no one, not even the artist himself, knew what records he was already breaking, and his heart grew heavy. And when once in a time some leisurely passer-by stopped, made merry over the old figure on the board and spoke of swindling, that was in its way the stupidest lie ever invented by indifference and inborn malice, since it was not the hunger artist who was cheating; he was working honestly, but the world was cheating him of his reward.

Many more days went by, however, and that too came to an end. An overseer's eye fell on the cage one day and he asked the attendants why this perfectly good stage should be left standing there unused with dirty straw inside it; nobody knew, until one man, helped out by the notice board, remembered about the hunger artist. They poked into the straw with sticks and found him in it. "Are you still fasting?" asked the overseer. "When on earth do you mean to stop?" "Forgive me, everybody," whispered the hunger artist; only the overseer, who had his ear to the bars, understood him. "Of course," said the overseer, and tapped his forehead with a finger to let the attendants know what state the man was in, "we forgive you." "I always wanted you to admire my fasting," said the hunger artist. "We do admire it," said the overseer, affably. "But you shouldn't admire it," said the hunger artist. "Well, then we don't admire it," said the overseer, "but why shouldn't we admire it?" "Because I have to fast, I can't help it," said the hunger artist. "What a fellow you are," said the overseer, "and why can't you help it?" "Because," said the hunger artist, lifting his head a little and speaking, with his lips pursed, as if for a kiss, right into the overseer's ear, so that no syllable might be lost, "because I couldn't find the food I liked. If I had found it, believe me, I should have made no fuss and stuffed myself like you or anyone else." These were his last words, but in his dimming eyes remained the firm though no longer proud persuasion that he was still continuing to fast.

"Well, clear this out now!" said the overseer, and they buried the hunger artist, straw and all. Into the cage they put a young panther. Even the most insensitive felt it refreshing to see this wild creature leaping around the cage that had so long been dreary. The panther was all right. The food he liked was brought him without hesitation by the attendants; he seemed not even to miss his freedom; his noble body, furnished almost to the bursting point with all that it needed, seemed to carry freedom around with it too; somewhere in his jaws it seemed to lurk; and the joy of life streamed with such ardent passion from his throat that for the onlookers it was not easy to stand the shock of it. But they braced themselves, crowded round the cage, and did not want ever to move away.

———

FRANZ KAFKA (1883–1924) *published only a few stories during his lifetime; like the artist in this story, who is buried "straw and all," Kafka asked, just before his death, to have all his manuscripts burned. His friend Max Brod instead edited and published six vol-*

umes of his writings. *These volumes, particularly* The Castle (1930),
The Trial (1937), *and* The Metamorphosis (1937) *have not only
affected virtually all modern writers but have in some important ways
helped us all to see our world more clearly. The Kafka world, one
in which man is at once helpless and guilty, in which man is alien
to his environment and a plaything of mysterious forces, seems to
many readers to be a starkly honest rendering of what lies behind
the surface of modern experience.*

1. *In this story, Kafka is dramatizing (among other things), the
   relationship between the artist and his audience. Why, instead
   of a starving painter, or writer, or musician, has Kafka decided
   to make the central figure an artist whose art is starvation itself? What does the hunger artist's performance offer an audience? Why ought we to expect his period of success to be
   brief?*

2. *Examine the relationship between the artist and his audience
   during the first section of the story, the old days when fasting
   was commercially successful. Why is there so much "suspicion"?
   What is the function of the "impresario" and what is his relation to the artist?*

3. *Why does the artist not want his performance to end? Why is
   there nonetheless a forty-day limit? Where is this conflict between artistic needs and commercial needs dramatized? Why is
   the artist so dissatisfied? So misunderstood?*

4. *The second section of the story moves to the present, after a
   shift in taste has forced the artist to join the circus in order to
   gain an audience. Describe his location at the circus; why has
   Kafka placed him there? Why do the crowds prefer the animals
   to the artist? What does Kafka mean when he says, "he was
   working honestly, but the world was cheating him of his reward"?*

5. *The last two paragraphs give us final statements by artist and
   audience. The artist declares he had to fast "because I couldn't
   find the food I liked." What is the artist here saying about his
   art? What assumptions about art—all art, of course, not fasting
   —are made here? The closing scene shows an excited crowd ad-
   miring the panther that has replaced the dead artist. What does
   the panther offer the crowd that the artist did not? Why is this
   message so readily accepted? What does the story assume to be
   the inevitable relationship between artist and audience?*

William Shakespeare

SHALL I COMPARE THEE TO A
SUMMER'S DAY?

> Shall I compare thee to a summer's day ?
> Thou art more lovely and more temperate :
> Rough winds do shake the darling buds of May,
> And summer's lease hath all too short a date :
> Sometime too hot the eye of heaven shines,
> And often is his gold complexion dimmed ;
> And every fair from fair sometime declines,
> By chance or nature's changing course untrimmed.
> But thy eternal summer shall not fade,
> Nor lose possession of that fair thou ow'st ,
> Nor shall death brag thou wander'st in his shade,
> When in eternal lines to time thou grow'st
> So long as men can breathe, or eyes can see,
> So long lives this, and this gives life to thee.

———

WILLIAM SHAKESPEARE (1564–1616) *was a professional actor and playwright; his plays were designed to please the "groundlings," the general public paying a penny for standing room, as well as the wealthy and educated, and hence were a kind of popular art for their day. Of course, his plays have long since been recognized as an unmatched artistic triumph. Many of his sonnets, such as this one, speak of the power of art to create new perceptions of reality, and hence new realities.*

1. *The first line focuses our attention on the act of writing a poem. This is to be a comparison of "thee" (the young man to whom the poem is addressed) with a particularly attractive version of nature, "a summer's day." Instead of listing the beauties of nature, however, the first eight lines list deficiencies in nature. What are these deficiencies?*

2. *The last six lines set out to demonstrate that "thou art more lovely and more temperate" than the summer's day. How can the poet speak of "thy eternal summer," when the young man of course must die? And how can the poet say the young man will not "lose possession of that fair thou ow'st" (that is, of the handsomeness he possesses) when, as line seven makes explicit, all things in nature "decline"? What is the "this" mentioned twice in the last line, and how does the existence of "this" prove the statement of line two?*

3. *What assumptions about man, nature, poetry, and the definition of reality are contained in this poem? What means does the poem use to urge you to accept its assumptions? To what extent do these assumptions agree or disagree with what you usually assume to be true? Why do you suppose this poem is sometimes misread as romantic praise of beauty, despite the obvious evidence to the contrary?*

Part Two UNDERSTANDING

IMPLICATIONS: ART AND BEHAVIOR

---

*A*ssumptions lie concealed behind an assertion. Implications, on the other hand, follow from an assertion; they are the unstated meanings that must be true if the assertion is true. Thus the bumper sticker "America: Love It or Leave It" assumes the existence of a group that does not "love" America. The assertion says that such a group should emigrate. But the slogan implies a threat against those who do not share a certain brand of patriotism. The exact nature of the threat is left vague, in the manner of implication. Yet the meaning is perfectly clear: you had better "love" America or suffer serious consequences.

An examination of what something "means" is often an examination of its implications. Why, for example, does Brer Rabbit usually come out on top in the Uncle Remus tales? Bernard Wolfe's answers not only tell us a great deal about the origin of the tales, but a great deal as well about American racism. David Riesman's analysis of an up-to-date children's story is evidence for his conclusions about the changing goals and character types in our society. It is the implications of these children's stories, what follows from the picture of the world they present, that reveal their meaning and make them of interest to grownups. To see what is there in popular art (or anything else) calls for close observation and concrete language; to see the assumptions behind what is there calls for insight into values, and the power to make abstractions about what is missing. The examination of implications demands not only these basic descriptive and analytic powers, but an added ability to discern possibilities and results. The most important meanings of what you read are often not stated, but implied, and the most important meanings of what you write often depend as well on your own awareness and control of what you imply.

75

Notice how carefully the writers in this section attend to the implications of their material:

> The media have created a picture of what boyhood and girlhood are like . . . and they force children either to accept or aggressively to resist this picture of themselves. —RIESMAN
>
> Today our ten-year-olds, in voting for MAD, are telling us in their own way that the TV image has ended the consumer phase of American culture. —McLUHAN
>
> Harris's inner split—and the South's, and white America's —is mirrored in the fantastic disparity between Remus's beaming face and Brer Rabbit's acts. —WOLFE
>
> We watch [King Kong] die, and by extension kill the ape within our bones. . . . —KENNEDY

Each of these typical sentences follows careful description and analysis of story; each sentence is an attempt to answer the reader's "so what?" The stories are worth reading, worth analyzing, these writers reply, because "by extension" they help us find out who we are. Our delight in King Kong implies an "ape within our bones"; the characters in Uncle Remus imply the racial ambivalences and conflicts in our society, etc. Writing that strikes us as good, interesting, relevant, meaningful, is usually writing filled with implications; we read, all of us, to find out how other people's ideas can help give meaning to our own lives.

Popular art for children is a particularly valuable topic to use for the study of implications. For the stories children read, or have read to them, give them a picture of what life is like; this picture must seem real and satisfying, or the stories die out. The eleven-year-old discovering the role of the teenager through "love" comic books, the sixteen-year-old reading Seventeen, *the college freshman reading* Playboy, *all have a great deal in common with the toddler hearing "The Ugly Duckling" or tales from Uncle Remus. Each reader is learning about how to behave in the world, each is receiving a myth, an "ideal" version of experience which has points of connection with the real world but by no means contains the whole truth. The meaning of the myths and their implications for those who find them satisfying are worth exploring, because we all tend to live by such myths; to inquire into children's literature is one way to see freshly our own values and codes of behavior.*

David Riesman feels that the children's literature he examines is designed to train children to be obedient employees of a system with flawed values. Marshall McLuhan feels the comics, particu-

larly Mad, *to be "a sure index of deep changes in our culture."
Bernard Wolfe, X. J. Kennedy, and Edward Field find that the
tales and film they analyze express deep-set human urges, largely
hostile ones. In Katherine Anne Porter's "The Circus," this familiar
form of popular art gives the child in the story (and us) a frightening moment of insight into the meaning of her world. All the writers
in this section share respect for and careful evaluation of their material; the implications of children's literature are not kid stuff.*

*If you are asked to analyze some form of children's literature,
you will find it interesting to return to the delights you remember
from your own childhood, particularly the unofficial stories or magazines you were not encouraged to read. Careful description of what
is there, and careful analysis of the assumed values in the stories,
should lead to a discussion of the implications of these stories; the
world children's books present is likely to contain assumptions and
reveal implications which tell us volumes about ourselves and our
society.*

David Riesman, Nathan Glazer, Reuel Denney

THE CHILD MARKET

A. *I like Superman better than the others because they can't do everything Superman can do. Batman can't fly and that is very important.*
Q. *Would you like to be able to fly?*
A. *I would like to be able to fly if everybody else did, but otherwise it would be kind of conspicuous.*

*—From an interview with a twelve-year-old girl.**

[I]n the era of incipient decline of population children begin their training as consumers at an increasingly young age. In America middle-class children have allowances of their own at four or five; they have, as opinion leaders in the home, some say in the family budget. The allowances are expected to be spent, whereas in the earlier era they were often used as cudgels of thrift. Moreover, the monopolistic competition characteristic of this era can afford, and is interested in, building up in the child habits of consumption he will employ as an adult. For he will live long, and so will the monopoly. Monopoly is, in fact, distinguished by this very ability to plan ahead, because it can afford specialists to do the planning as well as resources saved from profits to pay for it and its later implementation.

For all these reasons, then, it has become worth while for professional storytellers to concentrate on the child market; and as the mass media can afford specialists and market research on the particular age cultures and class cultures involved, the children are more heavily cultivated in their own terms than ever before. But while the educator in earlier eras might use the child's language to put across an adult message, today the child's language may be

Reprinted by permission of Yale University Press from *The Lonely Crowd* by David Riesman, Nathan Glazer, and Reuel Denney. Copyright © 1950 by Yale University Press.
* Katherine M. Wolfe and Marjorie Fiske, "The Children Talk About Comics," *Communications Research 1948–1949*, ed. Paul F. Lazarsfeld and Frank Stanton (New York, Harper, 1949), pp. 26–27.

used to put across the advertiser's and storyteller's idea of what children are like. No longer is it thought to be the child's job to understand the adult world as the adult sees it; for one thing, the world as the adult sees it today is perhaps a more complicated one.* Instead, the mass media ask the child to see the world as "the" child—that is, the *other* child—sees it. This is partly the result of the technical advances that make it possible for the movies to create the child world of Margaret O'Brien and her compeers, for the radio to have its array of Hardys, Aldriches, and other juveniles, and for advertising and cover art to make use of professional child models. The media have created a picture of what boyhood and girlhood are like (as during the war they created the picture of the GI, again using the considerably edited language of the soldier) and they force children either to accept or aggressively to resist this picture of themselves.

The child begins to be bombarded by radio and comics from the moment he can listen and just barely read. The bombardment —which of course inevitably over- and under-shoots—hits specifically at very narrow age-grades. For example, there seems to be for many children a regular gradation of comic-reading stages: from the animal stories like *Bugs Bunny* to invincible heroes like *Superman*, and from there to heroes like *Batman* who, human in make-up, are vulnerable, though of course they always win. The study from which the quotation at the head of this chapter is taken finds that the children themselves are aware of the progression, aware of those laggards who still read romper media when they should have graduated to blue jeans.

To be sure, the change from the preceding era of inner-direction in America is not abrupt; such changes never are. Formerly the mass media catered to the child market in at least three fields: school texts or homilies, magazines designed for children, and penny dreadfuls. But when these are compared with the contemporary media we are at once aware of differences. The appraisal of the market by the writers of this earlier literature was amateurish in comparison with market research today. Moeover, they aimed generally to spur work drives and stimulate mobility rather than to effect any socialization of taste. The English boys' weeklies, as Orwell describes them,† usually opposed liquor and tobacco—as did the clergyman authors of school and church readers. Such admonitions remind us of the "crime doesn't pay" lesson of the comics, a façade for messages of more importance. The boys' week-

---

* Certainly the adult literature is more complicated and/or more salacious on its top levels, as compared with the earlier era when both child and adult could read Mark Twain even at his most bitter, Dickens even at his most crude, H. G. Wells even at his most involved.
† George Orwell, *Dickens, Dali & Others* (New York, Reynal & Hitchcock, 1946), p. 76.

lies and their American counterparts were involved with training the young for the frontiers of production (including warfare), and as an incident of that training the embryo athlete might eschew smoke and drink. The comparable media today train the young for the frontiers of consumption—to tell the difference between Pepsi-Cola and Coca-Cola, as later between Old Golds and Chesterfields.

We may mark the change by citing an old nursery rhyme:

> "This little pig went to market;
> This little pig stayed at home.
> This little pig had roast beef;
> This little pig had none.
> This little pig went wee-wee-wee
> All the way home."

The rhyme may be taken as a paradigm of individuation and un-socialized behavior among children of an earlier era. Today, however, all little pigs go to market; none stay home; all have roast beef, if any do; and all say "we-we."

Winner Take All? · Yet perhaps the most important change is the shift in the situation in which listening and reading occur. In contrast with the lone reader of the era of inner-direction, we have the group of kids today, lying on the floor, reading and trading comics and preferences among comics, or listening to "The Lone Ranger." When reading and listening are not communal in fact, they are apt to be so in feeling: one is almost always conscious of the brooding omnipresence of the peer-group. Thus the Superman fan quoted at the head of the chapter cannot allow herself to iden-tify with Superman—the others would think her foolish—while they would not think her foolish for believing that flying is very important.

In a society dependent on tradition-direction children are, as we have seen, introduced to stories by adult storytellers. The latter do not feel themselves to be in critical competition with the young. Hence they can encourage, or a least patronize, children's unsophisticated reactions of alarm or excitement at the tales they are told—and, later on, encourage the youngster's own tall talk and tale embroidery. But the peer-groupers who read or listen together without the protective presence of adults are in no such cozy rela-tion of "listen my children and you shall hear . . ." They cannot afford to let go—to fly.

One correlate is that the comic book differs from the fairy tale in several important respects. In the fairy tale the protagonist is frequently an underdog figure, a younger child, an ugly duckling, a coimmoner, while the villain is frequently an authority figure, a king, a giant, a stepmother. In the comics the protagonist is apt to be an invulnerable or near-invulnerable adult who is equipped, if not with supernatural powers, at least with two guns and a tall, terrific physique. Magical aid comes to the underdog—who remains a peripheral character—only through the mediation of this figure. Thus, whereas Jack of *Jack and the Beanstalk* gains magical assistance chiefly through his own daring, curiosity, and luck, a comic-book Jack would gain magical assistance chiefly through an all-powerful helper. While vaguely similar themes may be found in the stories of Robin Hood and Sir Galahad, the comics show a quantitative increase in the role of the more or less invulnerable authority-hero.

The relative change in this pattern * is not the "fault" of the comics. These merely play into a style of reception that is fitted to peer-group reading. Indeed, if other-directed child comic fans read or hear stories that are not comics, they will read them as if they were comics. They will tend to focus on who won and to miss the internal complexities of the tale, of a moral sort or otherwise. If one asks them, then, how they distinguish the "good guys" from the "bad guys" in the mass media, it usually boils down to the fact that the former always win; they are good guys by definition.

But of course the child wants to anticipate the result and so looks for external clues which will help him pick the winner. In the comics this is seldom a problem: the good guys *look it*, being square-jawed, clear-eyed, tall men; the bad guys also look it, being, for reasons of piety, of no recognizable ethnic group but rather of a generally messy southern European frame—oafish and unshaven or cadaverous and oversmooth. But in movies (and in some comics with slinky beauties in them) this identification is not easy: the very types that are good guys in most comics may turn out to be villains after all. A striking example I have observed is the bafflement of several young comic fans at the movie portrayal of the Countess de Winter (Lana Turner) in *The Three Musketeers*. If she looked so nice, how could she be so mean?

Thus we come to a paradox. The other-directed child is trained to be sensitive to interpersonal relations, and often he understands these with a sophistication few adults had in the era of inner-direction. Yet he can be strikingly insensitive to problems of character as presented by his favorite storytellers; he tends to race through the story for its ending, or to read the ending first, and to miss just those problems of personal development that are not telltale clues to the outcome. It looks as though the situation of group

---

* Here, too, the abruptness of the change from inner-direction should not be exaggerated. Eliot Freidson, studying the ability of young children to remember stories, found them much more apt to recall a few traditional fairy tales like *Goldilocks* or *The Three Little Pigs* than either Golden Books or comics or movies. "Myth and the Child: an Aspect of Socialization" (Master's thesis, University of Chicago, 1949).

reading, of having to sit on the jury that passes out Hooper ratings, forces the pace for the other-directed child. He cannot afford to linger on "irrelevant" detail or to daydream about the heroes. To trade preferences in reading and listening he need know no more about the heroes than the stamp trader needs to know about the countries the stamps come from.

Fairy tales and the Frank Merriwell books also emphasize winning; hence it is important to see the precise differences introduced by the contemporary media as well as by the changed focus of the readers. One striking difference is that between the older ambition and newer "antagonistic cooperation." Ambition I define as the striving for clear goals characteristic of the period of inner-direction it may be a striving for fame or for goodness: to get the job, to win the battle, to build the bridge. Competition in the era depending on inner-direction is frequently ruthless, but at the same time people are in no doubt as to their place in the race—and that there is a race. If they feel guilt it is when they fail, not when they succeed. By contrast, "antagonistic cooperation" may be defined as an inculcated striving characteristic of the groups affected by other-direction. Here the goal is less important than the relationship to the "others." In this new-style competition people are often in doubt whether there is a race at all, and if so, what its goals are. Since they are supposed to be cooperative rather than rivalrous, they may well feel guilt about success and even a certain responsibility for others' failure.

Certainly, it is ambition that strikes us as an outstanding trait of the heroes of boys' literature in the era of inner-direction. Moreover, it is an ambition with which the child reader can identify, even if the particular goal—to fight Indians or find the treasure or North Pole or swim icy rivers or detect crime—is at the moment a remote one; that is, the reader could in fantasy emulate the moral qualities of the hero, such as his bravery and his self-control. Thus, while these heroes, like the modern heroes, almost invariably won, the reader was encouraged to be concerned not only with the final victorious outcome but with the inner struggles that preceded it and made it possible.

It is sometimes loosely said that the comic strip merely continues this older set of themes in a new medium, but the fact is that the themes change and the identifications change even more. Where, as often happens, children prefer comics in which the hero is not man but Superman or Plastic Man, possessing obviously unique powers, identification languishes: no amount of willpower, no correspondence course with Lionel Strongfort, will turn one into

Superman even in the wildest flight of fantasy. And such flights of fantasy appear to be less available today. Exposed to ever more sophisticated media, the children are too hep for "unrealistic" day-dreams; at the movies they soon learn the fine points and will criticize a Western because the hero fired seven shots running from his six-shooter. The media in turn encourage this realism with their color effects and sound effects, which exceed by far the realism of petty detail which Defoe and his successors strove for. The characters in much fiction of the era dependent on inner-direction were props—stereotypes of the sort indicated in the preceding section. In Jules Verne, for instance, it is the adventures, the mechanical details, not the characters, that are sharply delineated; the latter are loose-fitting uniforms into which many boys could fit themselves. The imaginative, tenebrous illustrations of an artist like Howard Pyle also left openings for identification on the part of the reader who wanted to picture himself as the hero.

Little of this looseness of fit remains for the imagination of the modern reader or listener to fill in. Though comic-strip and comic-book characterization is, if anything, less sharp, externals are pinned down conclusively: every detail of costuming and speech is given. This is the more necessary because, with so many mass-media heroes competing for attention, their portrayers must engage in marginal differentiation in search of their trade-mark. Bodies by Milton Caniff must be as instantly recognizable as bodies by Fisher.

There is paradox in the reception of this realism. On the one hand, every additional brush stroke of the comic-strip artist rules out identifications for millions; the small-breasted girl, for example, may find only disapproval for herself in the comics. On the other hand, the same realism is one source of the fear of being conspicuous in our little Supergirl cited at the chapter head. If she were Superman, she would be instantly recognizable. She would lack the privacy of narcissism permitted the reader of an earlier day who could gloat over the fact that he was M. Vidocq or Sherlock Holmes—only nobody knew it.

These generalizations need not be pushed too far. There are children—at least one has heard of them—who identify with Superman, or, more easily, with Terry or the Saint. Nor is it out of the question to identify, at the same time, on one level of consciousness with the hero and on another level with the person he rescues. And while the heroes of the comics are ageless, having discovered the secret of eternal youth, the growing child can move from one hero to another who better fits his own changing needs and aspirations. These counter-tendencies are encouraged by the gadgetry—Superman cloaks, and so on—that relates children to their radio, movie, and comic-book heroes. But it would be a mistake to assume that each wearer of a Superman cloak identifies with Superman; he may only be a fan, wearing his hero's colors.

Perhaps it is also significant that the comic book compresses into a few minutes' reading time a sequence which, in the earlier era, was dragged out in many pages of print. Think of the Count of Monte Cristo's years in jail, his suffering, his incredible patience, and the industry and study of the abbé's teaching; both his gain and his vengeance are moralized by these prolongations, and he is an old man when, after many chapters, he wins. By contrast, the comic-book or radio-drama hero wins almost effortlessly; the very curtailment of the telling time itself makes this more apparent. To be sure, like his movie counterpart, this hero does frequently get beaten up, but this adds to excitement, not to morality or inner change, and helps justify an even worse beating administered to the "crooks."

Still another aspect of this change is worth looking at. If one does not identify with the winner but is at the very same time preoccupied with the process of winning itself, as the best handle by which one grasps a story, one is prepared for the role of consumer of others' winnings. One is prepared, that is, for the adult role of betting on the right horse, with no interest in the jockey or horse or knowledge of what it takes to be either. The content of the identification is impoverished to the point where virtually the only bond between reader and hero is the fact of the hero's winning. The spectator—the same holds for a quiz game, a sport contest, and, as we shall see, a political contest—wants to become involved with the winner simply in order to make the contest meaningful: this hope of victory makes the event exciting, while the game or contest or story is not appreciated for its own sake.

The victory of the hero, then, is only ostensibly a moral one. To be sure, vestiges of older moralities hang on, often as conventions enforced by censorship or the fear of it. But morality in the sense of a literary character's development, rather than morality in the sense of being on the side of law and right, is not depicted. Consequently, morality tends to become an inference from winning. Just as in a whodunit all appear guilty until they are retroactively cleared by finding the real killer, so the victory of the hero retroactively justifies his deeds and misdeeds. "Winner take all" becomes a tautology.

Tootle: A Modern Cautionary Tale · Parents are sometimes apt to assume that comic books and the radio, as the cheapest and most widespread media, are the principal vehicles of these newer attitudes and values and that, in a home barricaded against Roy Rogers and

Steve Canyon, these patterns of audience response would also be excluded. The fact is, however, that many important themes of other-direction are introduced into the socializing and informative books of the non-comic variety which middle- and upper-middle-class children are given—conversely, these "educative" books are probably not without influence on the more socially conscious radio and comic-book artists. A whole range of these media teaches children the lesson given parents and teachers in many recent works on child development. The slant of that lesson is suggested by a passage from a book in use by teachers and PTA groups:

> The usual and desirable developmental picture is one of increasing self-control on the part of the individual children, of increasingly smooth social or play technics, and of an emergence at adolescence or early adulthood of higher forms of cooperation. The adolescent should have learned better "to take it" in group activity, should have developed an improved, though not yet perfect, self-control, and should have real insight into the needs and wishes of others.*

Tootle the Engine (text by Gertrude Crampton, pictures by Tibor Gergely) is a popular and in many ways charming volume in the "Little Golden Books" series. It is a cautionary tale even though it appears to be simply one of the many books about anthropomorphic vehicles—trucks, fire engines, taxicabs, tugboats, and so on—that are supposed to give a child a picture of real life. Tootle is a young engine who goes to engine school, where two main lessons are taught: stop at a red flag and "always stay on the track no matter what." Diligence in the lessons will result in the young engine's growing up to be a big streamliner. Tootle is obedient for a while and then one day discovers the delight of going off the tracks and finding flowers in the field. This violation of the rules cannot, however, be kept secret; there are telltale traces in the cowcatcher. Nevertheless, Tootle's play becomes more and more of a craving, and despite warnings he continues to go off the tracks and wander in the field. Finally the engine schoolmaster is desperate. He consults the mayor of the little town of Engineville, in which the school is located; the mayor calls a town meeting, and Tootle's failings are discussed—of course Tootle knows nothing of this. The meeting decides on a course of action, and the next time Tootle goes out for a spin alone and goes off the track he runs right into a red flag and halts. He turns in another direction only to encounter another red flag; still another—the result is the same. He turns and twists but can find no spot of grass in which a red flag does not

* M. E. Breckenridge and E. L. Vincent, *Child Development* (Philadelphia, W. B. Saunders, 1943), p. 456.

spring up, for all the citizens of the town have cooperated in this lesson.

Chastened and bewildered he looks toward the track, where the inviting green flag of his teacher gives him the signal to return. Confused by conditioned reflexes to stop signs, he is only too glad to use the track and tears happily up and down. He promises that he will never leave the track again, and he returns to the roundhouse to be rewarded by the cheers of the teachers and the citizenry and the assurance that he will indeed grow up to be a streamliner.

The story would seem to be an appropriate one for bringing up children in an other-directed mode of conformity. They learn it is bad to go off the tracks and play with flowers and that, in the long run, there is not only success and approval but even freedom to be found in following the green lights.* The moral is a very different one from that of *Little Red Riding Hood*. She, too, gets off the track on her trip to the grandmother; she is taught by a wolf about the beauties of nature—a veiled symbol for sex. Then, to be sure, she is eaten—a terrifying fate—but in the end she and grand-mother both are taken from the wolf's belly by the handsome woodchopper. The story, though it may be read as a cautionary tale, deals with real human passions, sexual and aggressive; it cer-tainly does not present the rewards of virtue in any unambiguous form or show the adult world in any wholly benevolent light. It is, therefore, essentially realistic, underneath the cover of fantasy, or, more accurately, owing to the quality of the fantasy.

There is, perhaps, a streak of similar realism in *Tootle*. There the adults play the role we have described earlier: they manipulate the child into conformity with the peer-group and then reward him for the behavior for which they have already set the stage. Moreover, the citizens of Engineville are tolerant of Tootle: they understand and do not get indignant. And while they gang up on him with red flags they do so for his benefit, and they reward him for his obedi-ence as if they had played no hand in bringing it about. Yet with all that, there is something overvarnished in this tale. The adult world (the teachers) is *not* that benevolent, the citizenry (the peer-group) *not* that participative and cooperative, the signals are *not* that clear, nor the rewards of being a streamliner that great or that certain. Nevertheless, the child may be impressed because it is all so nice—there is none of the grimness of Red Riding Hood. There is, therefore, a swindle about the whole thing—a fake like that the citizens put on for Tootle's benefit. At the end Tootle

---

* It is not made clear in the story what happens to Tootle's schoolmates in engine school. The peer-group relations of Tootle, either to the other engines or the other citizens of Engineville, are entirely amiable, and Tootle's winning can hardly mean that others fail. Who can be sure that Tootle would want to be a streamliner if others were not to be streamliners too?

has forgotten that he ever did like flowers anyway—how childish they are in comparison with the great big grown-up world of engines, signals, tracks, and meetings!

DAVID RIESMAN (1909–   ) *became a widely-known sociologist with his first book,* The Lonely Crowd (1950), *from which this excerpt is taken. His legal training and experience—Harvard Law School, clerk to Justice Brandeis, New York deputy-assistant district attorney—appears in his sociological writing as a keen regard for argument and evidence, for assumptions and implications. He has taught law and social sciences at the University of Chicago, Columbia, and other major universities. Later books include* Faces in the Crowd: Individual Studies in Character and Politics (1952) *and, most recently,* The Academic Revolution (1968).

In The Lonely Crowd, *Riesman defines three social types of character. Those who are "tradition directed" take their assumptions of behavior from "the various age and sex groups, the clans, castes, professions, and so forth—relations which have endured for centuries and are modified but slightly if at all, by successive generations." Tradition-directed cultures, such as the western Middle Ages, are followed by a period of "inner direction," such as "the society that emerged with the Renaissance and Reformation and that is only now vanishing." Inner-directed types early in life gain from their elders "generalized but nonetheless inescapably destined goals." In pursuit of these goals, this social type manages to live "without strict and self-evident tradition-direction," and his behavior needs to be individual and flexible. In the third period, one which Riesman sees now emerging, the "other directed" personality type predominates. This character type adopts the assumptions of his contemporaries as a source of goals and directions for behavior. "This mode of keeping in touch with others permits a close behavioral conformity, not through drill in behavior itself, as in the tradition-directed character, but rather through an exceptional sensitivity to the actions and wishes of others."*

1. *What is the difference between the "winning" of heroes of older tales (such as* Jack and the Beanstalk) *and the winning of the newer mass-media heroes? Riesman suggests large implications of this change in values: "the same holds for a quiz game, a sport contest, and . . . a political contest. . . ." What are some*

of these implications? How do these mass-media children's stories "train the young for the frontiers of consumption" by showing the heroes they do?

2. Riesman wrote The Lonely Crowd before TV had become a major force of popular culture for children. Does the emergence of children's programing during the last few decades support or deny the argument Riesman makes about the mass-media view of the world presented to children? Support what you say by careful analysis of a typical Saturday morning's programing.

3. Examine Riesman's procedure in his analysis of Tootle the Engine. What do the first two paragraphs do? What is the purpose of the next paragraph, the one that begins "The story would seem to be an appropriate one for bringing up children. . ."? The last paragraph offers an implicit comparison between the "real" world (that is, Riesman's assumptions about the world) and the world of Tootle; how does the comparison lead to the conclusion?

4. Choose another modern and original story from the Little Golden Books series. (Most American supermarkets stock representative titles.) Write an analysis of the story which includes a particular and detailed summary, an evaluation of its assumptions and implications, and a comparison between its world and what you see as the real world.

Marshall McLuhan

THE COMICS

It was thanks to the print that Dickens became a comic writer. He began as a provider of copy for a popular cartoonist. To consider the comics here, after "The Print," is to fix attention upon the persistent printlike, and even crude woodcut, characteristics of our twentieth-century comics. It is by no means easy to perceive how the same qualities of print and woodcut could reappear in the mosaic mesh of the TV image. TV is so difficult a subject for literary people that it has to be approached obliquely. From the three million dots per second on TV, the viewer is able to accept, in an iconic grasp, only a few dozen, seventy or so, from which to shape an image. The image thus made is as crude as that of the comics. It is for this reason that the print and the comics provide a useful approach to understanding the TV image, for they offer very little visual information or connected detail. Painters and sculptors, however, can easily understand TV, because they sense how very much tactile involvement is needed for the appreciation of plastic art.

The structural qualities of the print and woodcut obtain, also, in the cartoon, all of which share a participational and do-it-yourself character that pervades a wide variety of media experiences today. The print is clue to the comic cartoon, just as the cartoon is clue to understanding the TV image.

Many a wrinkled teenager recalls his fascination with that pride of the comics, the "Yellow Kid" of Richard F. Outcault. On first appearance, it was called "Hogan's Alley" in the New York *Sunday World*. It featured a variety of scenes of kids from the tenements, Maggie and Jiggs as children, as it were. This feature sold many papers in 1898 and thereafter. Hearst soon bought it, and began large-scale comic supplements. Comics (as already explained in the chapter on The Print), being low in definition, are a highly participational form of expression, perfectly adapted to the mosaic form of the newspaper. They provide, also, a sense of continuity from one day to the next. The individual news item is very low in information, and requires completion or fill-in by the reader, exactly as does the TV image, or the wirephoto. That is the reason why TV hit the comic-book world so hard. It was a real rival, rather than a complement. But TV hit the pictorial ad world even harder, dislodging the sharp and glossy, in favor of the shaggy, the sculptural, and the tactual. Hence the sudden eminence of *MAD* magazine which offers, merely, a ludicrous and cool replay of the forms of the hot media of photo, radio, and film. *MAD* is the old print and woodcut image that recurs in various media today. Its type of configuration will come to shape all of the acceptable TV offerings.

The biggest casualty of the TV impact was Al Capp's "Li'l Abner." For eighteen years Al Capp had kept Li'l Abner on the verge of matrimony. The sophisticated formula used with his characters was the reverse of that employed by the French novelist Stendhal, who said, "I simply involve my people in the consequences of their own stupidity and then give them brains so they can suffer." Al Capp, in effect, said, "I simply involve my people in the consequences of their own stupidity and then *take away* their brains so that they can do nothing about it." Their inability to help themselves created a sort of parody of all the other suspense comics. Al Capp pushed suspense into absurdity. But readers have long enjoyed the fact that the Dogpatch predicament of helpless ineptitude was a paradigm of the human situation, in general.

With the arrival of TV and its iconic mosaic image, the everyday life situations began to seem very square, indeed. Al Capp suddenly found that his kind of distortion no longer worked. He felt that Americans had lost their power to laugh at themselves. He was wrong. TV simply involved everybody in everybody more deeply than before. This cool medium, with its mandate of participation in depth, required Capp to refocus the Li'l Abner image. His confusion and dismay were a perfect match for the feelings of those in every major American enterprise. From *Life* to General Motors, and from the classroom to the Executive Suite, a refocusing of aims and images to permit ever more audience involvement and participation has been inevitable. Capp said: "But now America has changed. The humorist feels the change more, perhaps, than anyone. Now there are things about America we can't kid."

Depth involvement encourages everyone to take himself much more seriously than before. As TV cooled off the American audience, giving it new preferences and new orientation of sight and sound and touch and taste, Al Capp's wonderful brew also had to be toned down. There was no more need to kid Dick Tracy or the suspense routines. As *MAD* magazine discovered, the new audience found the scenes and themes of ordinary life as funny as anything in remote Dogpatch. *MAD* magazine simply transferred the world of ads into the world of the comic book, and it did this just when the TV image was beginning to eliminate the comic book by direct rivalry. At the same time, the TV image rendered the sharp and clear photographic image as blur and blear. TV cooled off the ad audience until the continuing vehemence of the ads and entertainment suited the program of the *MAD* magazine world very well. TV, in fact, turned the previous hot media of photo, film, and radio into a comic-strip world by simply featuring them as overheated packages. Today the ten-year-old clutches his or her *MAD* ("Build up your Ego with *MAD*") in the same way that the Russian beatnik treasures an old Presley tape obtained from a G.I. broadcast. If the "Voice of America" suddenly switched to jazz, the Kremlin would have reason to crumble. It would be almost as effective as if the Russian citizens had copies of Sears Roebuck catalogues to goggle at, instead of our dreary propaganda for the American way of life.

Picasso has long been a fan of American comics. The highbrow, from Joyce to Picasso, has long been devoted to American popular art because he finds in it an authentic imaginative reaction to official action. Genteel art, on the other hand, tends merely to evade and disapprove of the blatant modes of action in a powerful high definition, or "square," society. Genteel art is a kind of repeat of the specialized acrobatic feats of an industrialized world. Popular art is the clown reminding us of all the life and faculty that we have omitted from our daily routines. He ventures to perform the specialized routines of the society, acting as integral man. But integral man is quite inept in a specialist situation. This, at least, is one way to get at the art of the comics, and the art of the clown.

Today our ten-year-olds, in voting for *MAD*, are telling us in their own way that the TV image has ended the consumer phase of American culture. They are now telling us what the eighteen-year-old beatniks were first trying to say ten years ago. The pictorial consumer age is dead. The iconic age is upon us. We now toss to the Europeans the package that concerned us from 1922 to 1952. They, in turn, enter their first consumer age of standardized goods. We move into our first depth-age of art-and-producer orientation. America is Europeanizing on as extensive a pattern as Europe is Americanizing.

Where does this leave the older popular comics? What about "Blondie" and "Bringing Up Father"? Theirs was a pastoral world of primal innocence from which young America has clearly graduated. There was still adolescence in those days, and there were still remote ideals and private dreams, and visualizable goals, rather than vigorous and ever-present corporate postures for group participation.

The chapter on The Print indicated how the cartoon is a do-it-yourself form of experience that has developed an ever more vigorous life as the electric age advanced. Thus, all electric appliances, far from being labor-saving devices, are new forms of work, decentralized and made available to everybody. Such is, also, the world of the telephone and the TV image that demands so much more of its users than does radio or movie. As a simple consequence of this participational and do-it-yourself aspect of the electric technology, every kind of entertainment in the TV age favors the same kind of personal involvement. Hence the paradox that, in the TV age, Johnny can't read because reading, as customarily taught, is too superficial and consumerlike an activity. Therefore the highbrow paperback, because of its depth character, may appeal to youngsters who spurn ordinary narrative offerings. Teachers today frequently find that students who can't read a page of history are becoming experts in code and linguistic analysis. The problem, therefore, is not that Johnny can't read, but that, in an age of depth involvement, Johnny can't visualize distant goals.

The first comic books appeared in 1935. Not having anything connected or literary about them, and being as difficult to decipher as the *Book of Kells*, they caught on with the young. The elders of the tribe, who had never noticed that the ordinary newspaper was as frantic as a surrealist art exhibition, could hardly be expected to notice that the comic books were as exotic as eighth-century illuminations. So, having noticed nothing about the *form*, they could discern nothing of the *contents*, either. The mayhem and violence were all they noted. Therefore, with naïve literary logic, they waited for violence to flood the world. Or, alternatively, they attributed existing crime to the comics. The dimmest-witted convict learned to moan, "It wuz comic books done this to me."

Meantime, the violence of an industrial and mechanical environment had to be lived and given meaning and motive in the nerves and viscera of the young. To live and experience anything is to translate its direct impact into many indirect forms of awareness. We provided the young with a shrill and raucous asphalt jungle, beside which any tropical animal jungle was as quiet and tame as a rabbit hutch. We called this normal. We paid people to keep it at the highest pitch of intensity because it paid well. When the entertainment industries tried to provide a reasonable facsimile of the ordinary city vehemence, eyebrows were raised.

It was Al Capp who discovered that until TV, at least, any degree of Scragg mayhem or Phogbound morality was accepted as funny. *He* didn't think it was funny. He put in his strip just exactly what he saw around him. But our trained incapacity to relate one situation to another enabled his sardonic realism to be mistaken for humor. The more he showed the capacity of people to involve themselves in hideous difficulties, along with their entire inability to turn a hand to help themselves, the more they giggled. "Satire," said Swift, "is a glass in which we see every countenance but our own."

The comic strip and the ad, then, both belong to the world of games, to the world of models and extensions of situations elsewhere. MAD magazine, world of the woodcut, the print, and the cartoon, brought them together with other games and models from the world of entertainment. MAD is a kind of newspaper mosaic of the ad as entertainment, and entertainment as a form of madness. Above all, it is a print- and woodcut-form of expression and experience whose sudden appeal is a sure index of deep changes in our culture. Our need now is to understand the formal character of print, comic and cartoon, both as challenging and changing the consumer-culture of film, photo, and press. There is no single approach to this task, and no single observation or idea that can solve so complex a problem in changing human perception.

———

MARSHALL McLUHAN (1911–   ), *Director of the University of Toronto's Centre for Culture and Technology, developed a devoted following in the 1960s with his three major books,* The Gutenberg Galaxy (1962), Understanding Media (1964), *and* The Medium is the Massage (1967). *The Executive as Dropout* (with A. B. Nevitt) *is scheduled for publication in 1972. In his books and talks, McLuhan asserts the ending of the age of print (a "hot" medium, like photo, film, or radio), and the beginning of a new "cool" electronic age of low-definition media, such as TV, which call for a fuller imaginative participation by the popular audience. While a growing critical opposition sees his assertions as unsupported by evidence or argument, most readers value his insistence on the importance of popular art as a cultural force.*

1. *McLuhan sees* Mad *magazine and TV as positive forces. What makes them positive?*
2. *What is the distinction McLuhan draws between "genteel art" and "popular art"? Is it sound?*
3. *For McLuhan, the implications of the change he describes are great: "The pictorial consumer age is dead." What implications does McLuhan describe? What other implications do you see in the replacement of print ("consumerlike . . . activity") by the*

personal involvement of the "do-it-yourself aspect of the electric technology"?

4. McLuhan is famous for writing sentences with startling percep-tions below the surface: "all electric appliances, far from being labor-saving devices, are new forms of work, decentralized and made available to everybody." Choose this sentence, or some other from the essay, and examine closely its assumptions and implications.

5. Compare McLuhan on the comics with Orwell on the McGill postcards and Riesman on modern children's tales. Consider the tone of these essays, in particular: how positively or negatively do the writers react to the popular arts they examine? Why?

Bernard Wolfe

UNCLE REMUS AND THE
MALEVOLENT RABBIT

Aunt Jemima, Beulah, the Gold Dust Twins, "George" the Pullman-ad porter, Uncle Remus. . . . We like to picture the Negro as grinning at us. In Jack de Capitator, the bottle opener that looks like a gaping minstrel face, the grin is a kitchen utensil. At Mammy's Shack, the Seattle roadside inn built in the shape of a minstrel's head, you walk into the neon grin to get your hamburger. . . . And always the image of the Negro—as we create it—signifies some bounty—for us. Eternally the Negro gives—but (as they say in the theater) *really gives*—grinning from ear to ear.

Gifts without end, according to the billboards, movie screens, food labels, soap operas, magazine ads, singing commercials. Our daily bread: Cream O' Wheat, Uncle Ben's Rice, Wilson Ham ("The Ham What Am!"), those "happifyin'" Aunt Jemima pancakes for our "temptilatin'" breakfasts. Our daily drink, too: Carioca Puerto Rican Rum, Hiram Walker whiskey, Ballantine's Ale. Through McCallum and Propper, the Negro gives milady the new "dark Creole shades" in her sheer nylons; through the House of Vigny, her "grotesque" "fuzzy-wuzzy" bottles of Golliwogg colognes and perfumes. Shoeshines, snow-white laundry, comfortable lower berths, efficient handling of luggage; jazz, jive, jitterbugging, zoot, comedy, and the wonderful tales of Brer Rabbit to entrance the kiddies. Service with a smile. . . .

"The Negroes," writes Geoffrey Gorer, "are kept in their subservient position by the ultimate sanctions of fear and force, and this is well known to whites and Negroes alike. Nevertheless, the whites demand that the Negroes shall appear smiling, eager, and friendly in all their dealings with them."

But if the grin is extracted by force, may not the smiling face be a falseface—and just underneath is there not something else, often only half-hidden?

Reprinted from the July, 1949 issue of *Commentary* by permission of *Commentary* and Harold Matson Company, Inc. Copyright 1949 by *Commentary* and the American Jewish Committee.

Uncle Remus—a kind of blackface Will Rogers, complete with standard minstrel dialect and plantation shuffle—has had remarkable staying power in our popular culture, much more than Daddy Long Legs, say, or even Uncle Tom. Within the past two years alone he has inspired a full-length Disney feature, three Hit Parade songs, a widely circulated album of recorded dialect stories, a best-selling juvenile picture book, a syndicated comic strip. And the wily hero of his animal fables, Brer Rabbit—to whom Bugs Bunny and perhaps even Harvey owe more than a little—is today a much bigger headliner than Bambi or Black Beauty, outclassing even Donald Duck.

For almost seventy years, Uncle Remus has been the prototype of the Negro grinner-giver. Nothing ever clouds the "beaming countenance" of the "venerable old darky"; nothing ever interrupts the flow of his "hearty," "mellow," "cheerful and good-humored" voice as, decade after decade, he presents his Brer Rabbit stories to the nation.

But Remus too is a white man's brainchild: he was created in the columns of the Atlanta *Constitution*, back in the early 1880's, by a neurotic young Southern journalist named Joel Chandler Harris (1848–1908).

When Remus grins, Harris is pulling the strings; when he "gives" his folk stories, he is the ventriloquist's dummy on Harris's knee.

The setting for these stories never varies: the little white boy, son of "Miss Sally" and "Mars John," the plantation owners, comes "hopping and skipping" into the old Negro's cabin down in back of the "big house" and the story telling session gets under way. Remus's face "breaks up into little eddies of smiles"; he takes his admirer on his knee, "strokes the child's hair thoughtfully and caressingly," calls him "honey." The little boy "nestles closer" to his "sable patron" and listens with "open-eyed wonder."

No "sanctions of fear and force" here, Harris insists—the relationship between narrator and auditor is one of unmitigated tenderness. Remus "gives," with a "kindly beam" and a "most infectious chuckle"; the little boy receives with mingled "awe," "admiration," and "delight." But, if one looks more closely, within the magnanimous caress is an incredibly malevolent blow.

Of the several Remus collections published by Harris, the first and most famous is *Uncle Remus: His Songs and His Sayings*. Brer Rabbit appears twenty-six times in this book, encounters the Fox twenty times, soundly trounces him nineteen times. The Fox, on the other hand, achieves only two very minor triumphs—one over the Rabbit, another over the Sparrow. On only two other occasions is the Rabbit victimized even slightly, both times by animals as puny as himself (the Tarrypin, the Buzzard); but when he is pitted against adversaries as strong as the Fox (the Wolf, the Bear, once the whole Animal Kingdom) he emerges the unruffled winner. The Rabbit finally kills off all three of his powerful enemies. The Fox is made a thorough fool of by all the weakest animals—the Buzzard, the Tarrypin, the Bull-Frog.

All told, there are twenty-eight victories of the Weak over the Strong; ultimately all the Strong die violent deaths at the hands of the Weak; and there are, at most, two very insignificant victories of the Strong over the Weak. . . . Admittedly, folk symbols are seldom systematic, clean-cut, or specific; they are cultural shadows thrown by the unconscious, and the unconscious is not governed by the sharp-edged neatness of the filing cabinet. But still, on the basis of the tally-sheet alone, is it too far-fetched to take Brer Rabbit as a symbol—about as sharp as Southern sanctions would allow—of the Negro slave's festering hatred of the white man?

It depends, of course, on whether these are animals who maul and murder each other, or human beings disguised as animals. Here Harris and Remus seem to differ. "In dem days," Remus often starts, "de creeturs wuz santer'n 'roun' same like fokes." But for Harris—so he insists—this anthropomorphism is only incidental. What the stories depict, he tells us, is only the "roaring comedy of animal life."

Is it? These are very un-Aesopian creatures who speak a vaudeville dialect, hold candy-pulls, run for the legislature, fight and scheme over gold mines, compete for women in elaborate rituals of courtship and self-aggrandizement, sing plantation ditties about "Jim Crow," read the newspapers after supper, and kill and maim each other—not in gusts of endocrine Pavlov passion but cold-bloodedly, for prestige, plotting their crafty moves in advance and often using accomplices. . . . Harris sees no malice in all this, even when heads roll. Brer Rabbit, he explains, is moved not by "malice, but mischievousness." But Brer Rabbit "mischievously" scalds the Wolf to death, makes the innocent Possum die in a fire to cover his own crimes, tortures and probably murders the Bear by setting a swarm of bees on him—and, after causing the fatal beating of the Fox, carries his victim's head to Mrs. Fox and her children, hoping to trick them into eating it in their soup. . . .

One dramatic tension in these stories seems to be a gastronomic one: *Will the communal meal ever take place in the "Animal" Kingdom?*

The food-sharing issue is posed in the very first story. "I seed Brer B'ar yistiddy," the Fox tells the Rabbit as the story opens, "en he sorter rake me over de coals kaze you en me ain't make frens en live naborly." He then invites the Rabbit to supper—intending that his guest will be the main course in this "joint" feast. Brer Rabbit solemnly accepts the invitation, shows up, makes the Fox look ridiculous, and blithely scampers off: "En Brer Fox ain't kotch 'im yit, en w'at's mo', honey, he ain't gwine ter." The Rabbit can get along very well without the communal meal; but, it soon develops, Brer Fox and his associates can't live without it.

Without food-sharing, no community. Open warfare breaks out immediately after the Fox's hypocritical invitation; and the Rabbit is invariably the victor in the gory skirmishes. And after he kills and skins the Wolf, his other enemies are so cowed that now the communal meal finally seems about to take place: "de animals en de creeturs, dey kep' on gittin' mo' en mo' familious wid wunner nudder—bunchin' der perwishuns tergidder in de same shanty" and "takin' a snack" together too.

But Brer Rabbit isn't taken in. Knowing that the others are sharing their food with him out of fear, not genuine communality, he remains the complete cynic and continues to raid the Fox's goober patch and the Bear's persimmon orchard. Not until the closing episode does the Fox make a genuine food-sharing gesture —he crawls inside Bookay the Cow with Brer Rabbit and gratuitously shows him how to hack out all the beef he can carry. But the communal overture comes too late. In an act of the most supreme malevolence, the Rabbit betrays his benefactor to the farmer and stands by, "makin' like he mighty sorry," while the Fox is beaten to death. . . . And now the meal which aborted in the beginning, because the Fox's friendliness was only a ruse, almost does take place—with the Fox as the main course. Having brutally destroyed his arch enemy, Brer Rabbit tries to make Mrs. Fox cook a soup with her husband's head, and almost succeeds.

Remus is not an anthropomorphist by accident. His theme is a *human* one—neighborliness—and the communal meal is a symbol for it. His moral? There are no good neighbors in the world, neither equality nor fraternity. But the moral has an underside: the Rabbit can never be trapped.

Another tension runs through the stories: *Who gets the women?* In sex, Brer Rabbit is at his most aggressive—and his most invincible. Throughout he is engaged in murderous competition with the Fox and the other animals for the favors of "Miss Meadows en de gals."

In their sexual competition the Rabbit never fails to humiliate the Fox viciously. "I'll show Miss Meadows en de gals dat I'm de boss er Brer Fox," he decides. And he does: through the most elaborate trickery he persuades the Fox to put on a saddle, then rides him past Miss Meadows' house, digging his spurs in vigorously. . . . And in sex, it would seem, there are no false distinctions between creatures—all differences in status are irrelevant. At Miss Meadows' the feuds of the work-a-day world must be suspended, "kaze Miss Meadows, she done put her foot down, she did, en say dat w'en dey come ter her place dey hatter hang up a flag er truce at de front gate en 'bide by it."

The truce is all to the Rabbit's advantage, because if the competitors start from scratch in the sexual battle the best man must win—and the best man is invariably Brer Rabbit. The women themselves want the best man to win. Miss Meadows decides to get some peace by holding a contest and letting the winner have his pick of the girls. The Rabbit mulls the problem over. He sings ironically,

> Make a bow ter de Buzzard en den ter de Crow
> Takes a limber-toe gemmun fer ter jump Jim Crow.

Then, through a tricky scheme, he proceeds to outshine all the stronger contestants.

Food-sharing, sex-sharing—the Remus stories read like a catalogue of Southern racial taboos, all standing on their heads. The South, wearing the blinders of stereotype, has always tried to see the Negro as a "roaringly comic" domestic animal. Understandably; for animals of the tame or domestic variety are not menacing—they are capable only of mischief, never of malice. But the Negro slave, through his anthropomorphic Rabbit stories, seems to be hinting that even the frailest and most humble of "animals" can let fly with the most bloodthirsty aggressions. And these aggressions take place in the two most sacrosanct areas of Southern racial etiquette: the gastronomic and the erotic.

The South, with its "sanctions of fear and force," forbids Negroes to eat at the same table with whites. But Brer Rabbit, through an act of murder, *forces* Brer Fox and all his associates to share their food with him. The South enjoins the Negro, under penalty of death, from coming near the white man's women—although the white man has free access to the Negro's women. But Brer Rabbit flauntingly demonstrates his sexual superiority over all the other animals and, as the undisputed victor in the sexual competition, gets his choice of *all* the women.

And yet, despite these food and sex taboos, for two solid centuries—for the Rabbit stories existed long before Harris put them on paper—Southerners chuckled at the way the Rabbit terrorized all the other animals into the communal meal, roared at the Rabbit's guile in winning the girls away from the Fox *by jumping Jim Crow*. And they were endlessly intrigued by the O. Henry spasm of

the miraculous in the very last story, right after the Fox's death:
"Some say dat . . . Brer Rabbit married ole Miss Fox. . . ."

An interesting denouement, considering the sexual fears which
saturate the South's racial attitudes. Still more interesting that
Southern whites should even have countenanced it, let alone revelled in it. . . .

Significantly, the goal of eating and sex, as depicted in Uncle
Remus, is not instinct-gratification. The overriding drive is for
prestige—the South is a prestige-haunted land. And it is in that
potent intangible that the Rabbit is always paid off most handsomely for his exploits. Throughout, as he terrorizes the Strong, the
"sassy" Rabbit remains bland, unperturbed, sure of his invincibility.
When he humiliates the Fox by turning him into a saddle-horse, he
mounts him "same's ef he wuz king er de patter-rollers." ("Patter-
rollers," Harris cheerfully points out, were the white patrols that
terrorized Negro slaves so they wouldn't wander off the plantations.)

Brer Rabbit, in short, has all the jaunty topdog airs and attitudes which a slave can only dream of having. And, like the slave,
he has a supremely cynical view of the social world, since he sees it
from below. The South is the most etiquette-ridden region of the
country; and the Rabbit sees all forms of etiquette as hypocritical
and absurd. Creatures meet, address each other with unctuous
politeness, inquire after each other's families, pass the time of day
with oily clichés—and all the while they are plotting to humiliate,
rob, and assassinate each other. The Rabbit sees through it all; if
he is serene it is only because he can plot more rapidly and with
more deadly efficiency than any of the others.

The world, in Brer Rabbit's wary eyes, is a jungle. Life is a
battle-unto-the-death for food, sex, power, prestige, a battle without rules. There is only one reality in this life: who is on top? But
Brer Rabbit wastes no time lamenting the mad unneighborly
scramble for the top position. Because it is by no means ordained
that the Weak can never take over. In his topsy-turvy world, to all
practical purposes, the Weak *have* taken over. In one episode, the
Rabbit falls down a well in a bucket. He can get back up only by
enticing the Fox to climb into the other bucket. The Fox is
duped: he drops down and the Rabbit rises, singing as he passes
his enemy:

> Good-by, Brer Fox, take keer yo' cloze
> Fer dis is de way de worril goes
> Some goes up en some goes down
> You'll git ter de bottom all safe en soun'.

This is the theme song of the stories. The question remains, who sings it? The Rabbit is a creation of Uncle Remus's people; is it, then, Uncle Remus singing? But Uncle Remus is a creation of Joel Chandler Harris. . . .

There is a significant difference in ages—some hundreds of years—between Uncle Remus and Brer Rabbit. The Rabbit had been the hero of animal stories popular among Negroes from the early days of slavery; these were genuine folk tales told by Negroes to Negroes and handed down in oral form. Uncle Remus was added only when Harris, in packaging the stories—using the Negro grin for gift-wrapping—invented the Negro narrator to sustain the dialect.

Harris, then, fitted the hate-imbued folk materials into a framework, a white man's framework, of "love." He took over the animal characters and situations of the original stories and gave them a human setting: the loving and lovable Negro narrator, the adoring white auditor. Within this framework of love, the blow was heavily padded with caresses and the genuine folk was almost emasculated into the cute folksy.

Almost, but not quite. Harris all his life was torn between his furtive penchant for fiction and his profession of journalism. It was the would-be novelist in him who created Remus, the "giver" of interracial caresses; but the trained journalist in him, having too good an eye and ear, reported the energetic folk blow in the caress. Thus the curious tension in his versions between "human" form and "animal" content.

Before Harris, few Southerners had ever faced squarely the aggressive symbolism of Brer Rabbit, or the paradox of their delight in it. Of course: it was part of the Southerner's undissected myth—often shared by the Negroes—that his cherished childhood sessions in the slave quarters were bathed in two-way benevolence. But Harris, by writing the white South and its Negro tale-spinners into the stories, also wrote in its unfaced paradoxes. Thus his versions helped to rip open the racial myth—and, with it, the interracial grin.

What was the slippery rabbit-hero doing in these stories to begin with? Where did he come from? As soon as Harris wrote down the oral stories for mass consumption, these questions began to agitate many whites. The result was a whole literature devoted to proving the "un-American" genealogy of Brer Rabbit.

Why, one Southern writer asks, did the Negro pick the Rabbit for a hero? Could it be because the Rabbit was "symbolic of his own humble and helpless condition in comparison with his master the owner of the plantation"? Perhaps the Rabbit represents the Negro "in revolt at . . . his own subordinate and insignificant place in society"?

But no: if the Negro is capable of rebelling against society—American society—even symbolically, he is a menace. The Negro must be in revolt against *Nature*, against the "subordinate and insignificant place" assigned to him by biological fate, not America. The writer reassures himself: the Negro makes animals act "like a low order of human intelligence, such as the Negro himself [can] comprehend." The Negro naturally feels "more closely in touch with [the lower animals] than with the white man who [is] so superior to him in every respect." No threat in Brer Rabbit; his genealogy, having no *American* roots, is a technical matter for "the psychologist or the student of folklore."

However, uneasy questions were raised; and as they were raised they were directed at Harris. Readers sensed the symbolic taunts and threats in the Rabbit and insisted on knowing whether they were directed against white America—or against "Nature." Harris took refuge from this barrage of questions in two mutually contradictory formulas: (1) he was merely the "compiler" of these stories, a non-intellectual, a lowly humorist, ignorant of "folkloristic" matters; and (2) Brer Rabbit was most certainly, as Southerners intuited, an undiluted African.

"All that I know—all that we Southerners know—about it," Harris protested, "is that every old plantation mammy in the South is full of these stories." But, a sentence later, Harris decided there *was* one other thing he knew: "One thing is certain—the Negro did not get them from the whites; *probably they are of remote African origin*." And if they come from the Congo, they offer no symbolic blows to Americans; they are simply funny. So Harris warns the folklorists: "First let us have the folktales told as they were intended to be told, for the sake of amusement. . . ."

But if the folklorists *should* find in them something "of value to their pretensions"? Then "let it be picked out and preserved with as little cackling as possible."

The South wavered; it could not shake off the feeling that Brer Rabbit's overtones were more than just funny. And Harris, too, wavered. To a British folklorist editor he wrote, suddenly reversing himself, that the stories were "more important than humorous." And in the introduction to his book he explains that "however humorous it may be in effect, its intention is perfectly serious. . . . It seems to me that a volume written wholly in dialect must have its solemn, not to say melancholy features."

What was it that Harris sporadically found "important," "solemn," even "melancholy" here? It turns out to be the *Americanism* of Brer Rabbit: "it needs no scientific investigation," Harris continues in his introduction, "to show why he [the Negro] selects as his hero the weakest and most harmless of all animals. . . . It is not virtue that triumphs, but helplessness. . . . Indeed, the parallel between the case of the 'weakest' of all animals, who must, perforce, triumph through his shrewdness, and the humble condition of the slave raconteur, is not without its pathos."

A suggestive idea. But such a "parallel" could not have been worked out in the African jungle, before slavery; it implies that Brer Rabbit, after all, was born much closer to the Mississippi than to the Congo. . . . This crucial sentence does not occur in later editions. Instead we read: "It would be presumptious [*sic*] in me to offer an opinion as to the origins of these curious myth-stories; but, *if ethnologists should discover that they did not originate with the African, the proof to that effect should be accompanied with a good deal of persuasive eloquence.*"

In this pressing sentence we can see Harris's whole fragmented psyche mirrored. Like all the South, he was caught in a subjective tug-of-war: his intelligence groped for the venomous American slave crouching behind the Rabbit, but his beleaguered racial emotions, in self-defense, had to insist on the "Africanism" of Brer Rabbit—and of the Negro. Then Miss Sally and Mars John could relish his "quaint antics" without recognizing themselves as his targets.

Against the African origin of Brer Rabbit one may argue that he is an eloquent white folk-symbol too, closely related to the lamb as the epitome of Christian meekness (the Easter bunny). May not the Negro, in his conversion to Christianity, have learned the standard Christian animal symbols from the whites? Could not his constant tale-spinning about the Rabbit's malevolent triumphs somehow, in some devious way, suggest the ascent of Christ, the meekness that shall inherit the earth; suggest, even, that the meek may stop being meek and set about inheriting the earth without waiting on the Biblical timetable?

But, there *is* more definite evidence as to Brer Rabbit's non-African origins—skimpy, not conclusive, but highly suggestive. Folklore study indicates that if the Negro did have stories about a rabbit back in Africa, they were not these stories, and the rabbit was most decidedly not this rabbit. Brer Rabbit's truer ancestor, research suggests, hails from elsewhere.

"Most of these Negro stories," reported a Johns Hopkins ethnologist—one of the "cackling" folklorists— ". . . bear a striking resemblance to the large body of animal stories made on European soil, of which the most extensive is that known as the *Roman de Renard*. The episodes which form the substance of this French version circulated in the Middle Ages on the Flemish border. . . . The principal actors . . . are the fox, who plays the jokes, and the wolf, most frequently the victim of the fox."

In incident after incident, the Brer Rabbit situations parallel the Reynard the Fox situations: the same props appear, the same set-to's, the same ruses, the same supporting characters, often the same dialogue. But there is one big difference: "In *Uncle Remus* the parts are somewhat changed. Here the rabbit, who scarcely appears (under the name Couard) in the *Renard*, is the chief trickster. His usual butt is the fox. . . ."

In Christian symbolism, then, the rabbit is the essence of meekness and innocence. And in an important part of white folk culture he stands for the impotent, the cowardly, as against the cunning fox. Suddenly, with the beginning of slavery, the Negro begins to tell stories in which the rabbit, now the epitome of belligerence and guile, crops up as the *hero*, mercilessly badgering the fox.

Could the Negroes have got the Reynard fables from the whites? Not impossible. The stories originated among the Flemish peasants. During the 12th century they were written down in French, Latin, and German, in a variety of rhymed forms. The many written versions were then widely circulated throughout Western Europe. And more than a few of the first Negro slaves were brought to France, Spain, and Portugal; and some of their descendants were transplanted to America. Also, many early slaves were brought to plantations owned by Frenchmen—whether in the Louisiana Territory, the Acadian-French sections of North Carolina, or the West Indies.

And many white masters, of French and other backgrounds, told these delightful fox tales to their children. And, from the beginning of the slave trade, many Negroes—who may or may not have had pre-Christian rabbit fables of their own back in Africa—could have listened, smiling amiably, slowly absorbing the raw materials for the grinning folk "gift" that would one day be immortalized by Joel Chandler Harris, Walt Disney, Tin Pan Alley, and the comics. . . .

The Harris research technique, we learn, was first-hand and direct. Seeing a group of Negroes, he approaches and asks if they know any Brer Rabbit stories. The Negroes seem not to understand. Offhandedly, and in rich dialect, Harris tells one himself—as often as not, the famous "Tar-Baby" story. The Negroes are transfixed; then, suddenly, they break out in peals of laughter, kick their heels together, slap their thighs. Before long they are swapping Rabbit yarns with the white man as though he were their lifelong "hail-feller." "Curiously enough," Harris notes, "I have found few Ne-groes who will acknowledge to a stranger that they know anything of these legends; and yet to relate one of the stories is the surest road to their confidence and esteem."

Why the sudden hilarity? What magic folk-key causes these wary, taciturn Negroes to open up? Harris claims to have won their "esteem"; but perhaps he only guaranteed them immunity. He thinks he disarmed the Negroes—he may only have demonstrated that he, the white bossman, was disarmed.

And how much did the Negroes tell him when they "opened up"? Just how far did they really open up? Harris observes that "there are different versions of all the stories—the shrewd narrators of the mythology of the old plantation adapting themselves with ready tact to the years, tastes, and expectations of their juvenile audiences." But there seem to be gaps in Harris's own versions. At tantalizingly crucial points Uncle Remus will break off abruptly—"Some tells one tale en some tells nudder"—leaving the story dangling like a radio cliff-hanger. Did these gaps appear when the stories were told to Harris? When the slave is obliged to play the clown-entertainer and "give" his folk tales to his masters, young or old, his keen sense of the fitting might well delete the imper-missible and blur the dubious—and more out of self-preservation than tact.

Of course, the original oral stories would not express the slave's aggressions straightforwardly either. A Negro slave who yielded his mind fully to his race hatreds in an absolutely white-domi-nated situation must go mad; and the function of such folk symbols as Brer Rabbit is precisely to prevent inner explosions by siphon-ing off these hatreds before they can completely possess conscious-ness. Folk tales, like so much of folk culture, are part of an elabor-ate psychic drainage system—they make it possible for Uncle Tom to retain his façade of grinning Tomism and even, to some degree, to believe in it himself. But the slave's venom, while subterranean, must nonetheless have been *thrillingly* close to the surface and its symbolic disguises flimsier, its attacks less roundabout. Accordingly his protective instincts, sensing the danger in too shallow symbolism, would have necessarily wielded a meticulous, if unconscious, blue pencil in the stories told to white audiences.

Harris tried hard to convince himself that Uncle Remus was a full-fledged, dyed-in-the-denim Uncle Tom—he describes the "ven-erable sable patron" as an ex-slave "who has nothing but pleasant memories of the discipline of slavery." But Harris could not completely exorcise the menace in the Meek. How often Remus steps out of his clown-role to deliver unmistakable judgments on class, caste, and race! In those judgments the aggressions of this "white man's nigger" are astonishingly naked.

"Why the Negro Is Black" tells how the little boy makes the "curious" discovery that Remus's palms are white. The old man explains: "Dey wuz a time w'en all de w'ite folks 'us black—blacker dan me. . . . Niggers is niggers now, but de time wuz w'en we 'uz all niggers tergedder. . . ." How did some "niggers" get white? Simply by bathing in a pond which washed their pigmentation off and using up most of the waters, so that the latecomers could only dabble their hands and feet in it.

But the stragglers who were left with their dark skin tone are not trapped—they may be able to wriggle out of it. In "A Plantation Witch," Remus, explaining that there are witches everywhere in the world that "comes en conjus fokes," hints that these witches may be Negroes who have slipped out of their skins. And these witches conjure white folks from all sides, taking on the forms of owls, bats, dogs, cats—and rabbits.

And in "The Wonderful Tar-Baby Story"—advertised on the dust-jacket as the most famous of all the Remus stories—Remus reverts to the question of pigmentation. ("There are few Negroes that will fail to respond" to this one, Harris advises one of his folklore "legmen.") The Fox fashions a "baby" out of tar and places it on the side of the road; the Rabbit comes along and addresses the figure. Not getting any answer, he threatens: "Ef you don't take off dat hat en tell me howdy, I'm gwineter bus' you wide open." (Here the Rabbit's bluster reads like a parody of the white man's demand for the proper bowing-and-scraping etiquette from the Negro; it is a reflection of the satiric mimicry of the whites which the slaves often indulged in among themselves.) He hits the Tar-Baby—his fist sticks in the gooey tar. He hits it with the other hand, then kicks it—all four extremities are stuck.

This is "giving" in a new sense; tar, blackness, by its very yielding, traps. Interesting symbol, in a land where the mere possession of a black skin requires you, under penalty of death, to yield, to *give*, everywhere. The mark of supreme impotence suddenly acquires the power to render impotent, merely by its flaccidity, its inertness; it is almost a Gandhi-like symbol. There is a puzzle here: it is the Rabbit who is trapped. But in a later story, "How Mr. Rabbit Was Too Sharp for Mr. Fox," it turns out that the Rabbit, through another cagey maneuver, gets the Fox to set him free from the tartrap and thus avoids being eaten by his enemy. The Negro, in other words, is wily enough to escape from the engulfing pit of blackness, although his opponents, who set the trap, do their level best to keep him imprisoned in it. But it is not at all sure that anyone else who fell victim to this treacherous black yieldingness—the Fox, say—would be able to wriggle out so easily.

The story about "A Plantation Witch" frightens his young admirer so much that Remus has to take him by the hand and lead him home to the "big house." And for a long time the boy lies awake "expecting an unseemly visitation from some mysterious source." Many of the other stories, too, must have given him uneasy nights. For within the "gift" that Uncle Remus gives to Miss Sally's little boy is a nightmare, a nightmare in which whites are Negroes, the Weak torture and drown the Strong, mere blackness becomes black magic—and Negroes cavort with cosmic forces and the supernatural, zipping their skins off at will to prowl around the countryside terrorizing the whites, often in the guise of rabbits. . . .

Harris's career is one of the fabulous success stories of American literary history. Thanks to Uncle Remus, the obscure newspaperman was catapulted into the company of Mark Twain, Bret Harte, James Whitcomb Riley, and Petroleum V. Nasby; Andrew Carnegie and Theodore Roosevelt traveled to Atlanta to seek him out; he was quoted in Congress. And all the while he maintained—as in a letter to Twain—that "my book has no basis in literary merit to stand upon; I know it is the matter and not the manner that has attracted public attention . . . my relations towards Uncle Remus are similar to those that exist between an almanac-maker and the calendar. . . ."

But how was it that Harris could apply his saccharine manner to such matter, dress this malevolent material, these nightmares, in such sweetness and light? For one thing, of course, he was only recording the tottering racial myth of the post-bellum South, doing a paste-job on its fissioning falseface. As it happened, he was peculiarly suited for the job; for he was crammed full of pathological racial obsessions, over and above those that wrack the South and, to a lesser degree, all of white America.

Even Harris's worshipful biographer, his daughter-in-law, can't prevent his story from reading like a psychiatric recital of symptoms. The blush and the stammer were his whole way of life. From early childhood on, we are told, he was "painfully conscious of his social deficiencies" and his "lack of size"; he felt "handicapped by his tendency to stutter" and to "blush furiously," believed himself "much uglier than he really was"; in his own words, he had "an absolute horror of strangers."

During his induction into the typographical union, Harris stutters so badly that he has to be excused from the initiation ceremony; trapped in a room full of congenial strangers, he escapes by

jumping out of the window. "What a coarse ungainly boor I am,"
he laments, "how poor, small and insignificant. . . ." He wonders
if he is mad: "I am morbidly sensitive . . . it is an affliction—a
disease . . . the slightest rebuff tortures me beyond expression.
. . . It is worse than death itself. It is *horrible.*" Again, he specu-
lates about his "abnormal quality of mind . . . that lacks only
vehemence to become downright insanity. . . ." Harris's life, it
appears, was one long ballet of embarrassment.

"I am nursing a novel in my brain," Harris announced archly
more than once. All along he was consumed with the desire to turn
out some "long work" of fiction, but, except for two inept and
badly received efforts (published after his forty-eighth year), he
never succeeded. Over and over he complained bitterly of his grind-
ing life in the journalistic salt mines—but when the Century Company offered him a handsome income if he would devote all his
time to creative work, he refused. This refusal, according to his
daughter-in-law, "can be explained only by his abnormal lack of
confidence in himself as a 'literary man.'"
    The urge to create was strong in Harris, so strong that it gave
him no peace; and he could not create. That is the central fact in
his biography: his creative impulses were trapped behind a block
of congealed guilts, granite-strong; the works he produced were not
real gushings of the subjective but only those driblets that were
able to seep around the edges of the block.
    Harris's stammer—his literal choking on words—was like a
charade of the novelist *manqué* in him; his blush was the fitful
glow of his smothered self, a tic of the guilty blood. And that
smothered self had a name: Uncle Remus.
    Accused of plagiarizing folk materials, Harris replies indignantly:
"I shall not hesitate to draw on the oral stories I know for incidents.
. . . The greatest literary men, if you will remember, were very
poor inventors." Harris all his life was a very poor inventor; his
career was built on a merciless, systematic plagiarizing of the folk-
Negro. Small wonder, then, that the "plantation darky" was such a
provocative symbol for him. For, ironically, this lowly Negro was,
when viewed through the blinders of stereotype, almost the walking
image of Harris's ego-ideal—the un-selfconscious, "natural," free-
flowing, richly giving creator that Harris could never become. Indeed,
for Harris, as for many another white American, the Negro *seemed*
in every respect to be a negative print of his own uneasy self:
"happy-go-lucky," socializing, orally expressive, muscularly relaxed,
never bored or passive, unashamedly exhibitionistic, free from self-
pity even in his situation of concentrated pain, emotionally fluid.
And every time a Remus opened his mouth, every time he flashed

a grin, he wrote effortlessly another novel that was strangled a-born-ing in Harris.

"I despise and detest those false forms of society that compel people to suppress their thoughts," Harris wrote. But he was him-self the most inhibited and abashed of men. What fascinates him in the Rabbit stories, he confesses, is "the humor that lies between *what is perfectly decorous in appearance* and *what is wildly extrava-gant in suggestion.*" But, a thorough slave to decorum, he was incapable of the "wildly extravagant," whether in his love-making ("My love for you," he informs his future wife, "is . . . far re-moved from that wild passion that develops itself in young men in their teens . . . it is not at all wild or unreasoning.") or in his writing.

Harris, then, was *awed* by Uncle Remus. It was the awe of the sophisticate before the spontaneous, the straitjacketed before the nimble. But was the Negro what Harris thought him to be? It is certainly open to question, for another irony of the South is that the white man, under his pretense of racial omniscience, actually knows the Negro not at all—he knows only the falseface which he has forced on the Negro. It is the white man who manufactures the Negro grin. The stereotype reflects the looker, his thwartings and yearnings, not the person looked at; it is born out of intense subjec-tive need.

Harris's racial awe was only an offshoot of the problem that tormented him all his life: the problem of identifying himself. He was caught in the American who-am-I dilemma, one horn of which is white, the other often black. And there is abundant proof that, at least in one compartment of his being, Harris defined himself by identifying with the Negro.

As a child, Harris started the game of "Gully Minstrels" with his white playmates; and later in life, whenever he felt "blue" and wanted to relax, he would jump up and exclaim, "Let's have some fun—let's play minstrels!" Often, in letters and newspaper articles, and even in personal relations, he would *jokingly* refer to himself as "Uncle Remus," and when he started a one-man magazine, he decided to name it *Uncle Remus's Magazine* instead of *The Opti-mist!* Frequently he would lapse into a rich Negro dialect, to the delight of his admirers, from Andrew Carnegie down to the local trolley conductor. And, like Uncle Remus, he even toys with the idea that whites are only blanched Negroes: "Study a nigger right close," he has one of his characters say, "and you'll ketch a glimpse of how white folks would look and do without their trimmin's."

Harris seems to have been a man in permanent rebellion against his own skin. No wonder: for he was driven to "give," and it was impossible for him to give without first zipping out of his own decorous skin and slipping into Uncle Remus's. To him the artist and the Negro were synonymous.

And Harris virulently *hated* the Negro, too. "The colored people of Macon," he writes in his paper, "celebrated the birthday of Lincoln again on Wednesday. This is the third time since last October. . . ." And: "A negro pursued by an agile Macon police-man fell in a well the other day. He says he knocked the bottom out of the concern." Again: "There will have to be another amendment to the civil rights bill. A negro boy in Covington was attacked by a sow lately and narrowly escaped with his life. We will hear next that the sheep have banded together to mangle the downtrodden race."

The malice here is understandable. Can the frustrate—the "al-manac-maker"—ever love unequivocally the incarnation of his own taboo self—the "calendar"? What stillborn novelist can be undi-lutedly tender towards the objectivization of his squelched alter-ego, whose oral stories he feels impelled to "draw on" all his life?

Most likely, at least in Harris, the love went deeper than the hate—the hate was, in some measure, a *defense* against the love. "*Some goes up en some goes down.*" Who sings this theme song? A trio: the Rabbit, Remus, *and* Harris. Literally, it is only a rabbit and a fox who change places. Racially, the song symbolizes the ascent of the Negro "Weak" and the descent of the white "Strong."

But to Harris, on the deepest personal level, it must have meant: the collapse of the "perfectly decorous" (inhibition, etiquette, em-barrassment, the love that is never wild, the uncreative journalist-compiler, the blush and the stammer) and the triumph of the "wildly extravagant" (spontaneity, "naturalness," the unleashed sub-jective, creativity, "Miss Meadows en de gals," exhibitionism, the folk-novelist). The song must have been *deliciously* funny to him. . . .

The Remus stories are a monument to the South's ambivalence. Harris, the archetypical Southerner, sought the Negro's love, and pretended he had received it (Remus's grin). But he sought the Ne-gro's hate too (Brer Rabbit), and revelled in it in an unconscious orgy of masochism—punishing himself, possibly for not being the Negro, the stereotypical Negro, the unstinting giver.

Harris's inner split—and the South's, and white America's—is mirrored on the fantastic disparity between Remus's beaming face and Brer Rabbit's acts. And such aggressive acts increasingly ema-nate from the grin, along with the hamburgers, the shoeshines, the "happifyin'" pancakes.

Today Negro attack and counter-attack becomes more straightforward. The NAACP submits a brief to the United Nations, demanding a redress of grievances suffered by the Negro people at the hands of white America. The election newsreels showed Henry Wallace addressing audiences that were heavily sprinkled with Negroes, protected by husky, alert, *deadpan* bodyguards—Negroes. New York Negroes voted for Truman—but only after Truman went to Harlem. The Gandhi-like "Tar-Baby" begins to stir: Grant Reynolds and A. Philip Randolph, announcing to a Senate committee that they will refuse to be drafted in the next war, revealed, at the time, that many Negroes were joining their civil-disobedience organization—the first movement of passive resistance this country had seen.

Increasingly Negroes themselves reject the mediating smile of Remus, the indirection of the Rabbit. The present-day animated cartoon hero, Bugs Bunny, is, like Brer Rabbit, the meek suddenly grown cunning—but without Brer Rabbit's façade of politeness. "To pull a Bugs Bunny," meaning to spectacularly outwit someone, is an expression not infrequently heard in Harlem.

There is today on every level a mass repudiation of "Uncle Tomism." Significantly the Negro comedian is disappearing. For bad or good, the *Dark Laughter* that Sherwood Anderson heard all around white New Orleans is going or gone.

The grin is faltering, especially since the war. That may be one of the reasons why, once more, the beaming Negro butler and Pullman porter are making their amiable way across our billboards, food labels, and magazine ads—and Uncle Remus, "fetchin' a grin from year to year," is in the bigtime again.

BERNARD WOLFE (1915–   ) *writes fiction and screenplays, as well as studies of popular culture. His first book, with* Mezy Mezzrow, *was* Really the Blues *(1946); later works include* Limbo *(1952),* The Late Risers *(1954),* In Deep *(1957),* The Great Prince Died *(1959),* The Magic of Their Singing *(1961). He has contributed many essays to such periodicals as* The Nation, Esquire, Playboy, *and* Commentary, *where the "Uncle Remus" article first appeared in 1949.*

1. *This essay begins by examining assumptions: "may not the smiling face be a falseface—and just underneath is there not something else, often only half-hidden?" Like Riesman with Little Red Riding Hood, Wolfe takes the animal tales seriously; the assumptions will form the basis for a later series of implications of the utmost importance. List the assumptions he identifies that*

lie within *the stories* (e.g., "*There are no good neighbors in the world*").

2. *After looking closely at the assumptions in the tales, Wolfe turns to the implications that follow: "Food-sharing, sex-sharing—the Remus stories read like a catalogue of Southern racial taboos, all standing on their heads." List some of the implications Wolfe draws from the stories, about the South, Harris, America.*

3. *If this examination of the Uncle Remus tales is valid, it helps explain some of the developments in race relations in America since 1949, when Wolfe's essay was published. What has happened since then, and how does the essay help us see what these events mean? What does the essay suggest about the future?*

4. *Wolfe says folk symbols are "cultural shadows thrown by the unconscious. . . ." Do the Negro spirituals throw shadows similar to those of the Uncle Remus tales? Choose another animal myth in your culture whose implications are worth examining: Donald Duck, say, or Bambi, or Rudolph the Red-Nosed Reindeer, etc. Write an essay examining the assumptions in these tales, and showing their implications, their "cultural shadows."*

X. J. Kennedy

WHO KILLED KING KONG?

The ordeal and spectacular death of King Kong, the giant ape, undoubtedly have been witnessed by more Americans than have ever seen a performance of *Hamlet, Iphigenia at Aulis,* or even *Tobacco Road.* Since RKO-Radio Pictures first released *King Kong,* a quarter-century has gone by; yet year after year, from prints that grow more rain-beaten, from sound tracks that grow more tinny, ticket-buyers by thousands still pursue Kong's luckless fight against the forces of technology, tabloid journalism, and the DAR. They see him chloroformed to sleep, see him whisked from his jungle isle to New York and placed on show, see him burst his chains to roam the city (lugging a frightened blonde), at last to plunge from the spire of the Empire State Building, machine-gunned by model airplanes.

Though Kong may die, one begins to think his legend unkillable. No clearer proof of his hold upon the popular imagination may be seen than what emerged one catastrophic week in March 1955, when New York WOR-TV programmed *Kong* for seven evenings in a row (a total of sixteen showings). Many a rival network vice-president must have scowled when surveys showed that *Kong* —the 1933 B-picture—had lured away fat segments of the viewing populace from such powerful competitors as Ed Sullivan, Groucho Marx and Bishop Sheen.

But even television has failed to run *King Kong* into oblivion. Coffee-in-the-lobby cinemas still show the old hunk of hokum, with the apology that in its use of composite shots and animated models the film remains technically interesting. And no other monster in movie history has won so devoted a popular audience. None of the plodding mummies, the stultified draculas, the white-coated Lugosis * with their shiny pinball-machine laboratories, none of the invisible stranglers, berserk robots, or menaces from Mars has ever enjoyed so many resurrections.

Why does the American public refuse to let King Kong rest in

Reprinted from the Spring 1960 issue of *Dissent* by permission of the author and *Dissent.*
* The actor Bela Lugosi.

peace? It is true, I'll admit, that *Kong* outdid every monster movie before or since in sheer carnage. Producers Cooper and Schoedsack crammed into it dinosaurs, headhunters, riots, aerial battles, bullets, bombs, bloodletting. Heroine Fay Wray, whose function is mainly to scream, shuts her mouth for hardly one uninterrupted minute from first reel to last. It is also true that *Kong* is larded with good healthy sadism, for those whose joy it is to see the frantic girl dangled from cliffs and harried by pterodactyls. But it seems to me that the abiding appeal of the giant ape rests on other foundations.

Kong has, first of all, the attraction of being manlike. His simian nature gives him one huge advantage over giant ants and walking vegetables in that an audience may conceivably identify with him. Kong's appeal has the quality that established the Tarzan series as American myth—for what man doesn't secretly image himself a huge hairy howler against whom no other monster has a chance? If Tarzan recalls the ape in us, then Kong may well appeal to that great-granddaddy primordial brute from whose tribe we have all deteriorated.

Intentionally or not, the producers of *King Kong* encourage this identification by etching the character of Kong with keen sympathy. For the ape is a figure in a tradition familiar to moviegoers: the tradition of the pitiable monster. We think of Lon Chaney in the role of Quasimodo, of Karloff in the original *Frankenstein*. As we watch the Frankenstein monster's fumbling and disastrous attempts to befriend a flower-picking child, our sympathies are enlisted with the monster in his impenetrable loneliness. And so with Kong. As he roars in his chains, while barkers sell tickets to boobs who gape at him, we perhaps feel something more deep than pathos. We begin to sense something of the problem that engaged Eugene O'Neill in *The Hairy Ape*: the dilemma of a displaced animal spirit forced to live in a jungle built by machines.

King Kong, it is true, had special relevance in 1933. Landscapes of the depression are glimpsed early in the film when an impresario, seeking some desperate pretty girl to play the lead in a jungle movie, visits souplines and a Woman's Home Mission. In Fay Wray— who's been caught snitching an apple from a fruitstand—his search is ended. When he gives her a big feed and a movie contract, the girl is magic-carpeted out of the world of the National Recovery Act. And when, in the film's climax, Kong smashes that very Third Avenue landscape in which Fay had wandered hungry, audiences of 1933 may well have felt a personal satisfaction.

What is curious is that audiences of 1960 remain hooked. For in the heart of urban man, one suspects, lurks the impulse to fling a bomb. Though machines speed him to the scene of his daily grind, though IBM comptometers ("freeing the human mind from drudgery") enable him to drudge more efficiently once he arrives, there comes a moment when he wishes to turn upon his machines and kick hell out of them. He wants to hurl his combination radio-alarmclock out the bedroom window and listen to its smash. What subway commuter wouldn't love—just for once—to see the downtown express smack head-on into the uptown local? Such a wish is gratified in that memorable scene in *Kong* that opens with a wide-angle shot: interior of a railway car on the Third Avenue El. Straphangers are nodding, the literate refold their newspapers. Unknown to them, Kong has torn away a section of trestle toward which the train now speeds. The motorman spies Kong up ahead, jams on the brakes. Passengers hurtle together like so many peas in a pail. In a window of the car appear Kong's bloodshot eyes. Women shriek. Kong picks up the railway car as if it were a rat, flips it to the street and ties knots in it, or something. To any commuter the scene must appear one of the most satisfactory pieces of celluloid ever exposed.

Yet however violent his acts, Kong remains a gentleman. Remarkable is his sense of chivalry. Whenever a fresh boa constrictor threatens Fay, Kong first sees that the lady is safely parked, then manfully thrashes her attacker. (And she, the ingrate, runs away every time his back is turned.) Atop the Empire State Building, ignoring his pursuers, Kong places Fay on a ledge as tenderly as if she were a dozen eggs. He fondles her, then turns to face the Army Air Force. And Kong is perhaps the most disinterested lover since Cyrano: his attentions to the lady are utterly without hope of reward. After all, between a five-foot blonde and a fifty-foot ape, love can hardly be more than an intellectual flirtation. In his simian way King Kong is the hopelessly yearning lover of Petrarchan convention. His forced exit from his jungle, in chains, results directly from his single-minded pursuit of Fay. He smashes a Broadway theater when the notion enters his dull brain that the flashbulbs of photographers somehow endanger the lady. His perilous shinnying up a skyscraper to pluck Fay from her boudoir is an act of the kindliest of hearts. He's impossible to discourage even though the love of his life can't lay eyes on him without shrieking murder.

The tragedy of King Kong then, is to be the beast who at the end of the fable fails to turn into the handsome prince. This is the conviction that the scriptwriters would leave with us in the film's closing line. As Kong's corpse lies blocking traffic in the street, the entrepreneur who brought Kong to New York turns to the assembled reporters and proclaims: "That's your story, boys—it was Beauty killed the Beast!" But greater forces than those of the screaming Lady have combined to lay Kong low, if you ask me.

116 · X. J. Kennedy

Kong lives for a time as one of those persecuted near-animal souls bewildered in the middle of an industrial order, whose simple desires are thwarted at every turn. He climbs the Empire State Building because in all New York it's the closest thing he can find to the clifftop of his jungle isle. He dies, a pitiful dolt, and the army brass and publicity-men cackle over him. His death is the only possible outcome to as neat a tragic dilemma as you can ask for. The machine-guns do him in, while the manicured human hero (a nice clean Dartmouth boy) carries away Kong's sweetheart to the altar. O, the misery of it all. There's far more truth about upper-middle-class American life in *King Kong* than in the last seven dozen novels of John P. Marquand.

A Negro friend from Atlanta tells me that in movie houses in colored neighborhoods throughout the South, *Kong* does a constant business. They show the thing in Atlanta at least every year, presumably to the same audiences. Perhaps this popularity may simply be due to the fact that *Kong* is one of the most watchable movies ever constructed, but I wonder whether Negro audiences may not find some archetypical appeal in this serio-comic tale of a huge black powerful free spirit whom all the hardworking white policemen are out to kill.

Every day in the week on a screen somewhere in the world, King Kong relives his agony. Again and again he expires on the Empire State Building, as audiences of the devout assist his sacrifice. We watch him die, and by extension kill the ape within our bones, but these little deaths of ours occur in prosaic surroundings. We do not die on a tower, New York before our feet, nor do we give our lives to smash a few flying machines. It is not for us to bring to a momentary standstill the civilization in which we move. King Kong does this for us. And so we kill him again and again, in much-spliced celluloid, while the ape in us expires from day to day, obscure, in desperation.

———

Joseph Kennedy (1929–   ) has added the individualizing X to his name for effect. He first gained wide notice with a volume of poetry, Nude Descending a Staircase *(1961), and has since published much poetry and an important textbook,* An Introduction to Poetry *(second edition, 1971). He has taught at the universities of Michigan and North Carolina; Wellesley College; and, currently, Tufts University.*

1. *Describe the tone of this essay. What is the effect on the tone of sequences such as "Kong's luckless fight against the forces of*

technology, tabloid journalism, and the DAR [Daughters of the American Revolution]," or "the plodding mummies, the stultified draculas, the white-coated Lugosis with their pinball-machine laboratories"? When Kennedy says urban man sometimes "wishes to turn upon his machines and kick hell out of them," how is he asking you to relate to him and to his subject?

2. Despite the lightness of tone, Kennedy makes it clear he is speaking of serious matters: "in the heart of urban man, one suspects, lurks the impulse to fling a bomb." "Any commuter," Kennedy continues, must find the destruction of the railway car "one of the most satisfactory pieces of celluloid ever exposed." And his last sentence speaks of "the ape in us" dying in desperation. What assumptions is Kennedy making about the nature of man and about the way horror films speak to that nature?

3. What does Kennedy mean by "the truth about upper-middle-class American life in King Kong"? What are the implications about American society to be drawn from the immense popularity of this film?

Katherine Anne Porter

THE CIRCUS

The long planks set on trestles rose one above the other to a monstrous height and stretched dizzyingly in a wide oval ring. They were packed with people—"lak fleas on a dog's ear," said Dicey, holding Miranda's hand firmly and looking about her with disapproval. The white billows of enormous canvas sagged overhead, held up by three poles set evenly apart down the center. The family, when seated, occupied almost a whole section on one level.

On one side of them in a long row sat Father, sister Maria, brother Paul, Grandmother; great-aunt Keziah, cousin Keziah, and second-cousin Keziah, who had just come down from Kentucky on a visit; uncle Charles Breaux, cousin Charles Breaux, and aunt Marie-Anne Breaux. On the other side sat small cousin Lucie Breaux, big cousin Paul Gay, great-aunt Sally Gay (who took snuff and was therefore a disgrace to the family); two strange, extremely handsome young men who might be cousins but who were certainly in love with cousin Miranda Gay; and cousin Miranda Gay herself, a most dashing young lady with crisp silk skirts, a half dozen of them at once, a lovely perfume and wonderful black curly hair above enormous wild gray eyes, "like a colt's," Father said. Miranda hoped to be exactly like her when she grew up. Hanging to Dicey's arm she leaned out and waved to cousin Miranda, who waved back smiling, and the strange young men waved to her also. Miranda was most fearfully excited. It was her first circus; it might also be her last because the whole family had combined to persuade Grandmother to allow her to come with them. "Very well, this once," Grandmother said, "since it's a family reunion."

This once! This once! She could not look hard enough at everything. She even peeped down between the wide crevices of the piled-up plank seats, where she was astonished to see odd-looking, roughly dressed little boys peeping up from the dust below. They were squatted in little heaps, staring up quietly. She looked squarely into the eyes of one, who returned her a look so peculiar she gazed and gazed, trying to understand it. It was a bold grinning stare without any kind of friendliness in it. He was a thin, dirty little boy with a floppy old checkerboard cap pulled over crumpled red ears and dust-colored hair. As she gazed he nudged the little boy next to him, whispered, and the second little boy caught her eye. This was too much. Miranda pulled Dicey's sleeve. "Dicey, what are those little boys doing down there?" "Down where?" asked Dicey, but she seemed to know already, for she bent over and looked through the crevice, drew her knees together and her skirts around her, and said severely: "You jus mind yo' own business and stop throwin' yo' legs around that way. Don't you pay any mind. Plenty o' monkeys right here in the show widout you studyin dat kind."

An enormous brass band seemed to explode right at Miranda's ear. She jumped, quivered, thrilled blindly and almost forgot to breathe as sound and color and smell rushed together and poured through her skin and hair and beat in her head and hands and feet and pit of her stomach. "Oh," she called out in her panic, closing her eyes and seizing Dicey's hand hard. The flaring lights burned through her lids, a roar of laughter like rage drowned out the steady raging of the drums and horns. She opened her eyes . . . A creature in a blousy white overall with ruffles at the neck and ankles, with bone-white skull and chalk-white face, with tufted eyebrows far apart in the middle of his forehead, the lids in a black sharp angle, a long scarlet mouth stretching back into sunken cheeks, turned up at the corners in a perpetual bitter grimace of pain, astonishment, not smiling, pranced along a wire stretched down the center of the ring, balancing a long thin pole with little wheels at either end. Miranda thought at first he was walking on air, or flying, and this did not surprise her; but when she saw the wire, she was terrified. High above their heads the inhuman figure pranced, spinning the little wheels. He paused, slipped, the flapping white leg waved in space; he staggered, wobbled, slipped sidewise, plunged, and caught the wire with frantic knee, hanging there upside down, the other leg waving like a feeler above his head; slipped once more, caught by one frenzied heel, and swung back and forth like a scarf . . . The crowd roared with savage delight, shrieks of dreadful laughter like devils in delicious torment . . . Miranda shrieked too, with real pain, clutching at her stomach with her knees drawn up . . . The man on the wire, hanging by his foot, turned his head like a seal from side to side and blew sneering kisses from his cruel mouth. Then Miranda covered her eyes and screamed, the tears pouring over her cheeks and chin.

"Take her home," said her father, "get her out of here at once," but the laughter was not wiped from his face. He merely glanced at her and back to the ring. "Take her away, Dicey," called the Grandmother, from under her half-raised crepe veil. Dicey, rebelliously, very slowly, without taking her gaze from the white figure swaying on the wire, rose, seized the limp, suffering bundle, prodded and lumped her way over knees and feet, through the crowd, down the levels of the scaffolding, across a space of sandy tanbark, out through a flap in the tent. Miranda was crying steadily with an occasional hiccough. A dwarf was standing in the entrance, wearing a little woolly beard, a pointed cap, tight red breeches, long shoes with turned-up toes. He carried a thin white wand. Miranda almost touched him before she saw him, her distorted face with its open mouth and glistening tears almost level with his. He leaned forward and peered at her with kind, not-human golden eyes, like a near-sighted dog: then made a horrid grimace at her, imitating her own face. Miranda struck at him in sheer ill temper, screaming. Dicey drew her away quickly, but not before Miranda had seen in his face, suddenly, a look of haughty, remote displeasure, a true grown-up look. She knew it well. It chilled her with a new kind of fear: she had not believed he was really human.

"Raincheck, get your raincheck!" said a very disagreeable looking fellow as they passed. Dicey turned toward him almost in tears herself. "Mister, caint you see I won't be able to git back? I got this young un to see to . . . What good dat lil piece of paper goin to do *me*?" All the way home she was cross, and grumbled under her breath: little ole meany . . . little ole scare-cat . . . gret big baby . . . never go nowhere . . . never see nothin . . . come on here now, hurry up—always ruinin everything for othah folks . . . won't let anybody rest a minute, won't let anybody have any good times . . . come on here now, you wanted to go home and you're going there . . . snatching Miranda along, vicious but cautious, careful not to cross the line where Miranda could say outright: "Dicey did this or said this to me . . ." Dicey was allowed a certain freedom up to a point.

The family trooped into the house just before dark and scattered out all over it. From every room came the sound of chatter and laughter. The other children told Miranda what she had missed: wonderful little ponies with plumes and bells on their bridles, ridden by darling little monkeys in velvet jackets and peaked hats . . . trained white goats that danced . . . a baby elephant that crossed his front feet and leaned against his cage and opened his mouth to be fed, *such* a baby! . . . more clowns, funnier than the first one even . . . beautiful ladies with bright yellow hair, wearing white silk tights with red satin sashes had performed on white trapezes; they also had hung by their toes, but how gracefully,

like flying birds! Huge white horses had lolloped around and round
the ring with men and women dancing on their backs! One man
had swung by his teeth from the top of the tent and another had
put his head in a lion's mouth. Ah, what she had not missed! Everybody had been enjoying themselves while she was missing her first
big circus and spoiling the day for Dicey. Poor Dicey. Poor dear
Dicey. The other children who hadn't thought of Dicey until that
moment, mourned over her with sad mouths, their malicious eyes
watching Miranda squirm. Dicey had been looking forward for
weeks to this day! And then Miranda must get scared—"Can you
imagine being afraid of that funny old clown?" each one asked the
other, and then they smiled pityingly on Miranda . . .

Then too, it had been a very important occasion in another way:
it was the first time Grandmother had ever allowed herself to be
persuaded to go to the circus. One could not gather, from her rather
generalized opinions, whether there had been no circuses when she
was young, or there had been and it was not proper to see them. At
any rate for her usual sound reasons, Grandmother had never ap-
proved of circuses, and though she would not deny she had been
amused somewhat, still there had been sights and sounds in this
one which she maintained were, to say the least, not particularly
edifying to the young. Her son Harry, who came in while the children made an early supper, looked at their illuminated faces, all the
brothers and sisters and visiting cousins, and said, "This basket of
young doesn't seem to be much damaged." His mother said, "The
fruits of their present are in a future so far off, neither of us may
live to know whether harm has been done or not. That is the trouble," and she went on ladling out hot milk to pour over their but-
tered toast. Miranda was sitting silent, her underlip drooping. Her
father smiled at her. "You missed it, Baby," he said softly, "and
what good did that do you?"

Miranda burst again into tears: had to be taken away at last, and
her supper was brought up to her. Dicey was exasperated and silent.
Miranda could not eat. She tried, as if she were really remembering
them, to think of the beautiful wild beings in white satin and span-
gles and red sashes who danced and frolicked on the trapezes; of the
sweet little furry ponies and the lovely pet monkeys in their comical
clothes. She fell asleep, and her invented memories gave way before
her real ones, the bitter terrified face of the man in blowsy white
falling to his death—ah, the cruel joke!—and the terrible grimace
of the unsmiling dwarf. She screamed in her sleep and sat up crying
for deliverance from her torments.

Dicey came, her cross, sleepy eyes half-closed, her big dark
mouth pouted, thumping the floor with her thick bare feet. "I
swear," she said, in a violent hoarse whisper. "What the matter

with you? You need a good spankin, I *swear!* Wakin everybody up
like this . . ."

Miranda was completely subjugated by her fears. She had a way
of answering Dicey back. She would say, "Oh, hush up, Dicey." Or
she would say, "I don't have to mind *you.* I don't have to mind
anybody but my grandmother," which was provokingly true. And
she would say, "You don't know what you're talking about." The
day just past had changed that. Miranda sincerely did not want anybody, not even Dicey, to be cross with her. Ordinarily she did not
care how cross she made the harassed adults around her. Now if
Dicey must be cross, she still did not really care, if only Dicey might
not turn out the lights and leave her to the fathomless terrors of the
darkness where sleep could overtake her once more. She hugged
Dicey with both arms, crying, "Don't, don't leave me. *Don't* be so
angry! I c-c-can't b-bear it!"

Dicey lay down beside her with a long moaning sigh, which
meant that she was collecting her patience and making up her mind
to remember that she was a Christian and must bear her cross.
"Now you go to sleep," she said, in her usual warm being-good
voice. "Now you jes shut yo eyes and go to sleep. I ain't going to
leave you. Dicey ain't mad at nobody . . . *nobody* in the whole
worl' . . ."

———

KATHERINE ANNE PORTER (1890–   ) *gained fame as a writer with*
two volumes of short stories, Flowering Judas (1930), The Lean-
ing Tower and Other Stories (1944), *and the short novels in* Pale
Horse, Pale Rider (1939). *Although she never attended college as a*
student, the brilliance of these few short works made her a welcome
visitor and lecturer at many colleges and universities; she would oc-
casionally boast of making a better living on her promise as a writer
than many others did from their published books. This promise
seemed fulfilled in Ship of Fools (1962), *now her best-known work.*
Most recently, her Collected Essays and Occasional Writings (1970)
included interesting essays, letters, and poems from her entire career.
"My whole attempt," she wrote in a 1956 essay in that collection,
"has been to discover and understand human motives, human feel-
ings, to make a distillation of what human relations and experiences
my mind has been able to absorb."

1. *Miranda's terrors are at the center of the story. But the source,*
    meaning, and implications of these terrors are not very clear.

Look, for example, at the obvious causes for her crying fit at the circus: list the major ones. Describe the explanations of her tears given by the others in her family: the father, the grandmother, the other children, Dicey. Why is she carrying on so?

2. The fourth and fifth paragraphs of the story give us Miranda's perception of the circus; the seventh paragraph gives us the other children's view of it. Compare the language of these two descriptions of the circus; which is more accurate, which sees more? Why is Miranda even more frightened when she notices the "true grown-up look" on the dwarf's face? (You might expect her to be reassured, since "she had not believed he was really human.") Is there something genuinely, really frightening about the circus (any circus) which most people cover over or only half perceive? Miranda sees things (like the boys under the plank seats) that others routinely ignore. In what sense are her terrors childish? In what sense are they too grown up for the grownups?

3. Grandmother hints at serious implications of the circus experience: "The fruits of their present are in a future so far off, neither of us may live to know whether harm has been done or not." At the start of the story Miranda hopes to be exactly like her cousin Miranda Gay. How "Gay" is the child Miranda to grow up to be, with her kind of perceptions? "The day just past had changed that," along with much else. Are there suggestions that Miranda can see through the surface pretense of the family group into what is really going on? What are the implications of this story about sensitive people living in insensitive surroundings?

Edward Field

THE BRIDE OF FRANKENSTEIN

The Baron has decided to mate the monster,
to breed him perhaps,
in the interests of pure science, his only god.

So he goes up into his laboratory
which he has built in the tower of the castle
to be as near the interplanetary forces as possible,
and puts together the prettiest monster-woman you ever saw
with a body like a pin-up girl
and hardly any stitching at all
where he sewed on the head of a raped and murdered beauty
    queen.

He sets his liquids burping, and coils blinking and buzzing,
and waits for an electric storm to send through the equipment
the spark vital for life.
The storm breaks over the castle
and the equipment really goes crazy
like a kitchen full of modern appliances
as the lightning juice starts oozing right into that pretty corpse.

He goes to get the monster
so he will be right there when she opens her eyes,
for she might fall in love with the first thing she sees as
    ducklings do.
That monster is already straining at his chains and slurping,
ready to go right to it:
He has been well prepared for coupling
by his pinching leering keeper who's been saying for weeks,
"Ya gonna get a little nookie, kid,"
or "How do you go for some poontang, baby?"
All the evil in him is focused on this one thing now
as he is led into her very presence.

She awakens slowly,
she bats her eyes,
she gets up out of the equipment,
and finally she stands in all her seamed glory,
a monster princess with a hairdo like a fright wig,
lightning flashing in the background
like a halo and a wedding veil,
like a photographer snapping pictures of great moments.

She stands and stares with her electric eyes,
beginning to understand that in this life too
she was just another body to be raped.

The monster is ready to go:
He roars with joy at the sight of her,
so they let him loose and he goes right for those knockers.
And she starts screaming to break your heart
and you realize that she was just born:
In spite of her big tits she was just a baby.

But her instincts are right—
rather death than that green slobber:
She jumps off the parapet.
And then the monster's sex drive goes wild.

Thwarted, it turns to violence, demonstrating sublimation
    crudely;
and he wrecks the lab, those burping acids and buzzing coils,
overturning the control panel so the equipment goes off like
    a bomb,
and the stone castle crumbles and crashes in the storm
destroying them all . . . perhaps.

Perhaps somehow the Baron got out of that wreckage of his
    dreams
with his evil intact, if not his good looks,
and more wicked than ever went on with his thrilling career.
And perhaps even the monster lived
to roam the earth, his desire still ungratified;
and lovers out walking in shadowy and deserted places
will see his shape loom up over them, their doom—
and children sleeping in their beds
will wake up in the dark night screaming
as his hideous body grabs them.

———

EDWARD FIELD (1924–   ) *won the* Lamont Poetry *award for his first volume of poems* Stand Up, Friend, With Me *(1963). A second volume,* Variety Photoplays *(1967) confirmed his talent as a poet who commands the respect of fellow poets as well as that of those who normally dislike poetry.*

Mary Shelley's Frankenstein *(1818) tells of the evil Baron Frankenstein who constructs, then loses control of, a rather pitiable monster. The film (1931) made from the book is a classic horror movie, filled with the machinery and effects that have since become deadly familiar. Neither the book nor the 1931 film include a bride, but sequels added this and other embellishments. The poem apparently refers to the best of these sequels,* The Bride of Frankenstein *(1935), with Boris Karloff and Elsa Lanchester.*

1. What is the writer's attitude toward the characters and scenes he describes? Are we expected to take the Baron and his laboratory as "real" or as if we were watching a corny old film? In the third stanza, for instance, what is the effect of "burping," or "the equipment really goes crazy/like a kitchen full of modern appliances"? Where else in the poem do you see examples of this same tone?

2. Find places early in the poem where the writer, despite his smile at the old-fashioned machinery, asks us to see something serious behind the surface. Why are the bride's instincts "right"? In the fourth stanza, we are told the monster focuses his "evil"; just what is the nature of this evil?

3. The last two stanzas change tone, as they show the implications of "the monster's sex drive goes wild." What are the results in the film? In the real world of lovers' lanes and children's nightmares? Why is the writer now asking us to take the "evil intact" of the Baron and the "hideous body" of the monster so seriously?

4. Compare this poem with X. J. Kennedy's "Who Killed King Kong?" Point out similarities in tone, topic, conclusion; where are there significant differences? Which form, poem or essay, seems more apt for demonstrating assumptions? For implications? Why?

Part Three THE USES OF

EVIDENCE: ART AND POPULAR ART

In this section we turn directly to the esthetic question at the center of this book: What useful distinctions can or should be made between "art" and "popular art"? The question is complicated and does not yield easy answers; assumptions about the definition, value, and meaning of "art" lie behind most attempts to analyze popular art, and different assumptions usually lead to different conclusions. All the selections that follow deal with the question in one way or another and use analysis of particular forms of popular art to support their conclusions.

Thus in this section we also turn directly to the rhetorical topic this book has been presenting in different ways: the use of evidence to demonstrate conclusions. Good writers know they have to prove what they say, that the simple assertion of an idea is not enough to make ideas convincing. If you want to be believed, you must find ways to bring evidence to support the assertions you make.

Of course the formal study of evidence and proving is the immensely complex discipline known as logic. The study of logical categories and methods is valuable for a writer and is an invaluable aid in thinking straight. But whereas logicians are concerned for the validity (the internal correctness) or the truth of a proof, the writer has a less formal but still taxing job: he must be sure that his evidence is both suitable and satisfying for his purpose and for his audience.

You need to be clear in your own mind about the distinction between asserting your ideas and demonstrating them. You need also to be sure that you have isolated your most interesting and important assertions for careful demonstration. If you are asked to evaluate some form of popular art (the topic this section of the book suggests), you will have to come to some conclusions about the purpose and meaning of art as well as about the artistry of what you examine. These conclusions should be supported by facts and arguments as well as careful description and analysis of what you have seen both on and beneath the surface.

Notice, for example, how Joan Peyser sets out to demonstrate that the Beatles' later songs are in fact works of art:

> Despite the careful handling of so many diverse musical tools, the legend of how Beatle music is made persists: Lennon whistles to McCartney and McCartney whistles back to Lennon.
>
> In its essence the legend is accurate. But between the initial melodic impulse and the finished product more than cooperative whistling has taken place. When they record the men work a five-day week—from 7 P.M. to 2 A.M. They spent almost half a year recording their thirteenth album; it took 12 hours to make "Meet the Beatles." From 1964 on, they have had the services of a gifted, well-trained musician, George Martin, who translates their unorthodox ideas into recognizable symbols for the regular symphony orchestra musicians who now complement their forces. Within the past year the Beatles have made music for French horn, oboe, clarinet, bassoon, piano, harmonium, tamboura, and sitar. Not long ago Harrison said: "There's much more going on in our minds. There are things past drums and guitars which we must do. In the last two years we've been in a good vantage point inasmuch as people are used to buying our records. . . . We can do things that please us without conforming to the standard pop idea. We are not only involved in pop music but all music and there are many things to be investigated."

For an audience largely academic and largely unsympathetic to her central idea, Joan Peyser needs to accumulate a great deal of evidence in order to be convincing. (The essay was written for the Columbia Forum.) Thus we are first given a series of quiet facts: the recent album required about six months of long, hard work ("a five-day week—from 7 P.M. to 2 A.M."); the Beatles use "a gifted, well-trained musician, George Martin"; they use a regular symphony orchestra; they write music for eight specialized, named instruments, some of them exotic. The author chooses her facts to satisfy her reader's assumptions about art: it can begin with spontaneity, but requires immense labor; it calls for high craftmanship (Martin, the orchestra) as well as "unorthodox ideas"; it asks for expansion of form and media (all those instruments).

The quotation from Harrison also supports her case for the artistry of these musicians. He here specifically rejects the imitative role of the popular artist (" 'without conforming to the standard pop idea'") and allies himself with the avant garde of the music world (*"all music"*) seeking new forms of expression. In the face of all this evidence, her readers are now ready to entertain her assertion that "Sergeant Pepper" is "*a work of art that has sprung from unexpected, non-art roots.*" And the evidence that follows, the careful analysis of "Sergeant Pepper," is just as carefully calculated to support the central idea.

The Joan Peyser essay is the first of three dealing with the artistry of popular music. Reed Whittemore's review, which follows it, takes the opposite point of view, using much of the same evidence. And Robert Christgau's critical evaluation of the whole rock scene makes a series of hard judgments, again carefully supplying evidence. When you consider which of the three is the most convincing, you are largely evaluating their use of evidence; as you plan your own essay on the subject of popular art, consider as well your own use of evidence.

The essay in definition by Sir Herbert Read that opens this section takes its evidence from historical and cultural generalizations and from a tightly-woven argument. The analyses of films by Ralph Ellison not only takes its evidence from the films and the demonstrated assumptions behind them, but uses the felt experience of racism to support its basic idea. The Donald Barthelme piece on the Ed Sullivan variety show is an extreme example of the use of observation to support an argument; here the accumulation of evidence is so powerful that the conclusions don't even need to be stated.

Quotations, facts, analyses, arguments, definitions, descriptions —the ways of gathering evidence are beyond number. The appendix to this book gives you suggestions about locating and using sources so that your own individuality as thinker and writer remains. As you develop the habit of distinguishing clearly your own best ideas and then demonstrating them, you will develop the sense of what kind and amount of evidence is appropriate. And this conscious sense of obligation to your own ideas and your reader's response is the surest sign that you are developing into a writer.

Herbert Read

ART AND SOCIETY

"Art" and "society" are two of the vaguest concepts in modern language. In English the word "art" is so ambiguous that no two people will spontaneously define it in the same sense. Sophisticated people try to isolate some characteristic common to all the arts and soon find themselves involved in the science of art, in esthetics, finally in metaphysics. Simple people tend to identify art with one of the arts, usually painting. They are confused if they are asked to consider music or architecture as art. Common to both sophisticated and simple people is the assumption that whatever art may be, it is a specialist or professional activity of no direct concern to the average man.

"Society" is equally vague as a concept. A society may be taken to mean the total population of a country—it may even mean mankind as a whole. At the opposite extreme it may mean a few people who have come together for a common but special purpose—the members of a religious sect or a club. But just as we have a science of art—esthetics—that tries to bring order to a confused subject, so we have a science of society—sociology—that tries to give logical coherence to this second concept. The two rarely overlap, but there have been attempts to create a sociology of art, and various utopias and works such as Plato's *Politicus* are concerned with an art of society, with government or social organization conceived of as an art rather than as a science.

Very few philosophers—Plato is one of them—have seen that art and society are inseparable concepts—that society, as a viable organic entity, is somehow dependent on art as a binding, fusing, and energizing force. That has always been my own view of the relationship, and I should like to give some account of what such a relationship involves (or has involved in the past) and of the fatal consequences that follow from the absence of any such relationship in our contemporary civilization.

Both art and society in any concrete sense of the terms have their origin in man's relation to his natural environment. The earli-

Reprinted from *The Arts and Man* (1969) by Herbert Read. Reproduced with the permission of UNESCO.

est surviving works of art are the fairly numerous Paleolithic cave paintings and a few figurines in bone or ivory of the same period. We have no precise knowledge of the origins or purpose of these works of art, but no one supposes that they were works of art for art's sake. They may have had a magical or a religious function and as such were intimately related to the social structure of that time. This is also true of the art of all the succeeding civilizations of which we have historical evidence. If we examine the first records of the early civilizations of Sumer, Egypt, or the Middle East, we always find artifacts that still appeal to our esthetic sensibility—indeed, our knowledge of these societies is largely based on the evidence derived from surviving works of art.

All the way down the long perspective of history it is impossible to conceive of a society without art, or of an art without social significance, until we come to the modern epoch. We may next ask, how does it come about that modern societies have become insensitive to the arts? The hypothesis that at once suggests itself is that this fundamental change is, in some sense to be determined, a consequence of the sudden increase in the size of societies, a development that accompanies the industrialization of a country. It has always been a matter for wonder that the greatest epochs of art— Athens in the seventh and sixth centuries B.C., Western Europe in the twelfth and thirteenth centuries, the city-states of Italy in the fourteenth and fifteenth centuries—are associated with communities that, in comparison with the typical modern state, were minuscule. We tend to ignore this fact, to regard it as irrelevant, and even to assume that the biggest and most powerful nations must naturally, in due course, produce the greatest art. It is a conclusion for which history offers no support.

The most cursory consideration of the nature of the creative process in the arts will give us the explanation of this paradox. Whatever may be the nature of the relationship between art and society, the work of art itself is always the creation of an individual. It is true that there are arts, such as drama and dance and ritual, that are complex by nature and depend on a group of individuals for their execution or presentation; nevertheless, the unity that gives force and singularity and effectiveness to any one example of these arts is the creative intuition of a particular dramatist, choreographer, or architect.

But the individual does not work in a vacuum. The whole complexity of our problem arises from the fact that the artist is in some sense dependent on the community, not merely in the obvious economic sense, but in a sense that is far subtler and awaiting a psychological analysis. That would define two separate but interacting psychic entities: on the one hand the subjective ego of the artist, seeking to adjust itself to the external world of nature and society; on the other hand, society itself as an organism with its own laws of internal and external adjustment. Herein lies one of the basic paradoxes of human existence: Art is the pattern evolved in a complex interplay of personal and societal processes of adjustment.

There are certain evasions of the problem. The first is the one found in most democratic countries, that is to say in all those that have become aware of the problem. It is realized that art as a social activity has characterized the great social systems of the past, from prehistoric and primitive civilizations to the great aristocratic, ecclesiastic, and oligarchic societies of more recent times. This inevitable and apparently significant association of art and society is then seen to break down with the inception of the modern age—the age of industrialization, mass production, population explosion, and parliamentary democracy. Two deductions are then possible. The first, which prevailed generally during the nineteenth century, assumes that art is a thing of the past, and that a civilization such as ours can dispense with it. The second deduction, which is more and more characteristic of our own time, denies this historicist assumption, asserts that what is wrong with our present civilization can be diagnosed, and proceeds to recommend various remedies.

The most popular and in my opinion the most ineffective of these remedies is economic subsidy. It is pointed out, quite truly, that art in the past always had its patrons—the church in the Middle Ages, the princes and city councils of the Renaissance, the merchants of the seventeenth and eighteenth centuries. This is a superficial generalization that would not survive a scientific analysis —there is no demonstrable connection between the quality of art in any period and the quantity of patronage: Patrons for the most part have been whimsical, inconsistent, and sometimes positively tasteless or reactionary. But there is no need to examine this explanation of the present situation because the patronage at present enjoyed by the arts is probably greater in amount than at any previous time in European history. In the past fifty years vast sums have been expended on the purchase of Italian "old masters" and Impressionist paintings, and equally large sums have been spent on the building of museums, theaters, opera houses, concert halls, and so on, and on the subsidy of performances in such institutions. All to no effect on the basic problem, which is the creation of a vital democratic art to correspond to our democratic civilization. Our civilization, in its visual aspects, is chaotic; it is without a characteristic poetry, without a typical drama; its painting has sunk to a level of mindless incoherence and its architecture to "economic" functionalism that projects its own "brutalism" as an esthetic virtue.

There are exceptions to these generalizations, but nowhere in the world today is there a *style* of art that springs spontaneously from the basic social and economic realities of our way of life.

The first question to ask and the most profoundly disturbing one is whether there is an incompatibility between those basic realities (our system of economic production) and the spontaneous production of works of art. Before answering that question it is perhaps necessary to affirm that there is no change in the potentiality of the human race for the production of works of art. I am evading Hegel's suggestion that art, "on the side of its highest possibilities" (an important qualification), is a thing of the past. I proceed on the assumption that human nature, *in its potentialities*, does not change (or has not changed within measurable time). The world is full of frustrated artists, or rather of people whose creative instincts have been frustrated. Burckhardt pointed out that "there may now exist great men for things that do not exist." I refer not only to obvious geniuses who in spite of the times they live in give evidence of their genius in fragmented works of individualistic expressionism —the works of artists such as Picasso, Klee, Schoenberg, Stravinsky, Eliot—but also to all those potential artists who waste their talents in so-called commercial art (a contradiction in terms) and to all those sensitive children who give early proof of their potentialities and are then sacrificed like rams on the altars of industrial expediency. One of the most tragic injustices of our technological civilization is that the natural sensibility of men, which in other ages found an outlet in basic crafts, is now completely suppressed, or finds a pathetic outlet in some trivial "hobby."

I begin, therefore, by affirming with Burckhardt that "the arts are a faculty of man, a power and a creation. Imagination, their vital, central impulse, has at all times been regarded as divine." It is true that we must always distinguish (as Burckhardt does) between the doers and the seers, between the craftsmen and the visionaries. "To give tangible form to that which is inward, to represent it in such a way that we see it as the outward image of inward things—that is a most rare power. To re-create the external in external form—that is within the power of many."

We must examine our way of life—our social structure, our methods of production and distribution, the accumulation of capital, and the incidence of taxation—to decide whether it is not in these factors that we should look for an explanation of our esthetic impotence. To do this in detail would be a task for a book, not a brief essay, but I have written much on the subject in the past and would now only point briefly to three characteristics of our civilization that are patently inimical to the arts.

The first is the general phenomenon of alienation, which has been much written about since Hegel invented the term and Marx gave it political significance. The term is used to denote both a social and a psychological problem, but these are only two aspects of the same problem, the essence of which is the progressive divorce of human faculties from natural processes. Apart from the many social aspects of the problem (beginning with the division of labor and leading to the elimination of labor, or automation, and other consequences of the Industrial Revolution such as conurbation and congestion, disease and delinquency), there is a general effect, noticed by social philosophers such as Ruskin and Thoreau, but not greatly the concern of "scientific" sociologists, which might be described as the atrophy of sensibility. If seeing and handling, touching and hearing, and all the refinements of sensation that developed historically in the conquest of nature and the manipulation of material substances are not educed and trained from birth to maturity, the result is a being that hardly deserves to be called human: a dull-eyed, bored, and listless automaton whose one desire is for violence in some form or other—violent action, violent sounds, distractions of any kind that can penetrate to its deadened nerves.

The second feature, the decline of religious worship, is doubtless the inevitable consequence of a growth of scientific rationalism, and the fact that scientific progress has not been accompanied by any equivalent progress in ethical standards is frequently regretted. But it is not so often observed that the same forces that have destroyed the mystery of holiness have destroyed the mystery of beauty. I am not suggesting that this process of rationalization is reversible: The mind never gives up its materialistic conquests, short of world catastrophe. I am merely pointing to the obvious fact that the scope of scientific knowledge is still limited. The nature of the cosmos and the origins and purpose of human life remain as mysteries, and this means that science has by no means replaced the symbolic functions of art, which are still necessary "to overcome the resistance of the brutish world."

Thirdly, and most diffidently, one must mention a characteristic of our way of life which, however solidly based on our cherished ideals of democracy, is inimical to art. I have already mentioned the obvious fact that works of art are produced by individuals. It follows from this that the values of art are essentially aristocratic: They are not determined by a general level of esthetic sensibility, but by the best esthetic sensibility available at any particular time. This is a faculty possessed by relatively few people—the arbiters of taste, the critics and connoisseurs, and, above all, artists themselves —and the level of taste is determined by their intercourse. Whatever we may think of Carlyle's or Burckhardt's theory of the role of the great man in history—and Burckhardt pointed out that there are categories of great men, some of them of doubtful benefit to humanity—and however much importance we may give to the "grass roots" theory of art, nevertheless, the history of art is a graph traced between points that represent the appearance in history of a great artist. A Michelangelo or a Mozart may be the product of as-certainable forces, hereditary or social; but once he has created his works of art, the history of art departs from its previous course. I do not, of course, assume that the history of art is identical with the history of culture. Culture is not even the sum of all the arts, or of all the arts, customs, scientific and religious beliefs of a period. As T. S. Eliot once pointed out, all these parts into which a culture can be analyzed act upon each other, and a culture is something they create which is greater than the sum of their parts. Fully to under-stand one you have to understand all.

Unfortunately for art, a democratic society has its own categories of greatness that do not necessarily correspond to our defini-tions of culture. I do not refer so much to the heroes of war, poli-tics, or sport. These nonesthetic categories are common to all ages. I confine my observations to the arts, and there modern democracy has shown a total incapacity to distinguish between genius and talents. This is probably due to the strangeness or originality of genius—even in other ages, genius was not always immediately recognized at its true worth. But more recently technological ad-vances in methods of communication have conspired with an innate envy of originality to produce that typical famous man of our time, the pander. Whether as a columnist or a television "personality," this usurper appears before a public numbering millions and, by anticipating their opinions and prejudices, flatters them into con-currence and adulation. To see—actually to see—their own com-monplace thoughts and instinctive judgments voiced by an elo-quent jack-in-the-box gives people not merely the illusion that greatness is democratic, but also the greater illusion that truth need not be disturbing. For complacency (allied to complicity) is the ultimate ideal of a democratic way of life.

Art, on the other hand, is eternally disturbing, permanently revolutionary. It is so because the artist, to the degree of his great-ness, always confronts the unknown, and what he brings back from that confrontation is a novelty, a new symbol, a new vision of life, the outer image of inward things. His importance to society is not that he voices received opinions, or gives clear expression to the con-fused feelings of the masses—that is the function of the politician, the journalist, the demagogue. The artist is what the Germans call *ein Rüttler*, an upsetter of the established order. The greatest enemy of art is the collective mind, in any of its many manifestations. The collective mind is like water that always seeks the lowest level of gravity; the artist struggles out of this morass, to seek a higher level of individual sensibility and perception. The signals he sends back are often unintelligible to the multitude, but then come the philosophers and critics to interpret his message. On the basic works of one genius, a Homer, a Plato, a Dante, a Shakespeare, a Michelangelo, a Bach, a Mozart, we build not only outworks of interpretation and explication but also extensions and imitations, until the art of one individual pervades and gives name to an epoch.

From whatever angle we approach this problem of the function of the arts in contemporary society, it is evident that their proper function is inhibited by the nature of that society. The Hegelian contradiction between art and idea loses its force and application in a society that has no use for either—either for "the soul and its emotions" or for "a concrete sensuous phenomenon," the two dialectical entities which in a progressive civilization are fused into unity by the vital energy that is life itself in its creative evolution.

It may be said that I have placed my priorities in the wrong order (actually I am denying that there are any priorities in the process). It has been generally assumed—at least in my own country, where Matthew Arnold gave currency to the opinion—that "the exercise of the creative power in the production of great works of literature or art . . . is not at all epochs and under all conditions possible." Arnold limits his illustrations to literature, but his meaning is quite general. "The grand work of literary genius is a work of synthesis and exposition, not of analysis or discovery; its gift lies in the faculty of being happily inspired by a certain intellectual and spiritual atmosphere, by a certain order of ideas, when it finds itself in them; of dealing divinely with these ideas, presenting them in the most effective and attractive combinations—making beautiful works with them, in short." This is the intellectualist heresy derived no doubt from Goethe and indirectly from Hegel. While it is true that in the creation of a masterwork (in any of the arts) "two powers must concur, the power of the man and the power of the moment," the essence of any work of art does not lie in synthesis and exposition, nor even in analysis and discovery, but in realization and manifestation. What is realized is an image—"we must render the image of what we see, forgetting everything that existed before us" (Cézanne). The artist, whether he is a poet or a painter, a musician or a potter, "gives concrete shape to sensations and perceptions" (Cézanne again); and what he manifests is this shape, in colors, in words, in sounds. The rest is what Wittgenstein called "the language game" and has nothing to do with art.

But that manifested shape is the node from which in due course ideas spring, and the more precise, the more vital the work of art, the more powerful will be the ideas it suggests. Then we can say with Arnold that "the touch of truth is the touch of life, and there is a stir and growth everywhere." But the first necessity is that the artist should render the image; if there are no images there are no ideas, and a civilization slowly but inevitably dies.

I believe that there is only one way of saving our civilization and that is by so reforming its constituent societies that, in the sense of the phrases already defined, the concrete sensuous phenomena of art are once more spontaneously manifested in our daily lives. I have called this reform "education through art," and it now has advocates throughout the world. But what I have not sufficiently emphasized and what is not sufficiently realized by many of my fellow workers in this field is the revolutionary nature of the remedy. An education through art is not necessarily anti-scientific, for science itself depends on the clear manifestation of concrete sensuous phenomena, and is necessarily impeded by "the language game." But an education through art does not fit human beings for the mindless and mechanical actions of modern industry; it does not reconcile them to a leisure devoid of constructive purpose; it does not leave them satisfied with passive entertainment. It aims to create "stir and growth" everywhere, to substitute for conformity and imitation in each citizen an endowment of imaginative power "in a kind perfectly unborrowed and his own" (Coleridge).

To believe that art is born in intimacy is not a quietist philosophy; there is no necessary association between art and inactivity. It is true that at the practical level there is a general contradiction between extrovert activities and the calm needed for creative work of any kind. War and revolution destroy the constructive works of the artist. But at the same time we must admit with Burckhardt that "passion is the mother of great things" and the artist is stimulated by great events, although he takes no part in them and does not even celebrate them directly in his works.

There are few conclusions in this field that can claim scientific validity. Genius is a genetic chance and history a confused clamor, but life persists. It is a flame that rises and sinks, now flickers and now burns steadily, and the source of the oil that feeds it is invisible. But that source is always associated with the imagination, and a civilization that consistently denies the life of the imagination must sink into deeper and deeper barbarism.

Sir Herbert Read (1893–1968) *published his first book, a collection of poems,* Songs of Chaos, *in 1915. In a very active life, he* wrote over two dozen volumes of poetry, criticism, art history, and political theory. Reason and Romanticism (1926) is an important collection of literary criticism; The Meaning of Art (1931), Art Now (1933), and Concise History of Modern Painting (1959) established him as Britain's most influential writer on modern art. Education Through Art (1943) and The Grass Roots of Art (1946) show his interest in the social and educative function of art, an interest maintained in this essay written just before his death.

1. In his first paragraph, Read points to the problem of defining "art." Imbedded in his essay are a series of descriptions and definitions of art, and the function of the artist. List these assertions and define what Read means by art.

2. Toward the end of his essay, Read turns to popular art, that produced by "the collective mind, in any of its many manifestations." Why does he insist that popular art is not art at all? Reread Kafka's "A Hunger Artist" and compare Kafka's concept of art with Read's.

3. What kind of evidence does Read use to support his assertions? Does he use facts and data, generally, or other assertions? Choose one of his major assertions, and show how he supports it. Is his argument convincing? Why, or why not?

Joan Peyser

THE MUSIC OF SOUND, OR, THE BEATLES
AND THE BEATLESS

Many people ask what are Beatles? Why Beatles? Ugh,
Beatles? How did the name arrive? So we will tell you. It
came in a vision—a man appeared on a flaming pie and said
unto them, "From this day on you are Beatles with an 'A'."
Thank you, Mister Man, they said, thanking him.
    And so they were Beatles.

                            —John Lennon, 1960

           A thousand years ago small groups of uncul-
tivated, bizarrely dressed, oddly named musicians traveled from
town to town, singing and accompanying themselves on the vielle.
The most famous of these—Jumping Hare, Little String, Ladies
Praiser and Rainbow—were rewarded with such fame and luxury
that they were imitated by hordes of less gifted, envious men. During the late Middle Ages chronicles refer to "large armies of minstrels," the better ones playing for nobility while lesser troupes
entertained at peasant celebrations. Despite the demand for their
performances at all levels of society, these itinerant poet-musicians
were held in contempt throughout the era. The animus stemmed
principally from the Church, which held that their obvious secular
joie de vivre posed a threat to the spiritual welfare of its people.

    Once again, to a degree unparalleled since the fourteenth cen-
tury, Western society loves and rewards its itinerant minstrels. The
Beatles, royalty of rock and roll, were received by the Queen of
England ("she was like a mum to us"), have appeared on satellite
television with Alexander Calder, Van Cliburn, and Joan Miro
("we would rather be rich than famous—that is—more rich and
slightly less famous"), and live in a state of growing luxury ("we're
not rich by rich standards. I could not afford to run four Rolls
Royces like people do"). John Lennon, author of the last statement

and the first of the Beatles, owns one Rolls Royce equipped with folding bed, television set, writing desk and telephone. He also owns a mini-Cooper, a Ferrari, five stationary television sets, innumerable tape recorders and telephones and an 1874 carriage, yellow with wild flowers, drawn by two white horses in front with two more trotting at the rear—a $10,000 toy purchased for his four year old son. Like their medieval predecessors, the Beatles are considered subversive by respectable society. Lennon's flip comment about contemporary Christianity ("we're more popular than Jesus now") prompted an Alabama disk jockey to instruct his listeners to burn Beatle records. Mayors across the continent picked up the disk jockey's lead and at the beginning of the group's last American tour, in August 1966, protected citizens by banning Beatles from their cities.

Who would have thought that the pop music of the 1960s would develop into a force as vital as that of the jongleur of old? Starting simply as a vehicle for solo performers, rock and roll didn't differ radically from some of the popular music that had preceded it. Out of Negro rhythm and blues and country and western came Elvis Presley. The tunes were predictable, the 12-bar phrases symmetrical, and the lyric content primitive—"You ain't nothin' but a hound dog." When Presley was drafted, relieved adults predicted the end of an unattractive fad. They were wrong. Rock and roll did not die; it only changed. Presley, with his long sideburns, tight pants and suggestive gyrations, reached only one segment of the population, although a large one. The Beatles, bursting onto the scene in the early '60s with Edwardian clothes and English schoolboy haircuts, transformed the original primitive Negro sound, making it acceptable to the mass of young white people all over the world. They brought to prominence Group Rock, one of the most attractive symbols of our non-private, corporate, thoroughly electronic age. Now literally "armies of minstrels"—the Beach Boys, the Jefferson Airplane, the Grateful Dead, the Who, the Bee Gees, the Doors, the Mothers of Invention, the Buffalo Springfield, and so on—indicate the awesome potential of electronic sound. Even Bob Dylan, who provoked shouts of "traitor" when he plugged his guitar into an electronic amplifier at the Newport Jazz Festival several years ago, committed himself to the medium in which his generation is making its messages.

Meanwhile, although little noticed by the general public, similar developments have been taking place in the serious music of our time. The explosive electronics of the pop field has diverted attention from the fact that technology came to art music well before it came to rock. As early as 1922 the French-American composer, Edgard Varèse, declared that composer and electrician would have to labor together to produce new media of expression. Rejected by musicians and critics alike during the '30s and '40s, when accessibility of music was the keynote, Varèse's views began to gain recognition in the 1950s, and American universities and European radio stations built well-equipped laboratories to experiment with electronic techniques in sound. This gave rise in Europe to the works of Pierre Boulez and Karlheinz Stockhausen and in this country to the construction of machines such as the RCA Synthesizer, a complex, costly apparatus which generates its own sounds, and the Syn-Ket, an instrument which performs "live" electronic music. Columbia University has been in the forefront of the development of the electronic medium. Professors Otto Luening and Vladimir Ussachevsky of the Music Department deposited one of their electronic compositions in the Westinghouse Time Capsule, scheduled to be opened in the 70th century, and the RCA Synthesizer is housed at the Columbia-Princeton Electronic Music Center on 125th Street in Manhattan.

Despite the prestige and backing electronic art music has been given since the end of World War II, its audience has remained sharply limited. In contrast, electronic rock, within a few years, has attracted an audience of staggering size. Contemporary art and rock music share a medium; the crucial differences are stylistic. Art music has abandoned beat; rock has revived it. Art music is essentially non-vocal and abstract—a feature it has in common with cool contemporary jazz—whereas rock has become increasingly verbal and concrete. Finally, electronic art music, aimed at total control of its materials, is at least partly motivated by the desire to eliminate the performer; he is frequently seen as the potential distorter of the composer's idea. Electronic rock propels the performer into the spotlight; he is singer and instrumentalist and recently poet and composer as well. Art music has not yet sought inspiration from rock. Rock, as many writers have pointed out, has drawn upon everything from Gregorian chant to the most far-out techniques of the avant-garde.

Consider the history of the archetype of Group Rock. John Lennon, Paul McCartney, and George Harrison met in 1956 when they were in their mid-teens and, although none of them could read or write music, they began to play guitar together. Drummer Richard Starkey, now Ringo Starr, joined in 1962. The original group, with a few friends moving in and out of it, was one of many unsuccessful "skiffle" bands in Liverpool during the 1950s. They listened to everything from rhythm and blues to contemporary jazz and Presley. In a few years, imitating what they liked and improvising on what they heard, Lennon, McCartney, and Harrison recapitulated much of the current history of pop music, a feat impossible in any but the acoustically equipped society in which we live.

In the spring of 1960 the Beatles, in their first significant club engagement, discovered the value of noise. The group, flat broke, owned four guitars but only two amplifiers and the booking was in a wild club on a noisy street in Hamburg. How were they going to be heard? McCartney recalled: "We didn't worry about arrangements or anything. If we had trouble with our overworked amplifiers—we had to plug two guitars into one—I'd just chuck everything in and start leaping around the stage or rush to the piano and start playing some chords . . . it was noise and beat all the way." The Germans loved it. When the police evicted the group from one club (they stamped their way through the floor at one point), the audience followed them to the next. Within a year the late Brian Epstein, then a 26-year-old English businessman, offered to become their manager, and in the fall of '61 he became their official disciplinarian in charge of hair, clothes, and manners. "Meet the Beatles," their first album, appeared in 1964.

Twelve albums have been issued since then, the noise and beat progressively abating. Much as the medieval minstrel picked up artistic techniques from the more sophisticated *trouvère* of the period, the Beatles have appropriated the most artful devices available in their own time. Medieval modes and pentatonic scales appear in the songs of '64 and '65, a baroque trumpet sings out "Penny Lane," and a classical string quartet performs the hauntingly beautiful "Eleanor Rigby." George Harrison has studied with Ravi Shankar, the Indian sitar virtuoso, and first used the sitar in a song called "Norwegian Wood." All of his recent music and lyrics show the influence of Indian melody and Indian philosophy. Paul McCartney, studying music now in London, has become absorbed in the avant-garde works of Stockhausen and Luciano Berio. His attitude has changed: "I used to think that anyone doing anything weird was weird. I suddenly realised that anyone doing anything weird wasn't weird at all and that it was the people saying they were weird that were weird." Despite the careful handling of so many diverse musical tools, the legend of how Beatle music is made persists: Lennon whistles to McCartney and McCartney whistles back to Lennon.

In its essence the legend is accurate. But between the initial melodic impulse and the finished product more than cooperative whistling has taken place. When they record the men work a five-day week—from 7 P.M. to 2 A.M. They spent almost half a year recording their thirteenth album; it took 12 hours to make "Meet the Beatles." From 1964 on, they have had the services of a gifted, well-trained musician, George Martin, who translates their unorthodox ideas into recognizable symbols for the regular symphony orchestra musicians who now complement their forces. Within the past year the Beatles have made music for French horn, oboe, clarinet, bassoon, piano, harmonium, tamboura, and sitar. Not long ago Harrison said: "There's much more going on in our minds. There are things past drums and guitars which we must do. In the last two years we've been in a good vantage point inasmuch as people are used to buying our records. . . . We can do things that please us without conforming to the standard pop idea. We are not only involved in pop music but all music and there are many things to be investigated."

The audience has responded. Today's population is literally turned on to listening; the record business grossed $892,000,000 in 1966 and the greater part of that was from rock. The Beatles' thirteenth album, "Sergeant Pepper's Lonely Hearts Club Band," replete with dissonant sounds, unconventional phrasing and advanced electronic techniques had, within two weeks of its appearance, sold a million and a half copies in the United States alone. A salesman at Sam Goody's Manhattan record store compared the response to "Sergeant Pepper" to that which greeted the recording of Horowitz' initial return concert at Carnegie Hall.

"Sergeant Pepper" is an extraordinary work, not just comparable to a new sonata or opera, but far more important. It is a work of art that has sprung from unexpected, non-art roots. The salesman's comment was appropriate; "Sergeant Pepper" is to be listened to in the concert context and the Beatles set the tone right away. The beginning of the album simulates the sounds in a concert hall before a performance. Musicians tune instruments, people talk and move around, and an air of expectation prevails.

To the accompaniment of a distorted old-time English music hall sound, the Beatles begin Side I; their business is show business:

> It was twenty years ago today,
> Sergeant Pepper taught the band to play,
> They've been going in and out of style,
> But they're guaranteed to raise a smile. . . .

Side I is about illusion. The Beatles sing of particular methods people use to hide the truth from themselves. Ringo wears the stripes. He is Sergeant Pepper, the lonely outsider, the non-intellectual of the group who, as he concedes in the first song following the theme, gets by "with a little help from my friends." In a dialogue between the narrator and the sergeant, Ringo is asked:

> Would you believe in love at first sight,
> Yes I'm certain that it happens all the time.
> What do you see when you turn out the light,
> I can't tell you but I know it's mine.

Drugs are the subject of "I'm Fixing a Hole" and "Lucy in the Sky with Diamonds," an acrostic of LSD. Lavish verbal imagery and tonal distortions obtained by electronic manipulation suggest the visual hallucinations associated with "acid":

> Picture yourself in a boat on a river
> With tangerine trees and marmalade skies
> Somebody calls you, you answer quite slowly,
> A girl with kaleidoscope eyes.

More familiar refusals to face the truth are treated in "Getting Better," a conventional rationalization, and in "She's Leaving Home." After their daughter has fled the house her parents sing:

> We gave her most of our lives
> Sacrificed most of our lives
> We gave her everything money can buy. . . .

While the narrator chants, in contrapuntal fashion:

> She's leaving home after living alone
> For so many years.

Side I concludes with a return to the most obvious fiction of all: show business. The subject of the final song, Mr. Kite, was inspired by an old-time theater poster.

Side II begins with a piece by George Harrison. It is the album's longest song, built on Indian ragas, and explicitly describes what Side I was all about:

> We were talking—about the space
> between us all
> And the people—who hide themselves
> behind a wall of illusion
> Never glimpse the truth. . . .

The next three numbers treat life without drugs or hypocrisy. The Beatles sing of the sterile, ritualized roles people play. The first song wryly mocks the activities of an elderly couple:

> I could be handy mending a fuse
> When your lights have gone.
> You can knit a sweater by the fireside
> Sunday morning go for a ride,
> Doing the garden, digging the weeds,

> Who could ask for more.
> Will you still need me, will you still feed me,
> When I'm sixty-four.

The second is a spoof on romantic love. A whore in Liverpool, who procures through her daytime trade as a meter-maid, was the inspiration for "Lovely Rita."

> In a cap she looked much older
> And the bag across her shoulder
> Made her look a little like a military man. . . .

The third describes, in desolate terms, the dissonance of an ordinary day:

> Nothing to do to save his life call his wife in
> Nothing to say but what a day
> how's your boy been
> Nothing to do it's up to you
> I've got nothing to say but it's O.K.
> Good morning, good morning. . . .

There follows a reprise of the Sergeant Pepper theme—with a stunning difference. Sergeant Pepper is no longer the raucous fun man, promising smiles and good times. Avoiding the initial expression of these empty hopes the band starts shouting Hup, two, three, four, pounding out the beat and the ultimate truth of Sergeant Pepper's inner life:

> Sergeant Pepper's lonely.
> Sergeant Pepper's lonely.
> Sergeant Pepper's lonely.
> Sergeant Pepper's lonely.

Thus Lennon and McCartney, the group's guiding spirits, commit themselves to the philosophy that Eugene O'Neill expressed in "The Iceman Cometh"—that man cannot live without illusion. The last song, "A Day in the Life," suggests that man cannot live with it either. It is a moving work, a desperate reflection of contemporary life, a song *Newsweek* described as the Beatles' "Waste Land."

The piece is, in a sense, a *roman à clef*. Shortly before its composition a close friend of the Beatles, the 21-year-old son of a prominent British couple, smashed his car in the center of London while high on drugs. After telling of the accident, the narrator cites a film of the English army after it had won the war. In both instances the protagonist is removed from the core of the experience in much the manner of the central character in an Antonioni film. The only links with his friend's death are a news story and a photograph; the only connections with violent war, a film and a book. Lennon's voice, breaking with sadness, invites the listener: "I'd love to turn you on." The last word of this one line refrain leads into an electronic passage in which a large orchestra, recorded on tracks laid upon tracks, builds up to a growling controlled crescendo, simulating a drug-induced "trip." An alarm awakens the narrator who continues his story to the accompaniment of a nervous jazz idiom:

> Woke up, fell out of bed,
> Dragged a comb across my head
> Found my way upstairs and drank a cup,
> And looking up I noticed I was late.
> Found my coat and grabbed my hat
> Made the bus in seconds flat
> Found my way upstairs and had a smoke,
> Somebody spoke and I went into a dream. . . .

High pitched voices intone a series of open, sensuous chords more suggestive of "pot" than "acid," after which John returns, reflects on the emptiness of everyone (the holes in Albert Hall are people), and invites the listener on still another trip. The non-pitched sounds return, increase in volume and duration until they dissolve, with suddenness, into one resonant, depressing, seemingly interminable terminal tonic chord.

At the bottom of the album cover is a burial plot covered with red flowers arranged to spell BEATLES. The original Beatles of the 1950s, joyous and innocent, are dead. Above and to the left are four standing figures in dark ties and dark suits, Madame Tussaud's wax reproductions of Brian Epstein's carefully groomed group of the early '60s. Sergeant Pepper's Lonely Hearts Club Band is pictured in the center of the cover. Its members are adorned with colorful, psychedelic costumes and are devastatingly unsmiling. They are the Beatles of today. Sergeant Pepper's Band, Madame Tussaud's figures, and a host of others, including Shirley Temple, Mae West, Fred Astaire, W. C. Fields, Marilyn Monroe, Timothy Leary, Edgar Allen Poe, Tom Mix, Bob Dylan, Karlheinz Stockhausen, Tony Curtis, and Lawrence of Arabia look down at the grave below. All mourn the loss of the youthful Beatles, the group Lennon recently referred to as "those four jolly lads."

Dealing with identity, illusion, loneliness, and death, the Beatles represent their generation and its overwhelming sense of anomie. Refusing to accept the status quo and take square places in a "straight" society, they reach everyone from the Haight-Ashbury section of San Francisco to the Manhattan East Side discotheques.

In this respect they differ most dramatically from the art musician of our time. Contemporary art composers are committed to a style of composition that is, in its essence, opposed to a dramatic expressionism that has prevailed in art music for the last few hundred years. Music as drama grew, in part, from tonality, a musical system in which one note, the "key", serves as the focus of an entire work. This single focus is placed into conflict with other keys throughout the course of the piece; the juxtaposition and resolution of the resulting tonal conflict weaves a dramatic, extramusical meaning into the musical fabric of the composition.

During the years in which Picasso and Kandinsky shattered the single focus of perspective in painting, Schoenberg and Varèse shattered the single focus of tonality in music. Schoenberg did it by organizing a new musical arrangement in which all 12 tones of the chromatic scale are equal and Varèse went even farther—by opening his music to all sound, not just pitched sound. Although a number of present-day musicians continue to rely on a traditional, tonal base for composition, the significant musical action of the 1950s and '60s has centered on Milton Babbitt, John Cage, and the musicians working around both men. All make music that is intramusical; abstract, beatless and non-melodic, it reaches only those trained in the highly complex manner of what is referred to as new musical expression.

Babbitt's highly structured form and Cage's negation of traditional form have a common base; both are expressions of a belief that tonality is no longer valid, that there is no *a priori* order, no God-given frame of reference. The particular tonal-expressive tradition that began with Monteverdi in the seventeenth century and culminated in the dramatic works of Richard Wagner has been overthrown. It is inevitable that serious art musicians write music the way that they do. The battle against dramatic expressionism in art music has been waged and won.

But the Beatles never had anything to do with a war. They replaced revolution with affable irreverence. Born in Liverpool, they grew up among the constantly shifting population and extremely high crime rate of a large seaport, where the standards and taste of bourgeois London mattered little, and local guitar players enjoyed higher repute in the community than opera singers. Lennon, McCartney, Harrison, and Starr emerged from this milieu as the antithesis of British tradition, classless kids who began their meteoric rise not musically but socially, by overstating the clothing and hairstyles of the educated Eton boy. Brashness and confidence have always distinguished their conduct. In Buckingham Palace McCartney criticized the condition of the carpets. And at a Royal Command Performance in London Lennon directed the audience:

"People in the cheap seats can clap. The rest of you—rattle your jewelry!"

The Beatles' sense of freedom from the shackles of social tradition is matched by their freedom from the shackles of the hallowed styles of musical composition. Lennon, whose mother played the banjo (she died when he was 13) and McCartney, whose father had a jazz band 30 years ago, never had an awesome musical tradition to fight. At least 10 years younger than the youngest of the recognized art composers of our day (the oldest Beatle is 27), and a generation younger than Babbitt and Cage, the Beatles grew up with transistor radios next to their ears. Bach's "Art of the Fugue" and Schoenberg's "Method of Composing with Twelve Tones" had as little relevance to them as English imperialism and the White Man's Burden. Despite the use of styles and techniques from various periods throughout the history of music, the Beatles and their youthful colleagues are essentially ahistorical. Born after the social and musical revolutions of the twentieth century, able simply to relax and use all the musical tools available, they have created something moving and altogether new.

Are we entering an era in which musical high art, as we have known it, is coming to an end? The medieval poet-musician, who passed on his art through an oral tradition, has a contemporary analogue in the rock and roll performer. He is a central, contributing member of a society that is moving steadily away from notation and inexorably toward the preservation of the musical object on record and tape. No notational system is capable of reproducing the complex texture of a Beatle record or the sophisticated manipulations the sound engineer immobilizes on it. What is preserved in the music is the performance itself; the record is the message. Marshall McLuhan's thesis that the visually oriented and literate society of Western man is being replaced by an acoustically oriented, electronic society receives its firmest confirmation in the most logical field. The compositional tradition associated with notation that has prevailed since the beginning of the Renaissance is being replaced by an overwhelmingly oral tradition—in both art and rock music. Art music, for the moment, has excluded all but the most cerebral, specialized listeners. Rock is all embracing, having absorbed elements of blues, folk, jazz, and the serious avant-garde.

Few other groups are as good as the Beatles, of course. The quality of rock is about as uneven as the quality of the songs of the jongleur; a small percentage of it is very good. But the best of rock is moving with unprecedented speed into unexpected, more artistically interesting areas. Such a phenomenon has historical antecedents; vital popular forms have anticipated crucial stylistic changes in art music of the past. The street singers' *commedia del arte*, for instance, was in great part responsible for the flowering of the opera which, in turn, provided the source for the very dramatic expressionism that dominated art music until the second half of this century.

A few performers, composers, and scholars of traditional art music have begun to acknowledge that the boundaries between art and rock music are becoming less defined. Cathy Berberian, noted avant-garde singer for whom Igor Stravinsky, John Cage and Luciano Berio have written works, recently recorded an album of 12 Beatle songs, and commented that "Eleanor Rigby" was one of the most beautiful she had heard in years. And on CBS-TV Leonard Bernstein called the best of rock "irresistible." From the other end of the spectrum the Beatles, with their drooping Mexican mustaches, lugubrious faces, and increasingly bizzarre clothing, are heard exploring progressively more intellectual and artistic frames of reference. Paul told a reporter that he vaguely minds anyone knowing anything he doesn't know and John said he would rather have the attention of two hundred people who knew what he was doing than two million who had no idea what was going on.

Despite the similarities, there is a crucial difference between the breeds. Art musicians have reacted to the absence of structure and system in contemporary society by imposing a highly complex structure and system upon their creative work or by annihilating form altogether. The Beatles, on the other hand, have reacted to the same sterility in an extramusical way—by immersing themselves in Eastern mystical theology and experimenting with psychedelic drugs. Because the intramusical aspect of their songs is unaffected by historical considerations, esthetic ideology, or the search for a meaning in life, their lyric bouyancy remains intact. It is in striking evidence in the rollicking single, "All You Need Is Love"—a wild and beautiful distillation of their sole and pervasive antidote to mid-century despair.

———

JOAN PEYSER, *who is the author of* The New Music: the Sense Behind the Sound *(N.Y., 1971), holds the M.A. in musicology from Columbia University (1956). Her writing has appeared in* The New York Times, Opera News, American Record Guide, *and* Commentary. *Her article in* Commentary *(September 1961) attacking aspects of the Lincoln Center cultural complex in New York aroused a strong response. In reply she stressed her continuing concern for the humanity and vitality of art: "Surely one must criticize a 'culture symbol' that presents a gleaming, glistening, opulent exterior, and an inner life devoid of warmth and beauty and vitality."*

1. This is the first of three arguments about the artistry—or non-artistry—of pop music. Each argument makes a basic assumption about what art is; in each case, you need to discover this assumed definition. Here Peyser suggests her definition whenever she praises the art of the Beatles: "they have created something moving and altogether new," for instance. Define "art" as it is used in this essay. How does this definition compare with Herbert Read's?

2. Paul McCartney is quoted as saying, "I suddenly realised that anyone doing anything weird wasn't weird at all and that it was the people saying they were weird that were weird." Is this a statement of an artist or a popular artist? Why?

3. Choose a typical paragraph for a close examination of the way the author uses evidence. How, for instance, does she support her assertions about the dedication and hard work and sophistication of the later Beatles? Is her argument convincing? Why?

4. At the center of this essay is an analysis of "Sergeant Pepper." What is the purpose of the analysis? What does it prove? What is the relationship of the analysis to the section before it? The section after it? Describe the structure of the essay, with particular attention to the way the author asserts, then demonstrates her major ideas. Where are the implications of these ideas described? Is the whole argument convincing?

Reed Whittemore

THE BEATLES ILLUSTRATED LYRICS

"I was the kingpin of my age group," said John. "The sort of gang I led went in for things like shoplifting and pulling girls' knickers down."

"We had masters who just hit you with rulers, or told us a lot of shit about their holiday in Wales or what they did in the Army," said Paul. "Never once did anyone make it clear to me what I was being educated for."

George had school complaints too: "Some schizophrenic jerk just out of training school would just read out notes to you which you were expected to take down. . . . Useless, the lot of them. . . . They were trying to turn everybody into rows of little toffees."

Unlike the others poor Ringo didn't have a chance to rebel as a child, and he didn't have "the education to do anything clever" because he was sick all the time. He stole a few things from Woolworth's ("just silly plastic things") but he was a late bloomer and the last Beatle to join up. He felt out of things for a while but made the scene finally so that he received equal time in the authorized biography of the Beatles by Hunter Davies (1968).

The quotations above are from the biography, maybe the first authorized biography deliberately devised to make its subject(s) look bad. The sixties were needed before the full monetary rewards of promoting dropouts and dropoutness could be realized. The Beatles found out early where the new big money was—it was in good anti-bourgeois vice—and with remarkable prescience they then hung close to the appropriately dissentious fads, right through LSD and the mysterious East, until they reached their present rich old age of 28 (average). For as John put it in the *new* book, "You see we're influenced by whatever's going."

John might have added, had he not been modest (he *did* say once that they were bigger than Jesus, but that was in Nashville),

Reprinted from the November 8, 1969, issue of *The New Republic* by permission of the publisher. Copyright © 1969, Harrison-Blaine of New Jersey, Inc. Lyrics from "Michelle" and "Think for Yourself" copyright © 1965, Northern Songs Ltd., "Hold Me Tight," copyright © 1963, Northern Songs Ltd. Used by permission. All Rights Reserved. Lyrics from "Love Me Do," copyright 1962 Ardmore & Beechwood, Ltd., England, assigned 1963 Beechwood Music Corporation for USA and Canada. Used by permission.

that they were not only influenced but influences. One of my children was just four when the first Ed Sullivan Beatle program occurred, and the "yeah yeah yeah" in a stirring love song released him instantly from whatever small influence we had had upon him. His head began to bob, he stamped his feet, he went off to find a drum—and grow hair. He has never recovered.

The new book, containing most of the lyrics the Beatles have themselves written, is another instance of their clever tactics. The lyrics are not bad, but they would have looked naked and skinny by themselves, not revolutionary. Most of the Beatles' message of dissent, and most of the profit has been in their music, not their words. The problem of the book was to find something to accompany a lyric on a page, something equivalent to Beatle noise—a problem handsomely solved with pictures, hundreds of wild, sexy, psychedelic, *noisy* pictures.

Half the new artists of the now world were harnessed to the job, and the result is extremely now. The editor, Alan Aldridge, is himself a clever young now dropout with appropriately long hair, and he describes his occupation with a phrase that covers the book itself: graphic entertainment. In graphic entertainment as in music the Beatles obviously let whatever's going influence them, but as with music they will doubtless in turn encourage more of the same. The book, priced low for so much genuine nekkid art, will sell like hotcakes and breed dozens of publishing imitations, some perhaps even using Dante, or Shakespeare's sonnets. (Think! the Dark Lady! I shdnt have mentioned it.)

What is impressive about the *lyric* entertainment in the book is how simple and sentimental and corny most of it is without the accompanying dissonance. Those who take deep soundings into the meanings of Beatle words should pay more attention instead to the meaning of musical bronx cheers—which are where the big Beatle profundity lies. A few lyrics have innuendoes about drugs and sex, and a few are openly porn, notably "Why don't we do it in the road"; but mostly they are straightforward love songs out of the twenties. Tin Pan Alley had its innuendoes too, but people just laughed at them. Now in our age of revolution we are asked, by editor Aldridge among others, to revel in ambiguities and hidden meanings. The revel is simply not there; it is in a bright and mildly tricky verbal surface enforced by, of all things, rhyme and rhythm:

> Michelle ma belle
> Those are words that go together well.

And:

> It feels so right now, hold me tight,
> Tell me I'm the only one,

> And then I might
> Never be the lonely one.

Those are deep like Irving Berlin. Ah, but Aldridge would have me look in the *deep* songs such as those in the Sgt. Pepper album, where there are deepnesses about going on trips and even a bit of Liverpool phallic. Yes, and there is surrealism too, as in lines like "keeping her face in a jar by the door" (stupidly I thought that described a woman and her make-up). I have looked at these now, and I still think the lyrics are simple (I refuse to play them backwards). What impresses me is that the Beatles themselves keep saying they are simple. Their very first song, composed by John and Paul together, remains the model for at least a third of the poems. It begins, undeeply but pleasantly, with a clever little syntactical arrangement, its only distinguishing feature aside from the fourth line's "who-ho":

> Love, love me do,
> You know I love you.
> I'll always be true
> so please love me do, who ho love me do.

Another third of the poems is like the first third except that a good deal more is made of the "who ho" motif. I mean that this second third clearly deviates from the simple Romantic Love they began with, by jazzing the romance up. Nothing unusual here. Tin Pan Alley moved readily from elementary corn to corny wit like, "Strictly between us/ You're cuter than Venus/ And what's more you've got arms." Beatle wit, in the jazz tradition, is more forcefully a part of the music and the performance than the words; it's in the head wagging and the gestures and the klaxon-like sounds where there should be sweet violins—an early model would be Fats Domino singing "Blueberry Hill." Yet with the Beatles the dissonance will clearly be present on the page, as not in "Blueberry Hill." The following sour lyric, for example, would seem to be a sort of parody of romantic songs in which the girl is going away and the boy is heartbroken:

> Do what you want to do,
> And go where you're going to,
> think for yourself,
> 'cos I won't be there with you.

In songs like this the Beatles are in effect playing dropout from jukebox Romantic Love. They are playing tough with it. They are little boys throwing snowballs at a stovepipe hat. And yet they constantly pay their respects to it by keeping the "I love you's" and the simple rhymes and rhythms as a base.

The third third is of course the deep third, containing numbers with exotic imagery from the land of the lotos eaters, and a few ironic monologues or dialogues in which they play the parts of unpleasant bourgeois people ("Revolution," "Try To See It My Way," and "She's Leaving Home"). These songs are more than tricky. I respect them. Perhaps I cheat them by underplaying them and emphasizing the other two-thirds of the Beatle repertoire. The Beatles, I feel, can afford to be cheated. Anyway it was the deep-rooted conventionality of the first two-thirds of the selection that most impressed me. I was oddly taken back in my own mind, as I read these lyrics, to the old Orson Welles movie *Citizen Kane*, in which the mystery of the rich old man's last death-bed word, "Rosebud," as well as the mystery of what had made him tick all his life, is laboriously sustained to the very dramatic end when the flames of Kane's great house burning finally consume a small sled up in the attic. On the sled is the word "Rosebud."

Tin Pan Alley is the Beatles' rosebud, and a convincing rosebud it is for four young capitalists selling 225 million records and saving the British pound. But what should be the rosebud for four of the world's leading dissenters? Neither honest art nor thoroughgoing dissent has ever accommodated itself well to money and middle-class opportunism. The Beatles have ringed their art with layer upon layer of dissonance, but in the still heart of the lyrics the deep truth is revealed. Hell of a way to run a revolution.

REED WHITTEMORE (1919–   ) *is a poet, editor, and teacher. His poems have appeared in various periodicals and a series of volumes:* Heroes and Heroines (1946), An American Takes a Walk (1956), The Self-Made Man, And Other Poems (1959), The Boy From Iowa (1962), *etc. As editor of the* Carleton Miscellany *from 1960 to 1964, he brought it to the first rank of American literary quarterlies. His recent awards include an appointment as consultant in poetry to the Library of Congress (1964–65), and the Award of Merit Medal from the American Academy of Arts and Letters (1970). He is now a professor of English at the National Institute of Public Affairs in Washington, D.C., and literary editor of* The New Republic.

1. *Whittemore obviously differs sharply from Joan Peyser in his estimation of the Beatles. Does he proceed from a different conception of art, or does he share with her a common definition?*
2. *What evidence does Whittemore bring to support his view that the lyrics are "simple and sentimental and corny"? How much*

of the evidence is the same that Joan Peyser used to support the opposite conclusion? What are the differences in the evidence, and the use of evidence?

3. What is the evidence for Whittemore's denial of "honest art," and "thoroughgoing dissent" to the Beatles' poems? What kinds of "dissent" are and are not necessary for "honest art"?

4. Whose argument is more convincing, Whittemore's or Peyser's? Why?

Robert Christgau

ROCK LYRICS ARE POETRY (MAYBE)

Until it narrowed its programming, there was one hip radio station in New York, the station of the college kids and the bright suburban adolescents and the young professionals and the hippies—your station, if you're within range: WOR-FM. Not that there was much choice—AM radio in New York is antediluvian. But for a while, WOR-Stereo did seem to try. Its playlist was flexible and enormous and its deejays enjoyed much freedom. WOR was the home of the born-again Murray the K, with his "attitude music" and his tell-it-like-it-is (baby) cool, and coming up strong behind was the latetime (ten-to-two) jock, a spade named Rosko. Rosko emcees at the Village Theater, which is a story in itself, but not this one. This one is about Rosko and Kahlil Gibran, now-deceased author of a dozen or so quasi-poetic, pseudo-religious texts, the most famous of which is *The Prophet.**

Rosko quit WOR when the station decided to chase after the post-adolescent AM audience with a tight oldies playlist, but he had more in common with all the screaming-meemies than he probably suspected. Just like Cousin Brucie or B. M. R., he did not so much announce a show as preside over a ritual. Cultism is not confined to teenyboppers. All four jazz fans out there should remember Symphony Sid, who played virtually the same cuts night after night for literally years, announcing the same Stan Getz / Oscar Brown, Jr. / Nina Simone / Willie Bobo / Miles Davis in the same throat-cancer growl. Rosko did Sid one better. He played the same stuff every night, Beatles / Stones / Dylan, plus hip hits and various cult heroes—Richie Havens, Vanilla Fudge, Jimi Hendrix, Big Brother, Judy Collins. Then, to ice the cake, he would climax his show with a reverent reading from Kahlil Gibran. "And he who has deserved to drink from the ocean of life deserves to drink from

From *The Age of Rock* (N.Y.: Random House, 1969). Copyright 1967 by Robert Christgau. Reprinted by permission of the author and International Famous Agency.
* Already I can hear the screaming. You *like* Kahlil Gibran, right? So let's have it out. A critical essay—consider yourself forewarned—illumines nothing so much as the prejudices of its author. My tastes in music derive largely from Alan Freed and Thelonious Monk, but my tastes in poetry and philosophy were pounded into me by a phalanx of Ivy League professors. I think Kahlil Gibran is the worst kind of trash, much worse than Harold Robbins, say, because good people take him seriously.

your little stream"; "The soul unfolds itself, like a lotus of count-less petals"; "Vague and nebulous is the beginning of all things, but not their end, and I would fain have you remember me as a begin-ning," et cetera. In the background was poor Ravi Shankar, who hadn't been so ill-used since that nameless film poetaster discovered the quadruple-exposure raga. Rosko's fans loved it. They flooded the station with requests for printed versions, which Rosko an-swered with the sweet suggestion that they buy the book. A Gibran boomlet—you may even have been part of it.

I hope not. Admirers of books like *The Prophet* crave the en-thrallment of poetry without the labor. For poetry—the Greek *poiein* means to construct or make—involves labor, in the creation and the understanding. Perhaps even too much so. Ever since the Industrial Revolution moved art out of the mainstream and pro-duced the artistic rebel, whose avant-garde art comprises virtually all the good work in this century and much in the last, the arts have moved slowly and sadly beyond ordinary people. Artists have turned inward and concerned themselves with form. Not without superb results, either—whatever disservices they are done in the classroom, Proust, Yeats, Pollock, Stravinsky, and all the others have produced work which is not only marvelous technically, but very real emo-tionally, to those who know the language. The problem is, not many do—art is still not very respectable, and it's a lot more trou-ble than it used to be. What's worse, many who take the trouble succeed imperfectly, and turn to mass art or kitsch.

I want to say right now that none of the categories I'm going to be using are worth much. All but a few artists resist categories; the good ones usually confound them altogether. So a term like "rock" is impossibly vague; it denotes, if anything, something historical rather than aesthetic. "Mass art" and "kitsch" are pretty vague as well. Let's say that mass art is intended only to divert, entertain, pacify—Mantovani, Jacqueline Susann, *Muscle Beach Party*, etc. Kitsch is a more snobbish concept, and a more sophisticated prod-uct. It usually has the look of slightly out-of-date avant-garde in order to give its audience the illusion of aesthetic pleasure, what-ever that is. An important distinction, I think, is that many of the craftsmen who make kitsch believe thoroughly in what they are doing. That may be true of the creators of mass art, too, but their attitude is more businesslike—they don't worry about "art," only commercial appeal.

I think it is just because they didn't worry about art that many of the people who ground out the rock-and-roll of the fifties—not only the performers, but all the background people—were engaged (unconsciously, of course) in, making still another kind of art, folk art. If longevity is any criterion, then I say the Five Satins will be remembered longer than the Weavers, because consciousness tends to kill what is vital in folk art. Like any rule, this one is far from perfect. Paul Anka's songs were horrible even though he didn't worry about art; Pete Seeger did, and his stuff was good. Or take a better example. In 1944, James Agee wrote an essay called "Pseudo-Folk" that deplored contemporary jazz; Duke Ellington was marvelous in his way, Agee argued, but he was also effete, and gimme that Jelly Roll. Like everything Agee wrote, "Pseudo-Folk" was sensible and heartfelt. But as it was written a young alto-sax player named Charlie Parker was creating jazz that had all the vitality of folk art plus all the complexity and technical inventiveness of the "higher" arts. You never can tell.

The same kind of transformation may be occurring right now in what used to be called rock-and-roll. It is certainly fashionable to think so. But despite all the happy praise, no one really seems to understand what is going on. Here is Robert Shelton of the New York *Times:* "More than a few conservatives in and out of the academy will be quick to dismiss serious writing by pop stars as commercial gimmickry, box-office ploys and faddist ephemera. Time, I submit, will strain out the worthless and leave us with some valuable creative works, in music and in literature, by a wholesome group of new writers." Shelton's facts are okay, but there is something dreadfully wrong about his tone—wholesome indeed. Does time really "strain out the worthless," or is it merely that we judge what is present and what is past by two entirely different and entirely proper standards? Does Shelton want to imply that "commercial gimmickry, box-office ploys and faddist ephemera" are necessarily inconsistent with "valuable creative works"? The Beatles have long since pulverized that cliché. Another example comes from Leonard Bernstein, who told a nationwide TV audience, "Many of the lyrics, in their oblique allusions and wayout metaphors, are beginning to sound like real poems." In a way Bernstein was right. Many rock lyrics sound like poems, especially to those who don't read poetry, which is almost everyone. But then, so does Kahlil Gibran.

The songwriter who seems to sound most like a poet is Bob Dylan. Dylan is such an idiosyncratic genius that it is perilous to imitate him—his faults, at worst annoying and at best invigorating, ruin lesser talents. But imitation is irresistible. Who can withstand Paul Nelson of *Little Sandy Review*, who calls Dylan "the man who in every sense revolutionized modern poetry, American folk music, popular music, and the whole of modern-day thought"? Or Jack Newfield of the *Village Voice*, wandering on about "symbolic alienation . . . new plateaus for poetic, content-conscious songwriters . . . put poetry back into song . . . reworks T. S. Eliot's

classic line . . . bastard child of Chaplin, Celine and Hart Crane,"
while serving up tidbits from Dylan's corpus, some of which don't
look so tasty on a paper plate? However inoffensive "The ghost of
electricity howls in the bones of her face" sounds on vinyl, it is
silly without the music. Poems are read or said. Songs are sung.

Dylan gets away with it simply because there is so much there.
The refrain of "My Back Pages," his renunciation of political pro-
test—"I was so much older then, I'm younger than that now"—
may be the finest line he has ever written. Its opening—"Crimson
flames tied through my ears"—may be the worst. The song bulges
with metaphors and epithets, some apt, some stuck in to fill out the
meter. The tired trick of using a noun for a verb to spice things up
reaches an all-time low with the word (?) "foundationed." Dylan's
obsession with rhyme (which he has lately begun to parody: "Hear
the one with the mustache say, jeeze/I can't find my knees") com-
pels him to match "now" with "somehow" three times in six
stanzas. Twice this is totally gratuitous. But the third time—"Good
and bad, I define these terms, quite clear no doubt somehow"—
"somehow" becomes the final qualification in a series of qualifications, and works perfectly: a typical hit among misses.

"My Back Pages" is a bad poem. But it is a good song, supported by a memorable refrain. The music softens our demands,
the importance of what is being said somehow overbalances the
flaws, and Dylan's delivery—he sounds as if he's singing a hymn at
a funeral—adds a portentous edge not present just in the words.
Because it is a good song, "My Back Pages" can be done in other
ways. The Byrds' version depends on intricate, up-tempo music that
pushes the words into the background. However much they mean
to David Crosby, the lyrics—except for that refrain—could be gib-
berish and the song would still succeed. Repeat: Dylan is a songwriter, not a poet. A few of his most perfect efforts—"Don't Think
Twice," or "Just Like a Woman"—are tight enough to survive on
the page. But they are exceptions.

Such a rash judgment assumes that modern poets know what
they're doing. It respects the tradition that runs from Ezra Pound
and William Carlos Williams down to Charles Olson, Robert Creeley, and perhaps a dozen others, the tradition that regards Allen
Ginsberg as a good poet, perhaps, but a wildman. Dylan's work,
with its iambics, its clackety-clack rhymes, and its scattergun images, makes Ginsberg's look like a model of decorous diction. An
art advances through technical innovation. Modern American poetry
assumes (and sometimes eliminates) metaphoric ability, concen-
trating on the use of line and rhythm to approximate (or refine)
speech, the reduction of language to essentials, and "tone of voice."
Dylan's only innovation is that he sings, a good way to control

"tone of voice," but not enough to "revolutionize modern poetry." He may have started something just as good, but modern poetry is getting along fine, thank you.

It is fortunate that Dylan's most prominent disciple, Donovan, is not an imitator. His best stuff crosses Dylan's surrealist bent with the jazzy cleverness of thirties' songwriters like Cole Porter. Donovan makes demands on his listeners (tossing off an elliptical image like "To a leopard's you've been changin'" or devoting whole songs to his medieval fetish) and he delights in obscurity (everyone loves "Mellow Yellow" and "Sunshine Superman," but no one understands them—and don't tell me about bananas, but once again he is a songwriter, and in a much less equivocal way than Dylan. With a few tricks so well tried that they are legitimate *lingua franca*, at least for his special audience (that is us), he is working to deliver songwriting from superannuated sentimentalists like Johnny Mercer and shrewd camp followers like Tommy Boyce and Bobby Hart. In another way, Mick Jagger and Keith Richard are doing the same thing. They began by writing pungent pseudo-blues from their peculiar, ironic vantage—"Heart of Stone," "The Last Time," etc. Now, while sticking to old forms, they have allowed their sense of themselves to dominate their sense of blues tradition, producing a body of work that is as consistent and various as anything this side of Lennon-McCartney, but still song, not poetry. In the atmosphere that they and Donovan and especially Dylan have created, dozens of intelligent craftsmen—from folk-rockers like Marty Balin and John Sebastian to commercial talents like Neil Diamond and Mike Nesmith—are working down below to return popular songwriting to the honest stature it had in the thirties and beyond. The new songwriters are sentimental, not about the way the world is, but about their feelings toward it. That is a great step forward.

Dylan's influence has not always been so salutary. Lennon-McCartney and Jagger-Richard would have matured without him. But had there been no Dylan to successfully combine the vulgar and the felicitous, would we now be oppressed with the kind of vague, extravagant imagery and inane philosophizing that ruins so much good music and so impresses the Kahlil Gibran fans? I doubt it. Gary Brooker and Keith Read of Procol Harum, for an instance, obviously have a lot of talent. The opening of "Homburg" ("Your multilingual"—piano chord—"business friend") is my choice for line of the month, and the transformation of Bach in "A Whiter Shade of Pale" was brilliant and well executed. But is "A Whiter Shade of Pale" poetry? From the ads London placed in the trades, you might assume it was Shakespeare, newly unearthed. In fact there is a rumor that it was adapted from an Elizabethan poem. No matter. Full of obscure clichés ("skipped the light fandango";

"sixteen vestal virgins") with a clever (admittedly) title phrase
and refrain, the overall archaic feel reinforced by literary reference
("the miller told his tale"), it sold because it did such a successful
job of sounding like poetry, which, as we all know, is obscure,
literary, and sort of archaic. Pure kitsch. Not much better is the
self-indulgence of the Doors' Jim Morrison. "Twentieth Century-
Fox," "Break on Through," "People Are Strange" and "Soul
Kitchen," listed in ascending order of difficulty, all pretty much
succeed. But Morrison does not stop there. He ruins "Light My
Fire" with stuff like "our love becomes a funeral pyre"—Ugh!
what does that mean? Nothing, but the good old romantic association of love and death is there, and that's all Morrison wanted—and
noodles around in secondhand Freud in "The End." Morrison
obviously regards "The End" as a masterwork, and his admirers
agree. I wonder why. The music builds very nicely in an Oriental
kind of way, but the dramatic situation is tedious stuff. I suppose it
is redeemed by Morrison's histrionics and by the nebulousness that
passes for depth among so many lovers of rock poetry.

The Doors and Procol Harum are good groups. Each has given
me much pleasure. But I don't think "The End" and "A Whiter
Shade of Pale" are just bad tries. I think they grow out of a bad
idea, the idea that poetry—a concept not too well understood—can
be incorporated into rock. This idea is old fashioned and literary
in the worse sense. But young rock groups write "symbolic" lyrics
that they like only because they wrote them, and they set them to
music, and the cycle starts again. In a sense Morrison and Brooker-
Reed are responsible for these kids in the same way Dylan is for
them.

This phenomenon obviously has limitless depths (though in
fairness it should be said that most groups—most of the ones you
hear, anyway—avoid them), but I think its heights have been
reached by a songwriter who has in abundance the one quality that
Dylan, Morrison, and all their lessers lack. The songwriter is Paul
Simon, and the quality is taste. Simon is so tasteful the media
can't help but love him. Even Richard Goldstein has guessed that
"chances are he's brought you closer to the feel and texture of
modern poetry than anything since the big blackout." Goldstein
does pin down the reason for Simon and Garfunkel's popularity,
though: "They don't make waves."

Paul Simon's lyrics are the purest, highest, and most finely
wrought kitsch of our time. The lyrics I've been putting down are
not necessarily easy to write—bad poetry is often carefully worked,
the difference being that it's easier to perceive flaccidly—but the
labor that must go into one of Simon's songs is of another order of
magnitude. Melodies, harmonies, arrangements are scrupulously

fitted. Each song is perfect. And says nothing.

What saddens me is that Simon obviously seems to have a lot to say to the people who buy his records. But it's a shuck. Like Kahlil Gibran all he's really doing is scratching them where they itch, providing some temporary relief but coming nowhere near the root of the problem. Simon's content isn't modern, it is merely fashionable, and his form never jars the sensibilities. He is the only songwriter I can imagine admitting he writes about that all-American subject, the Alienation of Modern Man, in just those words. His songs have the texture of modern poetry only if modern poetry can be said to end with early Auden—Edwin Arlington Robinson is more like it. Poets don't write like Robinson any more because his technical effects have outlived their usefulness, which was to make people see things in a new way. And even in such old-fashioned terms, what Simon does is conventional and uninspired. An example is "For Emily, Wherever I May Find Her," in which "poetic" words—organdy, crinoline, juniper (words that suggest why Simon is so partial to turn-of-the-century verse) and "beautiful" images (softer-than-the-rain, wandered-lonely-streets) are used to describe a dream girl. Simon is no dope; he knows this is all a little corny, but that's okay because Emily is an impossible girl. Only in order for the trick to come off there has to be an ironic edge. There isn't, and "For Emily" is nothing more than a sophisticated popular song of the traditional-fantasy type.

This kind of mindless craft reaches a peak in Simon's supposed masterpiece, "The Dangling Conversation," which uses all the devices you learn about in English class—alliteration, alternating concretion and abstraction, even the use of images from poetry itself, a favorite ploy of poets who don't know much of anything else—to mourn wistfully about the classic plight of self-conscious man, his Inability to Communicate. Tom Phillips of the *New York Times* has called this song "one of Paul Simon's subtlest lyrics . . . a pitiless vision of self-consciousness and isolation." I don't hear the same song, I guess, because I think Simon's voice drips self-pity from every syllable (not only in this song, either). The Mantovani strings that reinforce the lyric capture its toughness perfectly. If Simon were just a little hipper, his couple would be discussing the failure of communication as they failed to communicate, rather than psychoanalysis or the state of the theatre. But he's not a little hipper.

Still, maybe he's getting there. A new album should be out shortly (there is one more track to record at this writing) and could be a surprise. Simon is going through changes. He has released almost nothing new since *Parsley, Sage, Rosemary and Thyme,* which contains "For Emily" and "Dangling Conversation." Last winter's "At the Zoo" is more concrete and less lugu-brious than his other work, just a whimsical song about Central Park Zoo, and despite an occasional kernel of corn ("It's a light and tumble journey"), the metaphors work because they are fun: "Zebras are reactionaries/Antelopes are missionaries," "Fakin' It" is more serious, but the colloquial diction that dominates the song —in the first, third, and fifth sections, there is no word that isn't among the most common in the language: "The girl does what she wants to do/She knows what she wants to do and I know I'm/ Fakin' it/I'm not really makin' it"—adds a casual feel; even when the verbiage becomes more Simonesque, it is seasoned with a dash of the colloquial: "A walk in the garden wears me down/Tangled in the fallen vines/Pickin' up the punch lines." In addition, the song contains an extraordinarily subtle switch. "I own a tailor's face and hands/I am the tailor's face and hands." No image-mon-gering there, just one little changeover, from a clever metaphor to a painful identification.

In an oblique and probably unconscious way, I think "Fakin' It" is true rock poetry, an extension of a very specific tradition. The pop that preceded rock, and still exists today, was full of what semanticist S. I. Hayakawa has listed as "wishful thinking, dreamy and ineffectual nostalgia, unrealistic fantasy, self-pity, and sentimental clichés masquerading as emotion." The blues, by con-trast, were "unsentimental and realistic." Rock-and-roll combined the gutless lyrics of pop with the sexual innuendo of blues music and delivery. What this meant in practice was that it had no lyrics at all. Most rock fans just ignored what inane content there was in favor of the sound and the big beat. So rock diction became im-becilically colloquial, nonsense syllables proliferated, and singers slurred because nobody cared. Be-bop-a-lula, you can really start to groove it, caught Aunt Mary something and she ducked back in the alley. In "Fakin' It," the basic-English diction, the eleven repetitions of the title, and that almost inaudible changeover not only avoid Simon's usual pretensions; combined with the big-beat arrangement, they create a mood that asks "Why should this mean anything?" Only it does.

It is by creating a mood that asks "Why should this mean any-thing?" that the so-called rock poets can really write poetry—poetry that not only says something, but says it as only rock music can. For once Marshall McLuhan's terminology tells us something: rock lyrics are a cool medium. Go ahead and mumble. Drown the voices in guitars. If somebody really wants to know what you're saying, he'll take the trouble, and in that trouble lies your art. On a crude level this permits the kind of one-to-one symbolism of pot songs like "Along Comes Mary" and "That Acapulco Gold." "Fakin' It" does other things with the same idea. But the only song-writers who seem really to have mastered it are John Phillips and Lennon-McCartney.

Phillips possesses a frightening talent. "San Francisco—Flow-ers in Your Hair," catering to every prurient longing implicit in teenage America's flirtation with the hippies without ever even mentioning the secret word, is a stunning piece of schlock. A song like "Once Was a Time I Thought" (as if to say to all those Swingle Singer fans, "You thought that was hard? We can do the whole number in fifty-eight seconds") is another example of the range of his ability. You have the feeling Phillips could write a suc-cessful musical, a Frank Sinatra hit, anything that sells, if he wanted to.

Perhaps you are one of those people who plays every new LP with the treble way up and the bass way down so you can ferret out all the secret symbolic meanings right away. Personally I think that spoils the fun, and I suspect any record that permits you to do that isn't fulfilling its first function, which pertains to music, or, more generally, noise. The Mamas and Papas' records are full of diversions—the contrapuntal arrangements, the idiot "yeahs," the orchestral improvisations, the rhyme schemes ("If you're entertain-ing any thought that you're gaining by causin' me all of this pain and makin' me blue, the joke's on you") and Phillips' trick of drawing out a few words with repetitions and pauses. Perhaps this isn't conscious. In songs like "California Dreamin'," "12:30" and many others, Phillips is obviously just a good lyricist (with a lot of tender respect for the fantasy world of pure pop that critics like Hayakawa derogate so easily). But his lyrics are rarely easy to under-stand. Maybe it's just me, but I wonder how many of you are aware that a minor track on the second album, "Strange Young Girls," is about LSD. No secret about it—there it is, right out in the open of the first stanza: "Strange young girls, colored with sadness/Eyes of innocence hiding their madness/Walking the Strip, sweet, soft, and placid/Off'ring their youth on the altar of acid." But you don't notice because there's so much else to listen to.

My favorite Phillips song is "Straight Shooter." By now, every-one knows "Straight Shooter" is about drugs. They printed it right in the *Times* and everything. But its genius is that it doesn't have to be—it works equally well as one of those undefined, meaningless love songs that have always been the staple of rock. Oh, there are a few little aberrations—baby is suspected of holding anything, not anyone, and the "half of it belongs to me" doesn't make sense. But this is rock-and-roll. It doesn't have to make sense. Even the "just get me high" has all sorts of respectable precedents, like the "I get highs" in "I Want to Hold Your Hand," which may be about spiritual high but is no drug song. In addition there is the irony of this bright, bouncy melody being all about some needle freak. It's a characteristic trick—Phillips likes to conceal the tone of a lyric in a paradoxical melody (the perfect example being the gentle-sounding "Got a Feelin' "). Every level of uncertainty makes the song more like the reality we actually perceive. Yet the whole effect occurs within a strict rock framework.

Phillips achieves rock feel with his arrangements. The lyrics themselves are closer to traditional pop—Rodgers and Hart's "My Heart Stood Still," on the second album, sounds less out of place than Bobby Freeman's "Do You Wanna Dance?" on the first. Lennon-McCartney do it with diction. Their early work is all pure rock—the songs are merely excuses for melody, beat and sound. Occasionally it shows a flash of the subtlety to come, as in the sexual insinuation of "Please Please Me" or the premise of "There's a Place" ("There, there's a place/Where I can go/When I feel low, when I feel blue/And it's my mind"). More often it is pure, meaningless sentiment, couched in the simplest possible terms. By the time of *A Hard Day's Night* the songs are more sophisticated musically, and a year later, in *Help!*, the boys are becoming pop songwriters. *Help!* itself is a perfect example. Words like "self-assured" and "insecure" are not out of rock diction, nor is the line: "My independence seems to vanish in the haze." This facet of their talent has culminated (for the moment) in songs like "Paperback Writer," "A Little Help from My Friends," and "When I'm Sixty-four," which show all the verbal facility of the best traditional pop and none of the sentimentality, and in deliberate exercises like "Michelle" and "Here, There and Everywhere," which show both.

Other songs like "Norwegian Wood," "Dr. Roberts," "Good Morning, Good Morning" are ambiguous despite an unerring justness of concrete detail; little conundrums, different from Dylanesque surrealism because they don't fit so neatly into a literary category (Edward Lear is their closest antecedent). Most of the songs since *Rubber Soul* are characterized by a similar obliqueness. Often the Beatles' "I" is much harder to pin down than the "I" in Donovan or Jagger-Richard, a difficulty that is reinforced by their filters, their ethereal harmonies, and their collective public identity. This concern with angle of attack is similar to that of poets like Creeley.

Lennon and McCartney are the only rock songwriters who combine high literacy (as high as Dylan's or Simon's) with an eye for concision and a truly contemporary sense of what fits. They seem less and less inclined to limit themselves to what I have defined as rock diction, and yet they continue to succeed—the simul-

taneous lushness and tightness of "Lucy in the Sky with Diamonds,"
for instance, is nothing short of extraordinary. They still get
startling mileage out of the banal colloquial—think of the "oh boy"
in "A Day in the Life," or the repeating qualifications in "Straw-
berry Fields Forever." But they have also written two songs which
are purely colloquial—"She Said She Said," and "All You Need Is
Love."

"She Said She Said" is at once one of the most difficult and
banal of Beatle songs. It is a concrete version of what in "The
Dangling Conversation" (despite all those details) remains abstract,
a conversation between a hung-up, self-important girl who says she
knows "what it's like to be dead" and her boy friend, who doesn't
want to know. (If Simon had written it, the boy would have argued
that he was the one who knew.) The song uses the same kind of
words that can be found in "She Loves You" (the quintessential
early Beatles song), yet says so much more. Its conceit, embodied in
the title, is meaningless; its actuality is a kind of ironic density
that no other songwriter (except Dylan at his best) approaches. One
of its ironies is the suggestion that callow philosophizing is every
bit as banal as the most primitive rock-and-roll.

"All You Need Is Love," deliberately written in basic English
so it could be translated, makes the connection clearer by quoting
from "She Loves You" while conveying the ironic message of the
title. Is love all you need? What kind of love? Universal love? Love
of country? Courtly love? "She Loves You" love? It's hard to tell.
The song employs rock-and-roll—dominant music, big beat, repeated refrain, simple diction—and transforms it into something
which, if not poetry, at least has a multifaceted poetic wholeness.
I think it is rock poetry in the truest sense.

Maybe I am being too strict. Modern poetry is doing very
well, thank you, on its own terms, but in terms of what it is doing
for us, and even for the speech from which it derives, it looks a bit
pallid. Never take the categories too seriously. It may be that the
new songwriters (not poets, please) lapse artistically, indulge their
little infatuations with language and ideas, and come up with a
product that could be much better if handled with a little less
energy and a little more caution. But energy is where it's at. And
songs—even though they are only songs—may soon be more important than poems, no matter that they are easier too.

Once there were bards and the bards did something wondrous
—they provided literature for the illiterate. The bards evolved into
poets and the poetry which had been their means became their end.
It didn't seem to matter much after a while, since everyone was
literate anyway. But semiliteracy, which is where people go when
they're not illiterate any more, is in some ways a worse blight.

The new songwriters think there should be bards again and they're right, but the bardic traditions are pretty faint. Too many of them are seduced by semiliteracy—mouthing other people's ideas in other people's words. But they are bards, and that is very good. Maybe soon it will be a lot better.

This essay was written (too fast, like most journalism) in the early fall of 1967 for *Cheetah*, now sadly departed. Though I haven't been able to resist a few stylistic fixes, I have left it mostly as is. If the piece seems dated to me now, in the fall of 1968, then any revisions would no doubt seem dated by the time they appeared. Journalism ought to survive with its limitations of time and place intact.

Nevertheless I feel compelled to put things in some small perspective and right a few wrongs. I'm probably guilty of overkill on Paul Simon, who has since gone on to his just reward as the writer of a Number One filmscore, but when I wrote this he was still taken seriously by people who deserved better. And though I love "Mrs. Robinson" and consider *Bookends* S&G's finest album, I don't think Simon has lived up to the promise I discerned in "Fakin' It." As for John Phillips, I am now convinced the Mamas and the Papas are destined to become high camp, but that doesn't change what they were and sometimes still are for us, and I stand by my praise.

What I describe as the poetry of rock has to do with surprise, and it is still relevant: the effect of a lyric by John Kay of Steppenwolf, say, or even Gerry Goffin and Carole King, is frequently enhanced by indirection. But since last fall there have been only two completely successful examples of this tradition, the ultimate test being how broadly they sold: Lennon-McCartney's "Hello Good-bye" and Peter Townshend's "I Can See for Miles." I am beginning to think such specimens will become increasingly rare. The technique is based on one overriding assumption: that no one takes rock seriously. It can only survive as long as that assumption is viable, if not as a present truth then as a living memory. But even the memory seems to be dying. It may be that the most lasting verbal effect of what I can only call the rock ambience may be a new eloquence in popular songwriting, typified by a figure like Randy Newman, whose work has little to do with rock per se.

The key figure in all this is Bob Dylan, who as a vocalist and a writer has pointed out all sorts of new directions for song. I think I misunderstood what Dylan did for those of us who always knew he was a rotten "poet." It was his very badness that attracted us. His overwriting was the equivalent in folk music of the happy energy of the Beatles. He loved language enough to misuse it. Of course, if he hadn't had the genius to use it brilliantly as well,

that would hardly have been a virtue. But he did, and so re-
vitalized areas of language that had seemed exhausted. The songwriter who has learned most from this is Leonard Cohen, with his
wry exultation in silly rhymes and inconsistent or overly consistent
images. It may be, by the way, that poets have learned something
from Dylan's freedom as well. In any case I know now that the
work of poets like Robert Creeley was no longer really central when
I wrote this. Anyone who would like to sample what has replaced
it should refer to *Bean Spasms*, by Ted Berrigan and Ron Padgett.

———

ROBERT CHRISTGAU (1942–   ) *writes about the rock scene with a
highly personal colloquial-scholarly style. "Tune Up, Turn Disestab-
lishmentarian, Drop Out," an article on rock performers who are
college drop-outs, appeared in* Esquire, *September 1967. For this
article, Christgau somehow accumulated the posed yearbook pictures
of thirty-two performers, printing them alongside hairy publicity
shots, just for laughs. "Anatomy of a Love Festival"* (Esquire, January 1968) *saw the Monterey International Pop Festival as beautiful, perhaps the last of the good ones, "the first powwow of the love
crowd, the perfect pastorale, chocked with music and warmhearted
people. . . . And chances are that by next summer it may have disappeared forever."*

1. *Reread Christgau's essay and mark every sentence that assumes
    or asserts a definition of art, or non-art. From analysis of these
    sentences, construct a definition of what constitutes art for
    Christgau. Compare this definition with the one explicitly set
    out by Read, and those assumed by Peyser and Whittemore.
    Despite differences in topic, style, and conclusion, what general
    areas of agreement do you see among them?*

2. *One of the sharpest distinctions Christgau makes between art
    and non-art is that real poetry "says something": "It is by creat-
    ing a mood that asks 'Why should this mean anything?' that
    the so-called rock poets can really write poetry. . . . If some-
    body really wants to know what you're saying, he'll take the
    trouble, and in that trouble lies your art." Why should art be
    "trouble"? Why is the easy message, the "inane philosophy,"
    the "scratching them where they itch" of Gibran and Simon
    not art?*

3. *Two kinds of bad art are under attack in this essay: "The new*

songwriters are sentimental, not about the way the world is, but about their feelings toward it. That is a great step forward." What does "sentimental" mean here? How is it related to meaninglessness? Which of the writers are guilty of being "sentimental" about "the way the world is"? What does that mean, and what are some examples? Which of the writers are not sentimental about the way the world is, but only about their feelings? Why is this "a great step forward"?

4. How does Christgau's sensitivity to the music that is part of the rock song modify his attack on meaningless lyrics? How does he deal with the argument that these lyrics ought not to have meaning, and hence ought not to be judged as poetry?

5. How convincing is Christgau's argument that rock lyrics should be judged in the context of modern poetry and by traditional artistic standards? What evidence does he use to support his case? Why is the essay so packed with names and quotations? Choose a typical assertion (as the assessment of Dylan, or Simon) and show how Christgau uses evidence and analysis to support what he says.

Ralph Ellison

THE SHADOW AND THE ACT

Faulkner has given us a metaphor. When, in the film *Intruder in the Dust*, the young Mississippian Chick Mallison falls into an ice-coated creek on a Negro's farm, he finds that he has plunged into the depth of a reality which constantly reveals itself as the reverse of what it had appeared before his plunge. Here the ice—white, brittle and eggshell-thin—symbolizes Chick's inherited views of the world, especially his Southern conception of Negroes. Emerging more shocked by the air than by the water, he finds himself locked in a moral struggle with the owner of the land, Lucas Beauchamp, the son of a slave, who, while aiding the boy, angers him by refusing to act toward him as Southern Negroes are expected to act.

To Lucas, Chick is not only a child but his guest. Thus he not only dries the boy's clothes, he insists that he eat the only food in the house, Lucas's own dinner. When Chick (whose white standards won't allow him to accept the hospitality of a Negro) attempts to pay him, Lucas refuses to accept the money. What follows is one of the most sharply amusing studies of Southern racial ethics to be seen anywhere. Asserting his whiteness, Chick throws the money on the floor, ordering Lucas to pick it up; Lucas, disdaining to quarrel with a child, has Chick's young Negro companion, Aleck Sander, return the coins.

Defeated but still determined, Chick later seeks to discharge his debt by sending Lucas and his wife a gift. Lucas replies by sending Chick a gallon of molasses by—outrage of all Southern Negro outrages!—a white boy on a mule. He is too much, and from that moment it becomes Chick's passion to repay his debt and to see Lucas for once "act like a nigger." The opportunity has come, he thinks, when Lucas is charged with shooting a white man in the back. But instead of humbling himself, Lucas (from his cell) tells, almost orders, Chick to prove him innocent by violating the white man's grave.

In the end we see Chick recognizing Lucas as the representative

Reprinted from *Shadow and Act*, by Ralph Ellison, by permission of Random House, Inc. Copyright 1949 by Ralph Ellison.

of those virtues of courage, pride, independence and patience that
are usually attributed only to white men—and, in his uncle's words,
accepting the Negro as "the keeper of our [the whites'] con-
sciences." This bit of dialogue, coming after the real murderer is
revealed as the slain man's own brother, is, when viewed historically, about the most remarkable concerning a Negro ever to come
out of Hollywood.

With this conversation, the falling into creeks, the digging up
of corpses and the confronting of lynch mobs that mark the plot,
all take on a new significance: Not only have we been watching the
consciousness of a young Southerner grow through the stages of a
superb mystery drama, we have participated in a process by which
the role of Negroes in American life has been given what, for the
movies, is a startling new definition.

To appreciate fully the significance of *Intruder in the Dust* in
the history of Hollywood we must go back to the film that is regarded as the archetype of the modern American motion picture,
The Birth of a Nation.

Originally entitled *The Clansman*, the film was inspired by another Southern novel, the Reverend Thomas Dixon's work of that
title, which also inspired Joseph Simmons to found the Knights of
the Ku Klux Klan. (What a role these malignant clergymen have
played in our lives!) Re-entitled *The Birth of a Nation* as an after-
thought, it was this film that forged the twin screen image of the
Negro as bestial rapist and grinning, eye-rolling clown—stereotypes
that are still with us today. Released during 1915, it resulted in
controversy, riots, heavy profits and the growth of the Klan. Of it
Terry Ramsaye, a historian of the American motion-picture industry, writes: "The picture . . . and the K.K.K. secret society,
which was the afterbirth of a nation, were sprouted from the same
root. In subsequent years they reacted upon each other to the large
profit of both. The film presented predigested dramatic experience and thrills. The society made the customers all actors in cos-
tume."

Usually *The Birth of a Nation* is discussed in terms of its contributions to cinema technique, but, as with every other technical
advance since the oceanic sailing ship, it became a further instrument in the dehumanization of the Negro. And while few films
have gone so far in projecting Negroes in a malignant light, few
before the 1940s showed any concern with depicting their humanity. Just the opposite. In the struggle against Negro freedom,
motion pictures have been one of the strongest instruments for
justifying some white Americans' anti-Negro attitudes and practices. Thus the South, through D. W. Griffith's genius, captured

the enormous myth-making potential of the film form almost from the beginning. While the Negro stereotypes by no means made all white men Klansmen the cinema did to the extent that audiences accepted its image of Negroes, make them participants in the South's racial ritual of keeping the Negro "in his place."

After Reconstruction the political question of what was to be done with Negroes, "solved" by the Hayes-Tilden deal of 1876, came down to the psychological question: "How can the Negro's humanity be evaded?" The problem, arising in a democracy that holds all men as created equal, was a highly moral one: democratic ideals had to be squared with anti-Negro practices. One answer was to *deny* the Negro's humanity—a pattern set long before 1915. But with the release of *The Birth of a Nation* the propagation of subhuman images of Negroes became financially and dramatically profitable. The Negro as scapegoat could be sold as entertainment, could even be exported. If the film became the main manipulator of the American dream, for Negroes that dream contained a strong dose of such stuff as nightmares are made of.

We are recalling all this not so much as a means of indicting Hollywood as by way of placing *Intruder in the Dust*, and such recent films as *Home of the Brave*, *Lost Boundaries* and *Pinky*, in perspective. To direct an attack upon Hollywood would indeed be to confuse portrayal with action, image with reality. In the beginning was not the shadow, but the act, and the province of Hollywood is not action, but illusion. Actually, the anti-Negro images of the films were (and are) acceptable because of the existence throughout the United States of an audience obsessed with an inner psychological need to view Negroes as less than men. Thus, psychologically and ethically, these negative images constitute justifications for all those acts, legal, emotional, economic and political, which we label Jim Crow. The anti-Negro image is thus a ritual object of which Hollywood is not the creator, but the manipulator. Its role has been that of justifying the widely held myth of Negro unhumanness and inferiority by offering entertaining rituals through which that myth could be reaffirmed.

The great significance of the definition of Lucas Beauchamp's role in *Intruder in the Dust* is that it makes explicit the nature of Hollywood's changed attitude toward Negroes. Form being, in the words of Kenneth Burke, "the psychology of the audience," what is taking place in the American movie patron's mind? Why these new attempts to redefine the Negro's role? What has happened to the audience's mode of thinking?

For one thing there was the war; for another there is the fact that the United States' position as a leader in world affairs is shaken by its treatment of Negroes. Thus the thinking of white

Americans is undergoing a process of change, and reflecting that change, we find that each of the films mentioned above deals with some basic and unusually negative assumption about Negroes: Are Negroes cowardly soldiers? (*Home of the Brave*); are Negroes the real polluters of the South? (*Intruder in the Dust*); have mulatto Negroes the right to pass as white, at the risk of having black babies, or if they have white-skinned children, of having to kill off their "white" identities by revealing to them that they are, alas, Negroes? (*Lost Boundaries*); and, finally, should Negro girls marry white men—or wonderful non sequitur—should they help their race? (*Pinky*).

Obviously these films are not *about* Negroes at all; they are about what whites think and feel about Negroes. And if they are taken as accurate reflectors of that thinking, it becomes apparent that there is much confusion. To make use of Faulkner's metaphor again, the film makers fell upon the eggshell ice but, unlike the child, weren't heavy enough to break it. And, being unable to break it, they were unable to discover the real direction of their film narratives. In varying degree, they were unwilling to dig into the grave to expose the culprit, and thus we find them using ingenious devices for evading the full human rights of their Negroes. The result represents a defeat not only of drama, but of purpose.

In *Home of the Brave*, for instance, a psychiatrist tells the Negro soldier that his hysterical paralysis is like that of any other soldier who has lived when his friends have died; and we hear the soldier pronounced cured; indeed, we see him walk away prepared to open a bar and restaurant with a white veteran. But here there is an evasion (and by *evasion* I refer to the manipulation of the audience's attention away from reality to focus it upon false issues), because the guilt from which the Negro is supposed to suffer springs from an incident in which, immediately after his friend has called him a "yellowbelly nigger," he has wished the friend dead—only to see the wish granted by a sniper's bullet.

What happens to this racial element in the motivation of his guilt? The psychiatrist ignores it, and becomes a sleight-of-hand artist who makes it vanish by repeating again that the Negro is like everybody else. Nor, I believe, is this accidental, for it is here exactly that we come to the question of whether Negroes can rightfully be expected to risk their lives in an army in which they are slandered and discriminated against. Psychiatry is not, I'm afraid, the answer. The soldier suffers from concrete acts, not hallucinations.

And so with the others. In *Lost Boundaries* the question evaded is whether a mulatto Negro has the right to practice the old American pragmatic philosophy of capitalizing upon one's as-

sets. For after all, whiteness *has* been given an economic and social
value in our culture; and for the doctor upon whose life the film is
based "passing" was the quickest and most certain means to success.

Yet Hollywood is uncertain about his right to do this. The film
does not render the true circumstances. In real life Dr. Albert
Johnson, the Negro doctor who "passed" as white, purchased the
thriving practice of a deceased physician in Gorham, New Hamp-
shire, for a thousand dollars. Instead, a fiction is introduced in the
film wherein Dr. Carter's initial motivation for "passing" arises
after he is refused an internship by dark Negroes in an Atlanta
hospital—because of his color! It just isn't real, since there are
thousands of mulattoes living as Negroes in the South, many of
them Negro leaders. The only functional purpose served by this
fiction is to gain sympathy for Carter by placing part of the blame
for his predicament upon black Negroes. Nor should the irony be
missed that part of the sentiment evoked when the Carters are wel-
comed back into the community is gained by painting Negro life as
horrible, a fate worse than a living death. It would seem that in the
eyes of Hollywood, it is only "white" Negroes who ever suffer—or
is it merely the "white" corpuscles of their blood?

Pinky, for instance, is the story of another suffering mulatto,
and the suffering grows out of a confusion between race and love.
If we attempt to reduce the heroine's problem to sentence form
we'd get something like this: "Should white-skinned Negro girls
marry white men, or should they inherit the plantations of old
white aristocrats (provided they can find any old aristocrats to will
them their plantations) or should they live in the South and open
nursery schools for black Negroes?" It doesn't follow, but neither
does the action. After sitting through a film concerned with interracial marriage, we see it suddenly become a courtroom battle over
whether Negroes have the right to inherit property.

Pinky wins the plantation, and her lover, who has read of the
fight in the Negro press, arrives and still loves her, race be hanged.
But now Pinky decides that to marry him would "violate the race"
and that she had better remain a Negro. Ironically, nothing is said
about the fact that her racial integrity, whatever that is, was violated
before she was born. Her parents are never mentioned in the film.
Following the will of the white aristocrat, who, before dying, advises her to "be true to herself," she opens a school for darker
Negroes.

But in real life the choice is not between loving or denying one's
race. Many couples manage to intermarry without violating their
integrity, and indeed their marriage becomes the concrete expression of their integrity. In the film Jeanne Crain floats about like a

sleepwalker, which seems to me to be exactly the way a girl so full of unreality would act. One thing is certain: no one is apt to mistake her for a Negro, not even a white one.

And yet, despite the absurdities with which these films are laden, they are all worth seeing, and if seen, capable of involving us emotionally. That they do is testimony to the deep centers of American emotion that they touch. Dealing with matters which, over the years, have been slowly charging up with guilt, they all display a vitality which escapes their slickest devices. And, naturally enough, one of the most interesting experiences connected with viewing them in predominantly white audiences is the profuse flow of tears and the sighs of profound emotional catharsis heard on all sides. It is as though there were some deep relief to be gained merely from seeing these subjects projected upon the screen.

It is here precisely that a danger lies. For the temptation toward self-congratulation which comes from seeing these films and sharing in their emotional release is apt to blind us to the true nature of what is unfolding—or failing to unfold—before our eyes. As an antidote to the sentimentality of these films, I suggest that they be seen in predominantly Negro audiences. For here, when the action goes phony, one will hear derisive laughter, not sobs. (Perhaps this is what Faulkner means about Negroes keeping the white man's conscience.) Seriously, *Intruder in the Dust* is the only film that could be shown in Harlem without arousing unintended laughter. For it is the only one of the four in which Negroes can make complete identification with their screen image. Interestingly, the factors that make this identification possible lie in its depiction not of racial but of human qualities.

Yet in the end, turning from art to life, we must even break with the definition of the Negro's role given us by Faulkner. For when it comes to conscience, we know that in this world each of us, black and white alike, must become the keeper of his own. This, in the deepest sense, is what these four films, taken as a group, should help us realize.

Faulkner himself seems to realize it. In the book *Intruder in the Dust*, Lucas attempts not so much to be the keeper of anyone else's conscience as to preserve his own life. Chick, in aiding Lucas, achieves that view of truth on which his own conscience depends.

RALPH ELLISON (1914–) *won the National Book Award for fiction with* Invisible Man (1952). *In 1965, a poll of two hundred writers, editors, and critics conducted by* Book Week *voted the book*

*the most distinguished novel published in the twenty years since
1945. The title and theme of his great novel concerns itself with
perception and the self—what happens to your humanity if you
are invisible? Similarly, Ellison's preface to his next book points to
the act of writing as a means of gaining perception: "The process of
acquiring technique is a process of modifying one's responses, of
learning to see and feel, to hear and observe, to evoke and evaluate."*

Ellison's second book, Shadow and Act *(1964), is a collection
of twenty essays on various subjects, continuing concern with his
identity as artist, as American, and as Black American. He has taught
at various colleges and universities: Bard, Chicago, Rutgers, and
Yale. He continues to work on a much-awaited second novel.*

1. What are the differences between the two films Ellison analyzes
   in the first part of his essay? Does he see Intruder in the Dust
   as a work of art? Is The Birth of a Nation art, or popular art?
   Why?

2. After 1915, Ellison tells us, "the film became the main manipulator of the American dream. . . ." What does he mean by
   this? Why did this dream become a nightmare for Blacks? To
   what extent did the "shadow" created by Hollywood enforce as
   well as echo the "act" of American racism?

3. Compare Bernard Wolfe's analysis of the Uncle Remus tales
   (in Part One) to Ellison's analysis of these films. How similar
   are their assumptions about art? About race? About the effects
   of popular art upon society? Do they draw the same kinds of
   implications? Be sure to give evidence for your conclusions.

4. If popular art in general justifies cultural myths, what other
   forms of popular art also reaffirm the "widely held myth of
   Negro unhumanness and inferiority by offering entertaining rituals"? Ellison speaks here, of course, of Hollywood films; can
   you find other examples in, say, popular songs, comics, radio or
   television, etc.? Give specific examples, with analysis, as evidence for your conclusions.

Donald Barthelme

AND NOW LET'S HEAR IT FOR
THE ED SULLIVAN SHOW!

Oh, do not ask, "What is it?"
Let us go and make our visit . . .

       The Ed Sullivan Show. Sunday night. Church
of the unchurched. Ed stands there. He looks great. Not unlike an
older, heavier Paul Newman. Sways a little from side to side. Gary
Lewis and the Playboys have just got off. Very strong act. Ed
clasps hands together. He's introducing somebody in the audience.
Who is it? Ed points with his left arm. "Broken every house
record at the Copa," Ed says of the man he's introducing. Who is
it? It's . . . Don Rickles! Rickles stands up. Eyes glint. Applause.
"I'm gonna make a big man outa you!" Ed says. Rickles hunches a
shoulder combatively. Eyes glint. Applause. Jerry Vale introduced.
Wives introduced. Applause. "When Mrs. Sullivan and I were in
Monte Carlo" (pause, neatly suppressed belch), "we saw them"
(pause, he's talking about the next act), "for the first time and
signed them instantly! The Kuban Cossacks! Named after the
River Kuban!"
 Three dancers appear in white fur hats, fur boots, what appear
to be velvet jump suits. They're great. Terrific Cossack stuff in
front of onion-dome flats. Kuban not the U.S.S.R.'s most imposing
river (512 miles, shorter than the Ob, shorter than the Bug) but
the dancers are remarkable. Sword dance of some sort with the
band playing galops. Front dancer balancing on one hand and
doing things with his feet. Great, terrific. Dancers support selves
with one hand, don and doff hats with other hand. XOPOWÓ!
(Non-Cyrillic approximation of Russian for "neat.") Double-
XOPOWÓ! Ed enters from left. Makes enthusiastic gesture with
hand. Triple-XOPOWÓ! Applause dies. Camera on Ed who has
hands knit before him. "Highlighting this past week in New York.
. . ." Something at the Garden. Can't make it out, a fight probably.

Ed introduces somebody in audience. Can't see who, he's standing
up behind a fat lady who's also standing up for purposes of her
own. Applause.

Pigmeat Markham comes on with cap and gown and gavel. His
tag line, "Here come de jedge," is pronounced and the crowd
roars but not so great a roar as you might expect. The line's wearing out. Still, Pigmeat looks good, working with two or three
stooges. Stooge asks Pigmeat why, if he's honest, he's acquired
two Cadillacs, etc. Pigmeat says: "Because I'm very *frugal*," and
whacks stooge on head with bladder. Lots of bladder work in sketch,
old-timey comedy. Stooge says: "Jedge, you got to know me."
Pigmeat: "Who are you?" Stooge: "I'm the man that introduced
you to your wife." Pigmeat shouts, *"Life!"* and whacks the stooge
on the head with the bladder. Very funny stuff, audience roars.
Then a fast commercial with Jo Anne Worley from Rowan and
Martin singing about Bold. Funny girl. Good commercial.

Ed brings on Doodletown Pipers, singing group. Great-looking
girls in tiny skirts. Great-looking legs on girls. They sing something
about "I hear the laughter" and "the sound of the future." Phras-
ing is excellent, attack excellent. Camera goes to atmospheric shots
of a park, kids playing, mothers and fathers lounging about, a
Sunday feeling. Shot of boys throwing the ball around. Shot of
black baby in swing. Shot of young mother's ass, very nice. Shot
of blonde mother cuddling kid. Shot of black father swinging kid.
Shot of a guy who looks like Rod McKuen lounging against a . . .
a what? A play sculpture. But it's not Rod McKuen. The Doodletown Pipers segue into another song. Something about hate and
fear, "You've got to be taught . . . hate and fear." They sound
great. Shot of integrated group sitting on play equipment. Shot of
young bespectacled father. Shot of young black man with young
white child. He looks into camera. Thoughtful gaze. Young mother
with daughter, absorbed. Nice-looking mother. Camera in tight on
mother and daughter. One more mother, a medium shot. Out on
shot of tiny black child asleep in swing. Wow!

Sullivan enters from left applauding. Makes gesture toward
Pipers, toward audience, toward Pipers. Applause. Everybody's having a good time! "I want you to welcome . . . George Carlin!"
Carlin is a comic. Carlin says he hates to look at the news. News
is depressing. Sample headlines: "Welcome Wagon Runs Over
Newcomer." Audience roars. "Pediatrician Dies of Childhood Disease." Audience roars but a weaker roar. Carlin is wearing a white
turtleneck, dark sideburns. Joke about youth asking father if he can
use the car. Youth says he's got a heavy date. Pa says, then why
don't you use the pickup? Joke about the difference between organized crime and unorganized crime. Unorganized crime is when a

guy holds you up on the street. Organized crime is when two guys hold you up on the street. Carlin is great, terrific, but his material is not so funny. A Central Park joke. Cops going into the park dressed as women to provoke molesters. Three hundred molesters arrested and two cops got engaged. More cop jokes. Carlin holds hands clasped together at waist. Says people wonder why the cops don't catch the Mafia. Says have you ever tried to catch a guy in a silk suit? Weak roar from audience. Carlin says do you suffer from nagging crime? Try the Police Department with new improved GL-70. No roar at all. A whicker, rather. Ed facing camera. "Coming up next . . . right after this important word." Commercial for Royal Electric Jetstar Typewriter. "She's typing faster and neater now." Capable-looking woman says to camera, "I have a Jetstar now that helps me at home where I have a business raising St. Bernards." Behind her a St. Bernard looks admiringly at Jetstar.

Ed's back. "England's famous Beatles" (pause, neatly capped belch) "first appeared on our shew . . . Mary Hopkin . . . Paul McCartney told her she must appear on our shew . . . the world-famous . . . Mary Hopkin!" Mary enters holding guitar. Sings something about "the morning of my life . . . ceiling of my room. . . ." Camera in tight on Mary. Pretty blonde, slightly plump face. Heavy applause for Mary. Camera goes to black, then Mary walking away in very short skirt, fine legs, a little heavy maybe. Mary in some sort of nightclub set for her big song, "Those Were the Days." Song is ersatz Kurt Weill but nevertheless a very nice song, very nostalgic, days gone by, tears rush into eyes (mine). In the background, period stills. Shot of some sort of Edwardian group activity, possibly lawn party, possible egg roll. Shot of biplane. Shot of racecourse. Camera on Mary's face. "Those were the days, my friends. . . ." Shot of fox hunting, shot of tea dance. Mary is bouncing a little with the song, just barely bouncing. Shot of what appears to be a French 75 firing. Shot of lady kissing dog on nose. Shot of horse. Camera in tight on Mary's mouth. Looks like huge wad of chewing gum in her mouth, but that can't be right, must be her tongue. Still on balloon ascension in background. Live girl sitting in left foreground gazing up at Mary, rapt. Mary in chaste high-collar dress with that short skirt. Effective. Mary finishes song. A real roar. Ed appears in three-quarter view turned toward the right, toward Mary. "Terrific!" Ed says. "Terrific!" Mary adjusts her breasts. "Terrific. And now, sitting out in the audience is the famous . . . Perle Mesta!" Perle stands, a contented-looking middle-aged lady. Perle bows. Applause.

Ed stares (enthralled) into camera. "Before we introduce singing Ed Ames and the first lady of the American theatre, Helen Hayes. . . . " A Pizza Spins commercial fades into a Tareyton Charcoal

Filter commercial. Then Ed comes back to plug Helen Hayes's new book, *On Reflection*. Miss Hayes is the first lady of the American theatre, he says. "We're very honored to. . . ." Miss Hayes sitting at a desk, Louis-something. She looks marvelous. Begins reading from the book. Great voice. Tons of dignity. "My dear Grandchildren. At this writing, it is no longer fashionable to have Faith; but your grandmother has never been famous for her chic, so she isn't bothered by the intellectual hemlines. I have always been concerned with the whole, not the fragments; the positive, not the negative; the words, not the spaces between them. . . ." Miss Hayes pauses. Hand on what appears to be a small silver teapot. "What can a grandmother offer. . . ." *She speaks very well!* "With the feast of millennia set before you, the saga of all mankind on your bookshelf . . . what could I give you? And then I knew. Of course. My own small footnote. The homemade bread at the banquet. The private joke in the divine comedy. Your roots." Head and shoulders shot of Miss Hayes. She looks up into the lighting grid. Music up softly on, "So my grandchildren . . . in highlights and shadows . . . bits and pieces . . . in recalled moments, mad scenes and acts of folly. . . ." Miss Hayes removes glasses, looks misty. "What are little grandchildren made of . . . some good and some bad from Mother and Dad . . . and laughs and wails from Grandmother's tales . . . I love you." She gazes down at book. Holds it. Camera pulls back. Music up. Applause.

Ed puts arm around Miss Hayes. Squeezes Miss Hayes. Applause. *Heavy* applause. Ed pats hands together joining applause. Waves hands toward Miss Hayes. More applause. It's a triumph! Ed seizes Miss Hayes's hands in his hands. Applause dies, reluctantly. Ed says ". . . but first, listen to this." Shot of building, cathedral of some kind. Organ music. Camera pans down facade past stained-glass windows, etc. Down a winding staircase. Music changes to rock. Shot of organ keyboard. Close shot of maker's nameplate, HAMMOND. Shot of grinning organist. Shot of hands on keyboard. "The sound of Hammond starts at $599.95." Ed introduces singer Ed Ames. Ames is wearing a long-skirted coat, holding hand mike. Good eyes, good eyebrows, muttonchop sideburns. Lace at his cuffs. Real riverboat-looking. He strolls about the set singing a Tom Jones-Harvey Schmidt number, something about the morning, sometimes in the morning, something. Then another song, "it takes my breath away," "how long have I waited," something something. Chorus comes in under him. Good song. Ames blinks in a sincere way. Introduces a song from the upcoming show *Dear World*. "A lovely new song," he says. "Kiss her now, while she's young. Kiss her now, while she's yours." Set behind him looks like one-by-two's nailed vertically four inches on centers. The song is sub-lovely but Ames's delivery is very comfortable, easy. Chorus comes in. Ah ah ah ah ah. Ames closes his eyes, sings something something something something; the song is sub-memorable. (Something memorable: early on Sunday morning a pornographic exhibition appeared mysteriously for eight minutes on television-station KPLM, Palm Springs, California. A naked man and woman did vile and imaginative things to each other for that length of time, then disappeared into the history of electricity. Unfortunately, the exhibition wasn't on a network. What we really want in this world, we can't have.)

Ed enters from left (what's over there? a bar? a Barcalounger? a book? stock ticker? model railroad?), shakes hands with Ames. Ames much taller, but amiable. Both back out of shot, in different directions. Camera straight ahead on Ed. "Before I tell you about next week's . . . show . . . please listen to this." Commercial for Silva Thins. Then a shot of old man with ship model, commercial for Total, the vitamin cereal. Then Ed. "Next week . . . a segment from . . . the new Beatles film . . . The Beatles were brought over here by us . . . in the beginning. . . . Good night!" Chopping gesture with hands to the left, to the right.

Music comes up. The crawl containing the credits is rolled over shots of Russian dancers dancing (XOPOWÓ!). Produced by Bob Precht. Directed by Tim Kiley. Music by Ray Bloch. Associate Producer Jack McGeehan. Settings Designed by Bill Bohnert. Production Manager Tony Jordan. Associate Director Bob Schwarz. Assistant to the Producer Ken Campbell. Program Coordinator Russ Petranto. Technical Director Charles Grenier. Audio Art Shine. Lighting Director Bill Greenfield. Production Supervisor Herb Benton. Stage Managers Ed Brinkman, Don Mayo. Set Director Ed Pasternak. Costumes Leslie Renfield. Graphic Arts Sam Cecere. Talent Coordinator Vince Calandra. Music Coordinator Bob Arthur. The Ed Sullivan Show is over. It has stopped.

DONALD BARTHELME *(1931–   ) began publishing fiction in the early 1960s, quickly gaining a coterie of admirers for his originality. His first collection of stories was* Come Back, Dr. Caligari *(1964). A novel,* Snow White *(1967) perplexed readers of The New Yorker (February 18, 1967), which printed it in full; one critic defined it as "a reality harboring a radical mistrust of language, writing, fiction, the imagination." Two collections of stories have followed:* Unspeakable Practices, Unnatural Acts *(1968), and* City Life *(1970). His former editor says "he writes just as he sees things"; he himself says*

"I try to avoid saying anything directly and just hope something emerges." His work now appears regularly in The New Yorker.

1. How does this piece differ from the usual description of a show? From a newspaper review? How does Barthelme feel about the show? What does he like? Why? Since there is virtually no direct evaluation, how do you know so clearly what the writer thinks?

2. One way to see what the piece is doing is to imagine it as an accumulation of evidence for unstated but implied conclusions. Here is the most popular of popular art forms in all its detailed glory; here is the bored yet stoic watcher taking it all—almost all? more than all?—in. What are the implied conclusions about the show? About the actors? About the audience? What evidence leads to these conclusions?

3. Why does Barthelme focus our attention on Ed's belches, the fat lady in the audience, Mary Hopkin's tongue ("Looks like huge wad of chewing gum"), and all the other repulsive physical details? Why does Barthelme end with the dreary list of production credits? What have all those people, with all those artistic titles, produced?

4. What does popular art aim to achieve? Does the Ed Sullivan show achieve it? What is the aim of art? Does Barthelme's piece achieve it? How does this piece demonstrate in itself some of the distinctions between art and popular art that Herbert Read, and others discuss?

Appendix

PERCEPTIVE REWRITING:

ASSUMPTIONS, EVIDENCE,

AND IMPLICATIONS

A professional writer knows that only a small part of his job is done when his first draft is finished; ten or fifteen revisions are not unusual, and to salvage large parts of a first draft is a kind of triumph. Certainly no writer is likely to do very successful writing unless he adopts some of the habits of the professional and learns to rewrite thoroughly and carefully.

No one can give a ready or easy formula for rewriting. The process of creation from conception through outlining through early drafts to a final outline and final draft is very complicated. Each writer must finally choose the procedures which best allow him to understand and demonstrate his best thoughts on his topic.

After all, revision is most valuable if it serves the writer as well as the reader. To replace a vague word or an incoherent paragraph with the precise word or a developed idea is not merely a matter of pleasing a more or less interested reader; it is thinking itself. Rewriting is usually a matter of finding out what you really want to say by a search for the right words and the most effective organization.

The concepts which this text is designed to teach offer a valuable way to conceive of rewriting an analytic, expository paper. Whatever method you use to revise your work, you need to be sure you have considered the assumptions made by your material and by your own writing; you need to attend to the implications of both your material and your own argument; and you need to consider whether you have used enough appropriate evidence to demonstrate your argument. Unless you have some developed control over assumption, implication, and evidence, no amount of rewriting will turn a poor paper into a good one.

The student paper printed here dramatically demonstrates the kind of change that can take place when these concepts enter into the rewriting process. The major change from first to final draft occurs as the writer examines the assumptions and implications of the love comics she analyzes. The first draft is a clear and interesting description of the comics, giving us a good sense of what they look like and how they present their "pseudo-lovelife and dreamworld." But there does not seem to be much point to the paper; the writer does not have a clear idea of why she is describing what she does, or why the comics seem to her damaging. Notice how this purposelessness appears in the opening sentences of paragraphs eight and nine: "Another interesting aspect of these comic books is . . ."; "The advertisements in these comic books are a little harder to figure out."

The first paragraph of an intermediate draft follows. It contains the basic ideas which enrich and deepen the final draft. The quest for assumptions led the writer to Erik Erikson's Childhood and Society (among other books), and to a group of ideas about the adolescent quest for identity models. Thought about the implications of the comics led to an examination of the goals they set up as ideal, and an evaluation of these goals.

Thus the final draft uses description (the whole point of the first draft) as evidence for ideas developed out of consideration of what the comics mean. Their "real harm," we are told, comes from the false identity models they contain and the "unrealistic, unattainable, and unworthy" goals they provide. An essay that was originally a sample of interesting, though pointless description emerges now as a thoughtful assessment of the effects of a popular form of popular art on growing up.

Jeanne Reynolds

THE "LOVE COMIC'S" VIEW OF ROMANCE

(draft one)

One form of popular art that is present among pre-teen and young teenage girls is the romance or love comic books. They come in a variety of titles, including the four that I happened to pick up: *Young Romance, Falling in Love, Girls' Romances*, and *Secret Hearts*. These are aimed mainly at girls between the ages of about eight and fifteen, who have had little or no experience in love and romance and are still dreaming of the day they will fall in love. A typical cover says on it: "Thrill to the true-to-love story of Wendy Winthrop, television model, as she pursues her heart in and out of the loopholes of her romantic career." * Through these "true-to-love" stories, these comic books create a sort of temporary dream world for the young girl to live in. She can place herself in the position of a character such as Wendy Winthrop and dream of when the same experiences will happen to her. One little eight-year-old said, in the book, *Seduction of the Innocent*, "I like to read the comic books about love because when I go to sleep at night I love to dream about love." † Now, this in itself would not really be extremely bad except for the fact that the romantic experiences presented in these comic books are unrealistic and overly dramatic.

First of all, an unattractive or homely person is never seen in these comic books. The girls are all extremely pretty and shapely, and the men are extraordinarily handsome and masculine. Another thing never seen in these stories is a poor person. All of the characters seem to be either upper-middle or upper class in society. These two characteristics tend to make these stories even more ideal, while at the same time making them more unrealistic.

Most of the stories in these comic books fit into one basic style. That is, a girl thinks she is in love, or has been in love, with one boy, but through a series of actions and events, invariably including

Reprinted by permission of the author.
* *Girls' Romances*, April, 1964.
† Fredric Wertham, *Seduction of the Innocent* (New York: Rinehart, 1954), p. 39.

heartache and indecision, she meets her true love. However, another style that I found a few examples of is that of two friends, one who always gets the boy she wants while the other looks on. But in the end, the underdog finally gets the boy she wants, in spite of her friend. This second style of story would probably serve to give hope to the readers who are not very popular with boys, while the first, more prominent style, would meet every girl's dreams and hopes.

Every love comic story, despite all of the heartache and despair within it, ends happily. "The love comic formula demands that the story end with reconciliation." * The heroine always gets the man she wants and everything is summed up with a kiss.

However, nothing beyond a kiss is ever suggested in these stories. There is no hint of sexual relations. Everything is pure and innocent, and no one makes a move to make it otherwise. This helps to keep these stories within the realm of having dream-like qualities; anything less innocent would destroy a young girl's conception of love.

The covers of these various love comic books tend to be pictorial representations of the emotional appeal within. They always show a picture from one of the stories and, without fail, this picture is always the most romantic and emotionally appealing one the publishers could find. Every cover shows a heartrending scene; out of the four comic books that I chose, all of them showed, among other characters, a girl with a pained expression on her face, and in three of them, she had a tear in her eye.

The titles of the stories within the comic books also have a definite emotional appeal. They include, "Love, Love Go Away!", "Reach for Happiness" (episode 24), "The Secret in My Past," "The Truth About Men," and "In the Name of Love." All of this is perfect bait for the young girl who is dreaming of when she'll fall in love.

Another interesting aspect of these comic books is the "Ann Landers"-type column found in the middle of each one. Under the title of "Counselor-at-Love" or "Romance Reporter," these big-sister type counselors answer questions from the lovelorn. Most of the letters tend to be from girls around the ages of thirteen to fifteen who are having problems with their love lives and think that the world is ending because of it. Or if this isn't their problem, then they are desperately in love with a boy and want advice as to how to make him notice them. The responses to these letters always seem to assume that these girls are perfectly mature enough to be in love and, thus, the answers proceed from there. Here again is the

---

* Wertham, p. 38.

audience of young girls who really don't know what love is all about but want so desperately to find out. And they think they are finding the answer in these comic books.

The advertisements in these comic books are a little harder to figure out, for they are quite diverse. Quite a few of them have to do with bettering of appearance, such as a Magic Nail Formula (which appeared in three of them), hairpieces (including a "Romantic-Exciting Fall!")*, a device for improving posture, and a hair-do tote bag. These ads seem to be aimed at the teen-age readers while an ad for a "fully-furnished doll house with complete doll family" † is aimed at the younger readers. But the most interesting ad that I found in one of these comic books was for this type of comic book itself. It offers special rates for a two-year subscription to these magazines that contain "stories dedicated to those who love and are loved," and "stories dedicated to those who want to be loved." ** Here again is just exactly what a young girl will fall for. The second part, especially, is a direct appeal to the inexperienced young girl.

Thus, it seems to me that all the parts of these magazines or "love" comics are in accord. Every aspect of them seems to be dedicated to the effort of creating a pseudo-lovelife and dream-world for the young girl.

---

* *Falling in Love*, Jan., 1969, and *Secret Hearts*, Jan., 1969, back covers.
† *Falling in Love*, inside back cover.
** *Girls' Romances*, inside back cover.

(draft two: revised first paragraph)

In American society, children between the ages of about eight and fifteen are beginning to strive for an identity. They need something to relate to and to give them some sort of identity model to follow. "Adolescence is the age of the final establishment of a dominant positive ego identity. It is then that a future within reach becomes part of the conscious life plan." In establishing this ego identity, adolescents are influenced by such media as television, books, and comic books. Young girls in this age bracket are especially influenced by the "Love" comic books which can be found on the market under such titles as, "Girls' Love," "Secret Hearts," "My Love," and others. These romance manuals create an exciting world for the young girl, one that she can put herself into and dream about. Thus, these magazines create a fantasy world, a pseudo love life for the reader. However, they try to convince the reader that they are realistic, true-to-life pictures of everyday occurrences. "Love comics . . . play up the angle that what they depict is real life. 'The girls are real people with real problems and real dramatic confessions,' says a typical issue. What do these 'real' girls want? 'More than anything in the world I wanted glamor, money, adventure. . . .' " The goals that these girls have are material and social; they want to be beautiful, rich and popular. What more could the young reader ask for? The heroine's goals become her goals.

(draft three)

Children between the ages of about eight and fifteen need something to relate to and to give them some sort of identity model to follow. Erik Erikson pointed this out in his book *Childhood and Society*, when he said, "Adolescence is the age of the final establishment of a dominant positive ego identity. It is then that a future within reach becomes part of the conscious life plan." [1] A child needs to establish this ego identity for himself before he can work out the rest of his life. Once he decides who he is and what he wants out of life, then he can work towards the accomplishment of this goal. In modern American society the adolescent is influenced in this task by many sources. Among these are his parents, educational institutions, peer groups, and the mass media. The media are able to present a very glamorous and exciting picture of what life can be like, and this can be very influential, especially for an adolescent who is attempting to form an ego identity.

One of the mass media that is important to adolescents and pre-adolescents is the comic book. Through these magazines, the young person can find an exciting fantasy world. Young girls often turn to the "love" comic for an answer to what it means to be one of today's teenagers, which includes being beautiful, popular, and romantic. These comic books, which can be found on the market under such titles as "Secret Hearts," "Girls' Love," "My Love," create a world that a young girl can put herself into and dream about. What's more, they try to convince the reader that they are realistic, true-to-life pictures of everyday occurrences. To do this, they present some common situations that almost anyone can identify with and use them to capture the readers' attention and confidence. For example, almost every issue of these comic books contains one or more heartbreak scenes within the stories. And since almost every young girl feels heartbreak at one time or another she can easily identify with this. Another common feature of the stories involves an argument between a teenager and her mother who is constantly griping or meddling. Here again, since most adolescents experience parental problems, this is a situation that is easy to identify with. So these magazines lead the young reader to

[1] Erik H. Erikson, *Childhood and Society* (New York: W. W. Norton, 1963), p. 306.

believe that what they represent is a realistic picture of life and love. The cover of *Girls' Romances* asks the reader to: "Thrill to the true-to-love story of Wendy Winthrop, television model, as she pursues her heart in and out of the loopholes of her romantic career." [2] But "true-to-love" and true-to-life Wendy Winthrop is a beautiful, voluptuous redhead who always gets the man she wants. And this is not realistic, but yet it is apt to lead the young reader to believe that there is an easy solution to everything, including love and romance, and this, of course, would be a false conclusion. The comic books create a pseudo-love-life for the adolescent. She is urged to identify with the various heroines of the stories, and in doing this, she loses her own identity. She wants to follow the model set by the heroine, and achieve the same goals that she achieves because they would allow her to live a perfect, "happily-ever-after" life. In one issue of *Secret Hearts*, the heroine exclaims, "More than anything in the world I want glamor, money, adventure . . .!" [3] What exciting goals these are for the adolescent reader! She, too, wants to be beautiful, rich, and popular. In the world of these comics, there is nothing more to ask for. Those goals of the heroine are presented as being the only ones worth working for; intellectual or social responsibilities play no part here at all. The comics seem to be saying that if a teenage girl is rich and beautiful, she will therefore be popular, and this is all she needs to succeed in life. This, of course, is not always the case but it is what the reader is led to believe and would like to believe. Thus, she is presented with a false identity model to follow which urges her towards superficial goals.

The stories presented in these magazines further their unreality. First of all, the only unattractive or homely person that is ever seen is a parent or another unimportant figure. Every major character is good-looking and well-endowed. Special attention is given to physical, sexual characteristics. This seems to change the dreamworld into something that is not altogether innocent. Dr. Frederick Wertham, who has studied the effects of comic books on children, sees their sexual implication as distinctly unhealthy: "Comic books stimulate children sexually. That is an elementary fact of my research. In comic books over and over again, in pictures and text, . . . attention is drawn to sexual characteristics and sexual actions." [4] This is quite obvious, not only from all the attention given to physical characteristics and the many passionate love scenes, but also, as Dr. Wertham says, from the text itself. One heroine in *Secret Heart* speaks of being ". . . in his arms, powerless to resist"; [5] another from *Girls' Love* says, ". . . his demand-

[2] *Girls' Romances*, April, 1964.
[3] *Secret Hearts*, March, 1971.
[4] Fredric Wertham, *Seduction of the Innocent* (New York: Rinehart, 1954), p. 175.
[5] *Secret Hearts*, March, 1971.

ing kisses wanted me to really be a *woman* . . . for the first time . . ." [6] One heroine even reveals a dream she has had, saying, ". . . the stranger 'invaded' my bedroom . . . I imagined my lips throbbing with the sudden surge of blood as his hungry mouth came nearer . . . nearer . . . nearer. . . ." [7] Dr. Wertham implies that scenes and language of this kind are harmful to the adolescent mind. But it seems to me that this problem is not nearly as serious as the unreality of these magazines. Dr. Wertham does not seem to see that what these comic books represent is not realistic and in this lies their real harm.

Another version of ugliness, the poor person, is also rarely shown. Every major character is beautifully dressed and neatly groomed and drives a modern sports car. And it has to be this way. If the comic is going to be an idealistic dream world for the reader, then there can be no poor people in this world. That would destroy its perfection. So here again, the comics are portraying an unrealistic situation and passing it off as real.

The plots of the various "love" stories seem to be very much the same. For example, Beverly Bennett, a professional model, is torn between the two men in her life, Don Larrimer, her photographer, and Paul Kent, a male model. Through a series of adventures, conflicts, and indecisions, Beverly finally chooses Paul as her one and only love.[8] Very rarely is there an unhappy ending. In most cases the heroine gets the man she wants and everything is summed up with a kiss. This way, the reader can feel happy and fulfilled, as if she too has found the man she loves. An unhappy ending would probably leave her with feelings of discouragement and frustration and she would soon turn to some other means of supplying herself with a happy and successful "love life."

The world of the "love" comic book is an exciting and romantic one and, thus, sets up goals that are just what the adolescent female reader wants or, at least, thinks she wants. But these can be harmful goals because they are, in so many cases, unrealistic, unattainable, and what's more, unworthy. Not everyone can reach physical perfection and material and social success, but the comic leads the reader to believe that this is really possible. And when she finally realizes that it is not possible, she may be very disappointed. The impressionable adolescent girl wants desperately to find out what love is all about and in turning to one, easy source of information, she sets up an unrealistic, easily destroyed dreamworld for herself. And with the destruction of the dreamworld comes the destruction of the identity model and all of its exciting goals. And so the adolescent is left back where she started: in search of a positive ego identity. And so she will try a new source for her day dreams, perhaps turning to other, more sophisticated magazines as she grows older. But in all of them she can find an ideal dreamworld to put herself into in order to find, at last, happiness and satisfaction in her "love life."

———

JEANNE REYNOLDS (1950–   ) *wrote and rewrote this paper as a student at the California State College, San Bernardino. She receives the B.A. as an English major in 1972, and plans to be an elementary-school teacher.*

1. *The first draft contains ten paragraphs. Aside from the first and last, each paragraph is a description of a different part of the comics. Which paragraph gives the most satisfying description? What concrete and particular details support this description? How does the paragraph relate to the idea of the essay stated in the first and last paragraphs? Which paragraph is weakest? Why? What is the value of this kind of essay organization? What are its weaknesses?*

2. *Read the statement about Responsible Use of Sources at the back of this book. Now consider the third sentence of draft two, the quotation from Erik Erikson (see footnote 1 of draft 2). Is this sentence plagiarism? What is wrong with using a source this way, even if the quotation is put within quotation marks? Would a footnote to Erikson here satisfy the writer's responsibility to the source and to herself? Is the source used properly in the third draft? Is the Fredric Wertham book used properly as a source in draft one? In draft three?*

3. *How does the first paragraph of draft two improve upon draft one? What new thinking is going on in this revision? Show where the new material of draft two appears in draft three.*

4. *Draft three has six paragraphs, even though it is noticeably longer than draft one with its ten paragraphs. Prepare outlines of both of these drafts and compare them. What has been left out of draft three? Why do you think this material was cut? What organizing idea has replaced the plan of draft one (see question 1)?*

5. *Has the writer in draft three made a convincing case that the comics are "harmful"? What has been done in the essay to make it convincing? What might make it more convincing, more satisfying, even more interesting?*

Note on Source Material in the Popular Arts

A good selected bibliography appears in The Popular Arts, ed. Irving and Harriet Deer (New York: Scribner's, 1967). This bibliography has brief sections for literature, movies and photography, music, radio and television, and the comics, as well as a useful listing of miscellaneous and general materials. A number of anthologies of readings in this area have been published in the last decade. The best of these remains Mass Culture: The Popular Arts in America, ed. Bernard Rosenberg and David Manning White (Glencoe, Ill.: Free Press, 1957); this collection has no bibliography but includes essays on best sellers, detective fiction, comics, cartoons, mass magazines, movies, TV—even "Card Playing as Mass Culture." Standing out from a great deal of sociological writing on this topic is Joseph Klapper's The Effects of Mass Communication (Glencoe, Ill.: Free Press, 1960), an excellent account of research into the social, sociological, and psychological effects of the various media, especially television. Culture for the Millions? Mass Media in Modern Society, ed. Norman Jacobs (Princeton, N.J.: Van Nostrand, 1961) is a collection of articles from the magazine Daedalus. The most recent and, in many ways, most valuable book is Russell Nye's The Unembarrassed Muse: The Popular Arts in America (New York: Dial, 1970).

Journals in the field include Mass Media and the Journal of Popular Culture. But most of the interesting writing during the last few years has appeared in the general-audience quality magazines, such as Daedalus, Dissent, The Partisan Review, Commentary, The New Republic, etc. The Reader's Guide to Periodical Literature (published since 1900) lists both author and subject for most of these recent articles.

But the basic source material for a paper on popular art must be, of course, the art itself.

Note on Responsible Use of Sources

Suppose you are writing a paper about popular art, and you have chosen to contrast two comics—Peanuts and Donald Duck—in order to show what it is that defines popular art. You feel a difference between the two comics, and you wonder if this difference is one between two forms of popular art or between popular art and art.

In the course of your reading of and about the comics, you come across a fine article by Abraham Kaplan called "The Aesthetics of the Popular Arts," where, among other things, you read:

> *All art selects what is significant and suppresses the trivial. But for popular art the criteria of significance are fixed by the needs of the standardization, by the editor of the digest and not by the Author of the reality to be grasped. Popular art is never a discovery, only a reaffirmation. Both producer and consumer of popular art confine themselves to what fits into their own schemes, rather than omitting only what is unnecessary to the grasp of the scheme of things. The world of popular art is bounded by the limited horizons of what we think we know already; it is two-dimensional because we are determined to view it without budging a step from where we stand.**

What Kaplan has to say is clearly useful for your paper. But how are you to use it?

Few students are deliberately dishonest and foolish enough to plan plagiarism, that is, to copy it word for word and hand it in as if it were original. But honest and sensible people still have trouble using sources properly and sometimes stumble unawares into plagiarism, unless they understand clearly how to incorporate other people's ideas into their own work.

For instance, one way to use Kaplan's material would be to copy

---

This Note is adapted with permission from an unpublished paper written by Professor Peter Schroeder.
* *The Journal of Aesthetics and Art Criticism,* XXIV (Spring, 1966), 354. The article, in various forms, is reprinted in several recent collections of material on popular art, including the first one referred to in the Note on Source Material.

what he says word for word and put a note at the end referring to page 354 of the Journal of Aesthetics. But even though the source is acknowledged, plagiarism is still going on, since Kaplan's words and ideas are put forward as your own; there is no sign that you are thinking about your topic or your source, and you thus defeat the whole point of the paper—to show what you have to say.

It is more honest, but only a little more responsible, to put the quotation in quotation marks; at least there is now no pretense. Another possibility would be to look at the passage, try to figure out what it is saying, and put it in your own words:

> One important difference between popular art and art is that popular art is never new, never discovers anything out of the standard scheme of things. So popular art doesn't challenge people to think differently.

But the idea is still Kaplan's. So you might, just to be safe, put a note at the end of the paraphrase. Perhaps some time you have strung together a series of such paraphrases, with occasional quotations, in the belief that you were doing a "research" paper with footnotes.

But no such procedures will fulfill your responsibilities as a writer. Just what do such footnotes mean? How much of what you say is yours, how much is Kaplan's, or is there any difference? The problem for a writer is to inform himself as fully as possible about his topic and his sources, then form his own opinion. The job is not only to understand Kaplan, but to come to some personal understanding of the material at hand (here, the comics). This means regarding Kaplan critically. If you end up agreeing with him, you should say so, explicitly. If not, point out where and why you differ.

So we return once more to the comics. What is different about the way the characters are conceived, for instance? Why are there no "grown-ups" in Peanuts, while the Disney comic establishes a father and an uncle? What kinds of responses do the two comics ask their readers to have? Do Kaplan's terms apply wholly? partially? not at all?

To think this way is to come to terms with the problems of writing a paper using sources. Perhaps in the end you write:

> The real art of Peanuts becomes clear when you put it next to the dreary stereotypes and stale plots that make up Donald Duck. Peanuts seems fresh and original, to have its own world with its own rules and systems of behavior, whereas the Disney comic, with its constant fussing about money and social class, seems a reduced and corrupted version of our own world. When

*Abraham Kaplan says "popular art is never a discovery, only a
reaffirmation" he points to exactly this distinction.* If we agree
with Kaplan, as I do, that art is defined by the way it makes us
see things from a new perspective, Peanuts appears to deserve
the respect it has received from philosophers and theologians,
not to speak of the general public. Donald Duck reveals to us
what we believe when we are not thinking or seeing clearly; it
reassures us. But Peanuts makes us expand our vision, and so is a
different kind of art.*

*The point is that in using sources we must not be simple sponges,
soaking up uncritically everything we read: we must distinguish between the opinion of the author we are reading and the opinion
which we ourselves, after careful consideration, come to hold. And
others' opinions cannot stand by themselves; the fact that a source
has said something is only one piece of evidence to help us demonstrate our own ideas.*

*Most notes refer to books (footnote 1, below), articles in books
(footnote 2), articles in periodicals (3), or previous notes (4). Here
is one example of each of these kinds of notes; if you memorize
these forms in detail you will need to refer to a handbook (such as
the Modern Language Association style sheet) only occasionally.*

*But the real problem, as we have seen, comes when we try to
sort out the ideas, opinions, interpretation of other people from
those we hold ourselves. Each of us has his own intellectual identity,
though most of our ideas inevitably come from sources outside us,
and a responsible use of sources recognizes that identity and distinguishes clearly between what we think and what our source thinks.
It is no sin to accept wholly another person's idea: "If we agree
with Kaplan, as I do. . . ." The sin is in not having sufficient respect for yourself as a thinking being, or as a student, to interpose
yourself between your sources and your writing (or thinking, for
your papers should be occasional crystallizations of a continuum of
reflection). It is lazy and irresponsible to pass off Kaplan's ideas (or
anyone else's ideas) as your own, without first making them your
own through a process of critical scrutiny. These ideas then enrich
the substance of what you have to say about your subject and become part of the evidence you bring to support your own assertions.*

---

* Kaplan, p. 354.
[1] Fredric Wertham, *Seduction of the Innocent* (New York: Rinehart, 1954), p. 10.
[2] Leslie A. Fiedler, "The Comics: Middle Against Both Ends," in *Modern Culture
and the Arts,* ed. James B. Hall and Barry Ulanov (New York: McGraw-Hill, 1967),
pp. 526–538.
[3] William Barrett, "American Fiction and American Values," *Partisan Review,* 18
(1951), 681–690.
[4] Wertham, p. 75.